Alfred Williams Momerie

Inspiration, and Other Sermons

Delivered in the Chapel of the Foundling Hospital

Alfred Williams Momerie

Inspiration, and Other Sermons
Delivered in the Chapel of the Foundling Hospital

ISBN/EAN: 9783337161385

Printed in Europe, USA, Canada, Australia, Japan

Cover: Foto ©Lupo / pixelio.de

More available books at **www.hansebooks.com**

INSPIRATION

AND OTHER SERMONS

Delivered in the Chapel of the Foundling Hospital

BY

ALFRED WILLIAMS MOMERIE

M.A., D.SC., LL.D.

LATE FELLOW OF ST JOHN'S COLLEGE, CAMBRIDGE;
PROFESSOR OF LOGIC AND METAPHYSICS
IN KING'S COLLEGE, LONDON

WILLIAM BLACKWOOD AND SONS
EDINBURGH AND LONDON
MDCCCLXXXIX

CONTENTS.

	PAGE
INSPIRATION—	
I. THE EVOLUTION OF THE BIBLE,	1
II. INACCURACIES OF THE BIBLE,	12
III. THE GENIUS OF THE JEWS FOR RIGHTEOUSNESS,	25
IV. CHRIST'S NEW DOCTRINE,	37
V. CHRIST'S NEW MOTIVE,	49
VI. THE PERSONALITY OF GOD,	63
THE CANON,	76
TRUE AND FALSE DISCONTENT—	
I. DISCONTENT IN REGARD TO PERSONAL CIRCUMSTANCES,	89
II. FALSE DISCONTENT IN REGARD TO KNOWLEDGE,	103
III. TRUE DISCONTENT IN REGARD TO KNOWLEDGE,	116
IV. FALSE DISCONTENT WITH THE WORLD AS A WHOLE — PESSIMISM. (*A*) THE PLEASURES OF LIFE,	127

V.	PESSIMISM (*continued*)—(B) THE NECESSITY FOR PAIN,	140
VI.	PESSIMISM (*continued*)—(B) THE NECESSITY FOR PAIN (*continued*),	151
VII.	PESSIMISM (*continued*)—(C) ITS FALSE IDEAL,	161
VIII.	PESSIMISM (*continued*)—(D) THE EVOLUTION OF LOVE,	172
IX.	TRUE DISCONTENT WITH THE WORLD,	183
	CHRISTMAS DAY,	196
	NEW YEAR'S DAY,	210
	"THANKSGIVING SERVICE" AT THE FOUNDLING,	219
	SCIENCE AND RELIGION,	231
	PATIENCE,	245
	THE SABBATH,	255
	REMARKS ON PREVIOUS SERMON,	267
	COTTER MORISON,	272

Inspiration.

I.

THE EVOLUTION OF THE BIBLE.

" God breathed into man's nostrils the breath of life; and man became a living soul."—GEN. ii. 7.

" Prophesying came not in old time by the will of man; but holy men of old spake as they were moved by the Holy Ghost."—2 PETER i. 21.

" All Scripture is given by inspiration of God, and is profitable for correction, for reproof," &c.—2 TIM. iii. 16.

" Search the Scriptures; for in them ye think ye have eternal life. But ye will not come to me, that ye might have life."—JOHN v. 39.

INSPIRATION means etymologically a breathing into—a breathing into man by God. It is distinctly the teaching of the Bible that all men are inspired. "God breathed into man's nostrils the breath of life; and man became a living soul." Our mind, soul, spirit, ego, self, personality—however we may please to term it—is, so to speak, the breath of God. You will observe that this expression is a metaphor,—a material metaphor for a spiritual fact. Mind is not, and cannot be, a chemical combination of gases. Our essential self is something very different from the breath of our lungs. What the old Hebrew writer meant was simply that our being was derived from God's,—that it was in kind identical with God's. Every man is inspired; every man is himself an inspiration; he has been, so to speak, begotten by God; he is the outcome of God; his real nature is in germ divine.

In germ divine. This limitation is necessary to cover the fact that there is such infinite diversity observable among men. The mind which any one possesses to start with, is but the germ of what it may eventually become. Its development is different in different individuals, so different that we are apt to forget their common origin. When compared with men of genius, average men seem commonplace and undivine. It is the former only whom we should generally speak of as inspired. And even in their case we should not apply the word indiscriminately to all they said and did, but we should restrict it to the most remarkable of their achievements.

There is another restriction which has become common among religious people. They have frequently thought to honour religion by depreciating everything else. God has nothing to do, they imagine, with the productions of art, with the discoveries of science, with the meditations of the philosopher, with the labours of the philanthropist. God, they believe—though curiously enough they think at the same time that He was the Creator of the world—God, they believe, is a religious Being only, and never influences men except for the purpose of conveying religious instruction. They therefore restrict the term inspiration to the most remarkable religious writers, and, I may add, to most remarkable religious writers of the past; for somehow or other, I cannot make out how, they have come to the conclusion that all inspiration is at an end. In Christendom the term is generally applied to Biblical writers, and denied to all others even though, in some cases, what they have written is practically the same.

Now I want you to examine this current doctrine. I would remark, in the first place, that it is the outcome of self-conceit. Men have delighted to imagine themselves the special favourites of the Almighty, to believe that He did for them what He would not do for others. But the more we study history, the more clear becomes the folly of all such notions, the more certain do we feel that, however much men's circumstances may differ, God's dealings with them are always and everywhere the same. An unjust Deity would be a contradiction in terms. Nothing but self-conceit could ever have led men to the conclusion that their own scriptures were not only superior to all others, but that they owed their origin to a *unique* act of mercy on the part of the Almighty.

Those who have adopted this irrational doctrine have tried to find reasons for it in the Scriptures themselves. In John v. 39 they read, "Search the Scriptures; for in them ye think ye have eternal life." The passage answered their purpose better by the omission of "ye think," which they accordingly proceeded to omit, and henceforth quoted the text as, "Search the Scriptures; for in them ye have eternal life." Now, as a matter of fact, Christ said just the opposite. Instead of "search," the translation should be "ye search"; and what Christ said was this, "Ye search the Scriptures; for in them *ye think* ye have eternal life: but ye have not; they testify of me, and ye will not come to me, that ye might have life." In other words, the religious life is something very different from the worship of a book. In this passage Christ is not praising, but emphatically condemning, bibliolatry.

There is another text by which the current view

of inspiration is supported—viz., 2 Tim. iii. 16, "All scripture is given by inspiration of God, and is profitable for correction, for reproof," &c. This also is a mistranslation. You know, of course, that the word scripture merely means writing, just as the word bible means book. In course of time these terms have come to be restricted to the writings and to the book, which we regard as the writings and the book *par excellence*. But it is constantly assumed that the restriction existed from the beginning, and that it is implied in this particular passage in Timothy. Now manifestly the assumption is absurd; for the writings which we call Scripture had not then been collected into a single whole; many of them had not even been written; the very epistle in which this text occurs, an epistle which now forms part of our Scriptures, was at the time in process of composition. It will save confusion if we translate the word, not scripture, but writing. But the important mistranslation is in what follows. The apostle does not say "every writing is given by inspiration of God, and is profitable;" but every writing given by inspiration of God is profitable. Whether it be given by inspiration must be critically determined in each particular case; but if it be inspired, then the apostle asserts it is profitable, whenever, wherever, by whomsoever it was written. This is in harmony with, whereas the mistranslation contradicts, the teaching of St James, that "every good and perfect gift cometh from the Father of lights."

There is only one other passage in the Bible which bears directly upon the question of inspiration—viz., 2 Peter i. 21, "Holy men of old spake as they were moved by the Holy Ghost." Of course they did; and so they will to the end of time!

Why, then, is it that we regard the Bible as pre-eminently inspired, more inspired than other books? Are we right in so regarding it? I think we are. But the reasons by which this view is justified are generally wrong.

Let us consider some of the grounds on which the common view might be often vindicated. And the first and most obvious is that of style. If the Bible be altogether unique in its origin, if it *literally* had God for its author, we should naturally expect the style to be different from that of other books, and not only different but superior. Now, when we examine the Bible, what do we find? Why, we find among its writers the same literary excellences and defects that exist among profane authors; we find all possible varieties of style, from the most primitive portions of the Pentateuch up to the perfect art of Job. No one can honestly say that the books of Kings or of Chronicles are better written, or indeed as well, as the histories of Thucydides or of Freeman. And even supposing we discovered in all the books of the Bible the same proofs of genius as we do in the Book of Job, still we have works in profane literature which in point of ability fall little, if at all, short of that great poem. The difference in artistic merit between Job and Faust, *e.g.*, is not such as to warrant the supposition that while Goethe wrote the one, God alone could have been author of the other.

Secondly, it may be said that, though the style and idiosyncrasies of the Scriptural writers were not interfered with, they were nevertheless divinely and miraculously compelled, one and all of them, to give a full, perfect, infallible representation of Deity. But when we come to examine the Bible carefully for ourselves, we see that the representation of the Deity differs from writer to writer, and from age to age. We find, what we find everywhere else, an *evolution* of the idea of God. Just look at 1 Sam. xv. 1-3. Samuel said unto Saul, " Hearken thou unto the voice of the voice of the Lord. Go and smite Amalek, and utterly destroy all that they have; slay both man and woman, infant and suckling, ox and sheep, camel and ass." If a modern general were to give such an order, he would be considered a monster of iniquity. But the early Jewish writers imagined that the cruelty and fierceness of their own savage natures were actually characteristics of the Deity. Or look at Numbers xv. 32-36: "While the children of Israel were in the wilderness, they found a man that gathered sticks upon the Sabbath-day. And they brought him to Moses and Aaron, and unto all the congregation. And they put him in ward, because it was not declared what should be done unto him. And the Lord said unto Moses, The man shall surely be put to death: all the congregation shall stone him with stones without the camp. And all the congregation brought him without the camp, and stoned him with stones, and he died; as the Lord commanded Moses." What do you suppose Christ would have thought of such proceedings?

Here, perhaps, I ought to say a word in extenuation of these early writers. At first sight it may appear as if they were dishonest, not to say blasphemous, in so boldly announcing that their own crude opinions were the opinions of the Lord, in justifying their own cruelty by the assertion that they were fulfilling the divine behests. But I must point out to you that by all such expressions as "Thus saith the Lord," they merely meant to assert the strength of their own conscientious convictions. We ourselves speak of conscience as the voice of God, and yet we know that we have sometimes done conscientiously what we afterwards discovered to be wrong. Many of the greatest crimes in history, such as the tortures of the Inquisition, have been perpetrated by those who felt perfectly certain that they were acting in harmony with the will of God. I do not want you to condemn these Old Testament writers; I only want you to see that their views of God were sometimes very low.

Further, let me ask you to notice, not only do we find in the Bible different theological views obtaining in different ages, but we also find them coexisting in the same age. The controversies between the priests and the prophets of Judaism, both of whom professed to believe in inspiration, were very much the same as between the Ritualists and Broad Churchmen of to-day. The priests observed to the very last the ceremonialism of early times; and they were perfectly satisfied when they had offered up the proper number of doves and oxen, when they had duly changed the shewbread, and lighted the proper number of lamps. The prophets looked upon all this with more or less of contempt. The sacrifices of God they taught, the only sacrifices worth offering, were a broken and contrite heart.

We cannot possibly overestimate the difference —it is practically infinite—between the God of Samuel who ordered the infants and sucklings to be slaughtered, and the God of the Psalmist whose tender mercies are over all His works; between the God of the patriarchs who was always repenting, and the God of the apostles who is the same yesterday, to-day and for ever, with whom is neither variableness nor shadow of turning; between the God of the Old Testament who walked in the garden in the cool of the day, and the God of the New Testament whom no man hath seen or can see; between the God of Leviticus who was so particular about the sacrificial furniture and utensils, and the God of the Acts who dwelleth not in temples made with hands; between the God who hardened Pharaoh's heart, and the God who will have all men to be saved.

The Bible, then, cannot be distinguished from other books by the uniformity of its teaching any more than by the uniformity of its style. Between the covers of this little volume we find opinions as diverse and contradictory as have ever existed in the world. And, in particular, we can trace in it the development of the idea of God from barbarism up to Hegel.

Meantime, let me commend to your consideration

one idea. The authors of Genesis discovered the truth—and the discovery redounds to their eternal glory—that the spirit of every man is in degree divine. If we forget this, however cultivated and clever we may think ourselves, we have really degenerated,—we are in this respect in more than antediluvian ignorance. The inspiration of the Almighty, however its manifestations may differ, is not restricted to any age or country;

> "The whole round world is every way
> Bound by gold chains about the feet of God."

Inspiration.

II.

INACCURACIES OF THE BIBLE.

WE are engaged in considering the subject of Inspiration. The view at one time held, even by persons of some amount of culture, is represented very well in the following words of Burgon's: "The Bible is none other than the voice of Him that sitteth on the throne. Every book of it, every chapter of it, every verse of it, every word of it, every syllable of it, every letter of it, is the direct utterance of the Most High. The Bible is none other than the word of God; not some part of it more, some part of it less, but all alike the utterance of Him who sitteth upon the throne, supreme, absolute, faultless, unerring." Or as Baylee put it, "The Bible cannot be less than verbally inspired. Every syllable is just what it would be had God spoken from heaven, without the intervention of any human agent."

Now I was beginning to explain to you last week that this theory of inspiration could not possibly be true. If God were in a literal sense the author of the Bible the style of composition must always be perfect, and therefore the same. Whereas, on the contrary, we find in the books of the Bible all possible varieties of style, more than sufficient to show that they must have been written in the ordinary way by men. Moreover, if God were literally the author of the Bible, it must contain one uniform representation of the Deity; or at any rate, the representations must be consistent with each other. But we find here — as elsewhere — contradictory ideas of God. The superhuman cruelty of the Jehovah of the Pentateuch, and the superhuman tenderness of the heavenly Father of Christ, could not possibly be attributes of one and the self-same Being.

To-day I pass on to another argument. If the Bible were in a literal sense the work of God, its statements must be always true, scientifically and historically true. But when we come to examine it, we find that it contains innumerable mistakes. And first of the scientific errors. I might give you dozens of illustrations, but one must suffice,—viz., the Scriptural account of the creation. The authors of the Pentateuch teach that the world was made in six days. Well, it was not. Science has long since proved that the process of creation must have occupied millions of years. The validity of the scientific doctrine is admitted nowadays even by those who are in other respects orthodox. These semi-orthodox persons are accustomed to say that the Scriptural writers, when they spoke of days, meant indefinite periods of time. But it is manifest that they intended nothing of the kind. The injunction to keep the fourth commandment was distinctly based on the six days' theory of creation. " Remember the Sabbath-day to keep it holy. For in six days the Lord made heaven and earth, the sea, and all that in them is, and rested the seventh day : *wherefore* the Lord blessed the seventh day, and hallowed it."

And even if we were willing to renounce the teaching of modern science, we should still be unable to accept the Biblical account of creation as correct, for it contains *within itself* a number of the most palpable contradictions. In fact, we have in the first two chapters of the Book of Genesis two distinct stories of creation. This is practically recognised in our lectionary. The first lesson on Septuagesima Sunday, takes in the first chapter and the first three verses of the second chapter. That is one account of creation. The other begins at the fourth verse and finishes with verse twenty-five. How these two different theories come to be placed together, I shall explain to you another day. But that they *are* different, and in many respects mutually destructive, is evident on the most cursory examination.

In the first account (i. 20, 24, 26), the birds and beasts are created before man. In the second (ii. 7, 19), man is created before the birds and beasts. In the first (i. 20), fowls are made out of the waters; in the second (ii. 19), out of the ground. In the first (i. 28), man and woman are created together, as the closing and completing work of the whole creation; created also, as is evidently implied, in the same kind of way, to be the complement of one another; and thus created they are blessed together. In the second (ii. 7, 8, 15, 22), the beasts and birds are created between the man and the woman. First, the man is made of the dust of the ground, and is placed by himself in the garden; then the beasts and birds are made and the man gives them names; and lastly, after all this, the woman is made out of one of his ribs, not as the complement, but only as a helpmate for the man. The Biblical account of the creation, therefore, is erroneous, not only because it contradicts the teaching of modern science, but because it contradicts itself.

In the face of all this, it is pitiful to see able men like Dr Kinns and Mr Gladstone wasting their time in elaborate attempts to reconcile the Pentateuch with science. These attempts are bound to end in the most ludicrous failure. If the sciences of geology and palæontology did not yet exist, the Scriptural account of the creation might still be seen to be erroneous, because it contains its own refutation. And even if it were otherwise, even if the authors of the Pentateuch did know as much science as we know, what then? The Bible would be a more interesting literary curiosity certainly, but its real value—as a book of moral and spiritual teaching—would not be one iota increased.

Once more, the historical inaccuracies in the Bible are as numerous and as striking as the scientific. This must be seen at once by any careful student. The fact is established by internal evidence. Different writers in the Bible often give contradictory accounts of the same event; and of two contradictory statements both cannot be true. Compare, *e.g.*, Gen. vi. 20 with Gen. vii. 3. "Of fowls after their kind, and of cattle after their kind, of every creeping thing of this earth after his kind, *two* of every sort shall come unto thee to keep them alive." "Of fowls also of the air by *sevens*, the male and the female to keep seed alive upon the face of all the earth." Or compare again the statements as to the number of people returned in David's census. In 2 Sam. xxiv. 9, Israel is reckoned at 800,000, and Judah at 500,000. In 1 Chron. xxi. 5, the return is 1,100,000 for Israel, and 470,000 for Judah. Or compare again the price which David paid for the threshing-floor. According to 2 Sam. xxiv. 24, it was fifty shekels of silver; according to 1 Chron. xxi. 25, six hundred shekels of gold.

And so of dates. In 1 Kings vi. 1, we read, "In the 480th year after the children of Israel were come out of the land of Egypt, in the fourth year of Solomon's reign." But according to all the other Scriptural reckonings, the fourth year of Solomon's reign would be almost 580 years after the exodus. In St Paul's speech in the New Testament, the period from Joshua to Samuel alone is given at 450 years. Some semi-orthodox commentators have suggested leaving out the obnoxious sentence. But it is needless to say this only hides the discrepancy from the English reader, and seems a disrespectful way of treating an inspired historian. It affords, however, an interesting example of the manner in which men sometimes play fast and loose with the theory of verbal inspiration.

Look again at the dates in connection with Hoshea, as you have them in the 2d Book of Kings. The writer has evidently been copying from two distinct documents, and he has not noticed the disagreement between them. In xv. 30, he tells us that Hoshea began to reign in Israel in the twentieth year of Jotham, king of Judah. This he takes from the records of the northern kingdom. In the next paragraph (v. 33), copying from the southern records, he tells us that Jotham only reigned sixteen years altogether. In chapter xvii. he goes back to the records of the northern kingdom, and tells us that Hoshea came to the throne in the reign of Ahaz, who was Jotham's successor. If now he had said in the fourth year of Ahaz, we could see our way through the difficulty, for the fourth year of Ahaz would be at any rate twenty years from the beginning of Jotham's reign. He says however, not in the fourth, but in the twelfth year of Ahaz, king of Judah. The dates here, you see, are hopelessly and inextricably confused.

Many of these discrepancies, no doubt, are accidental. But some of them are attributed by all eminent Hebraists to deliberate dishonesty. When the writings of the chronicler—that is to say, the author of the two books of Chronicles, Ezra and part of Nehemiah—are carefully examined, it appears that he has wilfully altered the older records. Those alterations were made for the most part in the interests of the clerical body, to which in all probability the writer belonged. He copies large portions, word for word, from the books of Kings and other existing scriptures, but by omissions, additions and alterations, he gives an entirely different representation of the whole course of events. Upon this, however, I need not dwell. It forms no part of my argument, which is simply this: the fact of historical discrepancies — and their existence cannot possibly be denied—disproves, once and for ever, the doctrine of Biblical infallibility.

The New Testament also contains a large number of discrepancies. Sometimes we are able to correct one writer by another; but in any case the fact remains that all the writers are not always accurate. One illustration must suffice. The synoptic gospels assume that the Lord's Supper was the Passover feast. St John shows that it was not. The mistake into which the synoptic writers fell was very natural. It was known that Christ went up to Jerusalem for the purpose of eating the Passover; it was known that he actually had a supper with

His disciples; and we need not be surprised, therefore, that the two were regarded as identical. In Matthew and Mark their identity is implied, in St Luke it is explicitly stated. In verse 15, Christ is represented as saying, "with desire I have desired to eat this Passover with you before I suffer." No reader of these narratives could for a moment doubt that Jesus actually ate the Passover. But He did not. He sent His disciples to make ready the Passover; the night before He had supper with them in the prepared room; and no doubt He said that He had desired to eat the Passover with them. But He did not eat it. He himself was that year to be a paschal Lamb; and on the afternoon of the day on which the feast would be kept — somewhere about the time when the lambs were killed—He was dying on the cross. All this is made very plain by St John. In chapter xviii. 28, we read how, in the evening after the last supper, the Jews led Jesus from Caiaphas to the Pretorium, "and they themselves entered not into the Pretorium that they might not be defiled, but might eat the Passover," which shows of course that the Passover was yet to be eaten. Evidently then the last supper, though St Luke represents Christ as calling it the Passover, was not the Passover, but took place the evening before.

Now an immense number of books have been written, an immense number of lives have been wasted, in the attempt to explain away these and similar contradictions. The task is absolutely hopeless. But even if not, the waste of time would be almost equally great. It is amusing to notice the pleasurable excitement amongst a certain class of persons when, by excavations or otherwise, it is proved that some of the events mentioned in the Bible did actually happen. What is the proof worth? It refutes the theory that all the Scriptural writers were deliberate liars. But inasmuch as no one ever held such a theory, it does not need to be refuted. And even if we could prove that every scientific and historical statement in the Bible was correct, the *real value* of the Book would not be in the least increased. If all the science and all the history were taken out of it, the Bible would still remain the best Book in the world. I shall speak to you hereafter of its essential worth, and explain to you why it may be regarded as pre-eminently—more than other literature—inspired. I do not want you to think less of the Bible than you have been accustomed to think, but only to think differently. I want you to exchange — those of you who have not already done so — a childish, slavish fetish-worship, for a rational, manly, ennobling reverence.

But, I hear some one say, it would have been better had I let the subject alone. Would it? I will tell you a story. When Dr William Smith was bringing out his Biblical Dictionary, being a prudent editor and understanding the taste of the public extremely well, he determined that the articles should contain as much science as was compatible with orthodoxy, and no more. The one on the Deluge was to be written by a man whom the Doctor considered safe, but when it was finished, it turned out to be quite heterodox. There was no time to procure another; so in that volume of the Dictionary, when we look for Deluge, we only discover, "see Flood." This gave time for a fresh writer to be found; but when his article was returned, it was worse than the first. It was not allowed to appear: Dr Smith simply wrote, "Flood, see Noah." How he managed with this article, I don't know. But probably by that time the public would stand a little more science. Now, in the editor of a dictionary, I admire such conduct; it shows great business capacity. But in a clergyman we expect something more than business capacity, at least I do. It is a clergyman's duty—if he be fit for his office—to *teach* the people committed to his charge. It is his duty, so far as in him lies, to remove their prejudices, to correct their errors, to give them ever deeper and fuller views of truth.

I know the discussion of a subject like the present is apt to give offence, and that to two very different classes. There are some devout persons who have been accustomed from their infancy to regard the Bible as infallible, and when this infallibility has been disproved they feel shocked and stunned, they imagine that they should no longer love the Bible as they did. For these persons I have great sympathy; and I hope to show them, before I have done the present course, that, in spite of all its faults, the Bible does stand alone, unique in the literature of the world. But there is another class of persons for whom I confess I have no sympathy. They are not devout, but only lethargic. They have a lazy disinclination to look difficulties in the face, a cowardly fear of investigating their beliefs, a puerile dread of what is stigmatised as doubt. They flatter themselves that they already know as much as is necessary for salvation, and they are determined never, if they can help it, to know anything more. A new idea disturbs, startles, terrifies them. It is the correct thing, they consider, to hold that there are no discrepancies in the Bible, and rather than discover any, they would be content never to open this book again. Of course upon such people my work is quite thrown away. I am sorry for that, but it is not my fault.

I will conclude with some verses of Dean Alford's, addressed more particularly to clergymen:—

"Speak thou the Truth. Let others fence
 And trim their words for pay;
In pleasant sunshine of pretence
 Let others bask their day.

Guard thou the Fact; though clouds of night
 Down on thy watch-tower stoop;
Though thou should see thine heart's delight
 Borne from thee by their swoop.

Face thou the wind; though safer seem
 In shelter to abide;
We were not made to sit and dream;
 The safe must first be tried."

Inspiration.

III.

THE GENIUS OF THE JEWS FOR RIGHTEOUSNESS.

I SHOULD like to express for myself and you our sense of sorrow and bereavement. The Emperor William is dead. He died, it is true, in a good old age. A more illustrious career no man ever had; his work will undoubtedly live after him; but nevertheless his death is a loss—if not an irreparable loss—to the whole human race. It has been quaintly but not untruly said of him, that he made the present century a success. When he came to the throne Prussia was but a second-rate power; and now the destiny of Europe, the future of the world for many years to come, is centred in the Prussian capital. He was in all respects a great man. Great, first of all, from his strong sense of duty. In an essay which he wrote to his father at the time of his confirmation, he said, "To be an indefatigable learner and striver for the good of my country shall be the one aim of my public life." And so it always was. He was great enough to see that it was possible and desirable to make Germany into a nation, and great enough to work steadily for this end, even though it lost him for a time the confidence and goodwill of his subjects. He knew that his subjects would believe in him at the last. He was great in discovering, and still greater in allowing himself to be guided by the ablest statesman of perhaps any age. He was great, last of all, in his kindliness. He had not only the bearing and the intellect, but he had also the heart of a king. His people now feel as if they have lost their friend, their father. You can judge the man he was by the way in which he died. He was lying on his simple camp-bed. He talked a good deal about the army and other affairs of State. Some one asked him if he was not tired, to which he replied, "I have no time at present to feel tired." He spoke of his Fritz, his dear Fritz. He listened with pleasure while they read him the 23d Psalm, and after the fourth verse he exclaimed, "Das ist schön." A noble life! A beautiful death! A glorious entrance into a higher state! "The kings of the earth do bring their glory and honour into it."

We have now to resume our discussion as to the inspiration of the Bible. It has sometimes been maintained that the Bible came direct from God, that He was its author in the same literal sense in which Newton was the author of the 'Principia,' or Cervantes of 'Don Quixote.' I have explained to you that this cannot be. We find in the Scriptures the same diversities of style, the same variety and even inconsistency of teaching, the same scientific and historical inaccuracies, which we should find in any other collection of books written in different ages, by different individuals, under different circumstances. And let me ask you to notice this is no mere assertion of mine, it is no whim of the Broad Church party, but a simple fact, which can be verified by every one of you. You have only to read the Bible to discover that it contradicts itself. I have given you a few illustrations; I might have given you many more, but you can easily find them for yourselves. And one such instance of contradiction alone is sufficient to prove for ever the human origin of the Bible.

"The human origin of the Bible," I hear some one repeat. "At that rate it cannot be inspired at all, it must be a worthless book, an imposture, a fraud. To study it would be a waste of time; it cannot possibly do us any good; it has no right to any authority over our lives." Softly, my good sir; not so fast if you please. Why is it men always will persist in rushing from one extreme to its opposite? Why is it that, when they have got rid of one error, they are seldom satisfied till they have acquired another greater error in its stead? I will tell you why. Because they are but half educated, and have studied only one side of the subject. In men's attitude towards the Bible we find an illustration of the common tendency to extremes. Generally speaking, it is either worshipped as a deity, or trampled in the dust. I want to-day to point out what seems to me the true *via media*. Of course this is to some extent a verbal question. If you will mean by inspired, written or dictated by God in such a way as to exclude all possibility of mistake, then it is evident from what I have already said that the inspiration of the Bible must be denied by every intelligent and honest man, by every one who does not wilfully shut his eyes to much of the contents of the book which he professes to reverence as throughout equally divine. But there is no need to define the word in this absurd fashion: there is nothing either in the Bible or out of it to warrant such a definition. Let us see if there be not some other idea involved in the word inspiration which would justify even the most advanced of us in speaking of the Bible as inspired.

Now I reminded you the other day that, according to the teaching of the Book of Genesis, every man is in a sense inspired, is himself an inspiration. "God breathed into man the breath of life, and man became a living soul." Every man is in germ divine. It is manifest that if this Scriptural statement be correct, the inspiration of the Bible can only be a question of degree. If every man is inspired, the authors of the Bible may have been more inspired than their fellows, but that is all. And what do we mean by being more inspired? Simply that their work stands on a higher level, shows more genius, possesses greater value,—is in a word diviner, than the ordinary work of ordinary men. Generally we do not speak of more or less inspiration. We restrict the term to the more remarkable cases. We should speak of a poet as being inspired when he composed his greatest poems. We even apply the term to ourselves in certain exceptional circumstances. When, for example, a very bright idea comes into our head, we are so surprised to find it there, the phenomenon is such an unusual one, that we say "it must have been an inspiration." Now let us ask, bearing in mind the way in which the word is used in common speech, is there anything in the Bible which would justify us in regarding it as pre-eminently and in a paramount degree inspired? Is there anything which would justify us in distinguishing it from other inspired books? Is there anything which would justify us in applying to it the term "inspired" in a special and unique sense? Yes, there is. The term inspiration, which we are accustomed to apply to anything signally valuable in our own mental or spiritual experience, which we apply more legitimately and in a deeper sense to the remarkable achievements of thinkers like Newton or poets like Shakespeare, may be applied most legitimately and in the deepest sense of all to the Bible, for it is the most remarkable, the most valuable, the divinest production of the human race.

A statement like this is not generally much noticed when uttered from a pulpit in church. People think it is the sort of thing a clergyman is expected to say, and which, therefore, he must say. But those of you who know me at all, are well aware that I am not accustomed to say things because I am expected to say them. Besides, this is a statement which can be proved, and which indeed has been proved. The best proof of it has been given by a layman, the late lamented Matthew Arnold, in his 'Literature and Dogma.' There is one important point in which I do not agree with him, and which I think is a very serious mistake.[1] But this notwithstanding, he has done more than any one else to establish, beyond all possibility of contradiction, the infinite and eternal value of the Bible.

Matthew Arnold's proof, summed up in a sentence, is this: The Bible, more than any other book in the world, more than all other books in the world put together, will help us to attain to that righteousness of conduct upon which our wellbeing mainly depends. Let me explain. Our wellbeing depends upon many things. It will be enhanced no doubt to a certain extent by our ability to surround ourselves with the highest productions of art, by our making ourselves acquainted with the results of scientific research, by our entering on a serious and profound study of philosophy. But it will be determined far more by the way in which we behave in the common and commonplace affairs of everyday life. Our eating and drinking and amusements, our attitude towards the varied instincts and impulses of our nature, the way in which we treat the members of our family, of our community, of our race,—in one word, our conduct—that is the largest part of our existence. Conduct, says Matthew

[1] See pp. 65-75.

Arnold, forms on the very lowest estimate at least three-fourths of life. Upon conduct, therefore, our wellbeing must mainly depend.

Now for rightness of conduct—that is, for righteousness — the Jews had an enthusiasm which reached the point of genius. Open the Bible almost where you will, and you come upon such sentences as these: "Keep judgment and do righteousness;" "Cease to do evil, learn to do well;" "Offer the sacrifice of righteousness." A sentence which sums up the New Testament, and assigns the ground whereon the Christian Church stands, is this, "Let every one that nameth the name of Christ depart from iniquity." And the Old Testament may be summed up in the same kind of way; "O ye that love the Lord, see that ye hate the thing that is evil;" "To him that ordereth his conversation aright shall be shown the salvation of God." The Old Testament, no one will deny, is filled with the words and thoughts of righteousness. "In the way of righteousness is life, and in the pathway thereof there is no death." "Righteousness tendeth to life." "He that pursueth evil, pursueth it to his own death." "The way of transgressors is hard." Nobody will deny that these texts may stand for the fundamental and ever-recurring idea of the Old Testament. No people ever felt so strongly as the

Hebrews the supreme importance of conduct. No people ever felt so strongly that succeeding, going right, hitting the mark in this great concern, was the way of peace, the highest possible satisfaction. " He that keepeth the law, happy is he. Its ways are ways of pleasantness, and all its paths are peace. If thou hadst walked in its ways, thou shouldst have dwelt in peace for ever." The law of righteousness was to be the supreme object of their thoughts. " Let its words be in thy heart; thou shalt teach them to thy children; thou shalt talk of them when thou sittest in thine house, and when thou walkest by the way, when thou liest down and when thou risest up." That they might keep them ever in mind, they wore them, went about with them, made talismans of them. " Bind them upon thy fingers, bind them about thy neck, write them on the table of thy heart." "Take fast hold of her," they said of the doctrine of righteousness, " let her not go; keep her, for she is thy life."

"It may be said that other nations, too, had something of the idea of the importance of righteousness. They had; but to feel it enough to make the world feel it, it was necessary to be *possessed* with it. It is not enough to have been visited by such an idea at times, to have had it occasionally forced upon one's mind by the teaching of experience. No! 'He that hath the bride is the bridegroom.' The idea belongs to him who has most loved it. Common prudence can say, Honesty is the best policy. But Israel and the Bible are filled with religious joy." "O Lord, what love have I unto Thy law; all the day long is my study in it. Thy testimonies are the joy of my heart." Righteousness they regarded as the very essence of religion. To fear the Lord was to depart from evil. This was understanding; this was wisdom; this was the best possession. "She is more precious than rubies, and all the things thou canst desire are not to be compared unto her."

It is a fact then, past all possibility of dispute, that the Jews had a genius for righteousness such as never existed in the world before or since. Men need the Bible as much to-day as they did eighteen centuries ago. It is as essential to human wellbeing as food, or raiment, or home. It has been from the dawn of history, so far as we can see it is likely long to remain, the most important factor in the education of the race. "Every one is aware how those who want to cultivate any sense or endowment in themselves, must be habitually conversant with the works of people who have been eminent for that sense, must study them, catch inspiration from them. Only in this way can progress be made. And as long as the world lasts, all who want to make progress in righteousness will come to Israel for inspiration, as to the people who have had the sense for righteousness strongest and most glowing; and in hearing and reading the words Israel has uttered, those who care for conduct, will find a force and a stimulus they could find nowhere else. As well imagine a man with a sense for sculpture not cultivating it by the help of the remains of Greek art, or a man with a sense for poetry not cultivating it by the help of Homer and Danté, as a man with a sense for conduct not cultivating it by the help of the Bible. And this sense for conduct is a sense which the generality of men have far more decidedly than they have the sense for art or for science. At any rate, whether this or that man has it decidedly or not, it is the sense which has to do with three-fourths of human life."

"This does truly constitute for Israel a most extraordinary distinction. In spite of all which in them and their character is unattractive, nay, repellent, this petty, insignificant, unamiable people deserve their great place in the world's regard, and are likely to have it more as the world goes on rather than less. It is secured to them by the facts of human nature, and by the unalterable nature of things." More than one of their own prophets possessed in an eminent degree that most remarkable characteristic of genius—faith, and predicted the eternal pre-eminence of Israel as the teacher and inspirer of righteousness. "God hath commanded to bless, and it cannot be reversed. He hath not beheld iniquity in Jacob, neither hath He seen perverseness in Israel. Gentiles shall come to thy light, and kings to the brightness of thy rising. Darkness shall cover the earth, and gross darkness the people; but the glory of the Lord shall be seen upon *thee*."

Inspiration.

IV.

CHRIST'S NEW DOCTRINE.

IN many respects, as we have already seen, the Scriptures do not differ from any other collection of human writings. The different authors write in different styles; they hold different, and often inconsistent, opinions; one writer contradicts another, and not unfrequently the same writer contradicts himself; the science in the Bible is all wrong; the history is full of inaccuracies; and even the moral and religious teaching is sometimes barbarous and degraded. I have given you numerous illustrations of all this. With many of them, if you have read your Bibles carefully, you must have been already perfectly familiar. Whatever then we mean by the inspiration of the Bible, we cannot mean that it was written by God. To allow ourselves, even for a moment, to entertain such an idea would be blasphemy.

But I went on to explain to you, that though in this sense the inspiration of the Bible must be denied, there was another sense in which it might be most emphatically affirmed. We apply the term inspiration in common life to the most remarkable achievements of genius, to all the best creations of the human mind. A great poem or a great discovery we should speak of as inspired. We feel that the ordinary, average, typical man would have been incapable of it. The poet, the discoverer, the thinker, seem to us to live more in communion with the Infinite, seem to us to have received the best that is in them direct from God. It is one of the deepest instincts of the race, that every good and perfect gift cometh from above.

Now I pointed out to you that the word inspiration, understood in this sense, may be more fittingly applied to the Bible than to any other production of the human race; for, notwithstanding all its faults, mistakes and shortcomings, it is the most remarkable and the most valuable book in the whole of the world's literature. This assertion, as we saw, was no matter of mere opinion; it can be demonstrated; it has been demonstrated by

Matthew Arnold. Our wellbeing depends mainly upon the rightness of our conduct, upon what is called, in the language of religion, righteousness. And the Jews had a genius for righteousness which has never been equalled, much less surpassed. Just as the artist receives instruction and stimulus by studying the remains of Greek art, so the man who wishes to excel in conduct will turn naturally to the Bible for help. The old Hebrew seers prophesied, thousands of years ago, the eternal pre-eminence of Israel as a teacher and inspirer of righteousness; and the experience of the race from then to now has confirmed the truth of the prediction. The Bible always has been, there seems every prospect that it always will be, the most powerful instrument in the world for the creation and development of righteousness.

All this would be true if we possessed only the books of the Old Testament, from which last Sunday my illustrations were mostly taken. Many of the pre-Christian psalmists and prophets possessed an enthusiasm, a love, a passion for righteousness, which could scarcely be surpassed; and no man can ponder over their burning words without catching something of the spirit of their devotion. But in the development of righteousness, the New Testament has an important and peculiar part to play, the nature of which I propose now to explain to you.

The New Testament may practically be summed up in the one word, Christ. Let us see now precisely what it was that Christ accomplished. What was His relation to that problem of righteousness, which the best of the Jews had been for ages attempting to solve?

Christ did two things. He gave to the world a new doctrine and a new motive. Many sermons, of course, might be preached upon each of these topics, but I have already frequently discussed them with you, and I need therefore do little more than recall to your mind what I have formerly said. To-day I shall speak of the new doctrine, and next Sunday of the new motive.

And first of Christ's new doctrine. He taught what had never been taught before, and what is but little understood even yet,—the doctrine of righteousness through love. He adopted the golden rule, which had been already laid down by Hillel, and He carried it further in His own new commandment. That this new commandment was intended by Him to be fundamental and all-inclusive, can be doubted only by those who, in wilfulness or ignorance, disregard the plain teaching of the gospels. In the farewell address which St John records, Christ three times enunciates this commandment as a summary of all that He requires from men, and declares that their obedience to it would be a sufficient test of their genuine discipleship. (1) "A new commandment I give unto you, that ye love one another;" (2) "This is my commandment, that ye love one another;" (3) "These things I command you, that ye love one another. By this shall all men know that ye are my disciples, if ye have love one to another." If it be objected that the Gospel of St John was of much later origin than the synoptics, and contains a good deal that came from Alexandria rather than from Palestine, I admit it; but I reply, the objection is here irrelevant. No doubt the metaphysics of the Gospel of St John is Alexandrian, but we may be quite sure that the new commandment belongs to the original tradition. In all that the synoptic evangelists tell us of the teaching of Christ, this commandment is everywhere implied. And St Matthew goes even further than St John; for he asserts that obedience to the new commandment will not only be the test of our discipleship here, but that it will also determine our destiny hereafter. "When the Son of man shall come in His glory, . . . before Him shall be gathered all nations; and He shall separate them one from another. . . . Then shall the King say unto them on His right hand, Come, ye blessed of my Father, inherit the kingdom prepared for you from the foundation of the world: for I was an hungered, and ye gave me meat: I was thirsty, and ye gave me drink: I was a stranger, and ye took me in: naked, and ye clothed me: I was sick, and ye visited me: I was in prison, and ye came unto me. Inasmuch as ye have done it unto one of the least of these my brethren, ye have done it unto me." It is strange that those who have read this passage hundreds and thousands of times, should still believe in the doctrine of "justification by faith." The simple teaching of the Nazarene has been obscured by the misty writings of theologians. But if we set these aside, and look simply to the gospels themselves, the fact is seen to be indisputable, that Christ regarded all sin as a form of selfishness, that He represented unselfishness as the whole duty of man, that for the kingdom of righteousness which He sought to establish He laid down but a single law—the law of brotherhood, that His one distinctive doctrine was the doctrine of righteousness through love.

It needs, I think, but a little reflection to perceive the reasonableness and the value of this doctrine. At first sight it seems strange that Christ should thus reduce all sins to sin against one's neighbour—'that is to selfishness, and that He should say nothing of sins against God or of sins against ourself. But if you think for a little, you will see that selfishness implies and includes all other forms of sin. Every sin against one's neighbour is indirectly a sin against one's self. Our welfare must depend upon our recognition of facts, and we *are* brethren whether we know it or not. We are parts of a great organism in which, if one member suffers, all the members suffer. It can be well with us therefore only in proportion as we remember the solidarity—the essential oneness—of the race. And further, sinning against one's neighbour is really sinning against God. To injure any created being is to injure the Creator Himself, whose glory consists in the welfare of His creatures. So that every sin we are capable of committing may be justly regarded as a sin of selfishness; for in committing it, we act as if we were mere isolated units—as if the entire universe, and even God Himself, existed merely for our private gratification. Contrariwise, perfect unselfishness would be perfect sinlessness. It would help us to do our duty towards ourselves. A man cannot injure himself without injuring the entire organism of which he forms a part. The more therefore that we love our neighbours, the more—paradoxical as it may sound—we shall love ourselves; we shall be very jealous for our perfection when we remember that it is necessary for the perfection of the race. And further, unselfishness would help us to do our duty towards God. Apart from human love there can be no genuine love of God. "If a man loveth not his brother whom he hath *seen*, how can he love God whom he hath not seen?" "That is not first which is spiritual, but that which is natural, and afterwards that which is spiritual." And long before we come to love God consciously as God, unselfishness will help us to serve Him. The service of man, whether we know it or not, is in reality the service of God. There is only one thing we can do for the Almighty, and that is to perfect ourselves and our race. Many so-called infidels and atheists are amongst the most zealous servants of God. There are many who—

> "Adore and worship when they know it not;
> Pious beyond the intention of their thought,
> Devout beyond the meaning of their will."

Since then selfishness includes, and unselfishness excludes, all sin, it is manifest that the eradication of selfishness by the development of love is the one thing necessary for our salvation. It will help us to perfect ourselves, it will help us to perfect our race, it will help us to glorify God. "He that loveth is born of God; he cannot sin, because he is born of God."

And this doctrine is not only profoundly true, but it possesses the greatest practical utility. It is useful because of, and in proportion to, its extreme simplicity. Men have generally been bewildered by the problem of evil. It seems so vast, so complex; there are an infinite number of ways in which it is possible to do wrong. Priests and moralists have laid down innumerable laws for the regulation of human life. But the task was hopeless: it could never be completed. All their general principles were sometimes inapplicable; and in the life of every man each day's experience brought something new, something for which no commandment had been provided. In despair they began to restrict their attention chiefly to ceremonial acts, in regard to which uniformity seemed more likely to be attained. This was especially the case in the time of Christ. "The details of sacrifice and ritualistic purity were elaborated with microscopic nicety." One would have thought that the Levitical law was minute enough, but the Pharisees were always refining upon it. The cooking of a kid in its mother's milk was forbidden; whereupon the rabbis forbade the eating of a kid and milk on the same day, lest by accident the milk should be that of the kid's mother, and in the stomach of the eater kid and milk be cooked together. Months and years were spent in the discussion of questions which, from an ethical point of view, were quite meaningless and absurd. For example, it was long a burning question as to what should be done when the Passover had commenced, if the sacrificial knife had not been properly placed. Hillel was made leader of the great Sanhedrim, because he decided the point satisfactorily. The rabbis exercised themselves much—like some friends of ours in the present day—over matters of "Lord's Day observance." Was it lawful to eat an egg which had been laid on the Sabbath? Was it lawful on that day to untie a knot with both hands? If a sheep fell into a tank, should it be taken out, or fed in the tank until the next day? If a cow calved upon the Sabbath-day, should the cow be led to the water, or should the water be carried to the cow? There were never-ending casuistical discussions about Levitical purity and defilement. Did the flesh only of a carcass defile, or also the hide and the bones? Did contact with all the books of the Gentiles defile, or only contact with their sacred books? Which hand should be washed first? Should ablution stop at the wrist? Should the hands be held up or down? These refinements reached their acme in the idea that even the Scriptures were outwardly impure because written upon animal skins. No wonder the Sadducees said, "The Pharisees will wash the face of the sun;" they might have added, "and remain all the while themselves impure." If their commandments had been everywhere scrupulously obeyed, the evil in the world would not have been one iota diminished.

It was Christ's aim to deliver men once and for ever from the slavery of ritualism, and introduce them into the glorious liberty of the children of God. He taught that there was nothing wrong but selfishness, that there was but one duty—that of love. Several attempts had been made before Christ, notably amongst the Hebrew prophets, to find a simple expression which would summarise the whole of human duty. For example, "What doth the Lord thy God require of thee but to do justice, love mercy, and to walk humbly with thy God?" But here simplicity was gained at the expense of completeness. It is manifest that the virtues of justice, mercy and humility do not cover the whole field of human existence, whereas the new commandment is all-comprehensive in its scope. We cannot conceive circumstances to which it would not apply. Christianity includes everything that is reasonable and beautiful and good in other religions; but it supplements and supersedes them all. The great doctrine of righteousness through love makes it, in the very nature of things, the final religion for time and for eternity. What other religions sought, Christianity has found.

> "There is, we know, one primitive and sure
>   Religion pure—
> Unchanged in spirit, though its forms and codes
>   Wear myriad modes—
> Contains all creeds within its mighty span,—
> The love for God displayed in love for man."

Inspiration.

V.

CHRIST'S NEW MOTIVE.

IN discussing the question of inspiration we have seen that, while in some respects the Bible resembles every other collection of human writings, it nevertheless possesses one characteristic which renders it unique. A great many extraordinary qualities have been improperly ascribed to it, but it really has one inestimable merit which will alone suffice to place it at the head of all the literature of the race. Among the Jews there once existed a genius for righteousness which has never been equalled; and even now there is more moral stimulus to be derived from their writings than from anything else the world contains. This would be true if we possessed the Old Testament alone. It is impossible for any one to read the best utterances of the psalmists and of the prophets without catching something of their enthusiasm for righteousness. In the last sermon I was beginning to explain to you the special function of the New Testament. We saw that Christ taught an original doctrine—the doctrine viz., of righteousness through love. The one radical defect of human nature is selfishness: and on the contrary complete unselfishness is nothing less than complete righteousness. In fully discharging their duty to others, men will at the same time be perfecting their own nature, and rendering to the Deity the most acceptable service. The whole duty of man, therefore, Christ summed up under the law of love.

Now this doctrine is profoundly true. I gave you last Sunday a popular exposition of its *rationale*. You will find a philosophical exposition of it in Hegel. But theory is one thing and practice is another. We may perceive the correctness and even the beauty of a doctrine, and yet find difficulty in applying it. As St Paul puts it, we may "delight in the law of God after the inward man, and yet find another law in our members warring against the law of the mind, and bringing it into captivity unto the law of sin which is in our members." In the well-known words of the Roman poet—

"Video meliora proboque; pejora sequor."

It was not enough, therefore, for Christ to lay down the new doctrine; it was not enough to teach men the kind of disposition which they ought to acquire: it was necessary that He should help them to acquire it. And He did. He gave men a new motive. Let us see.

The first thing that must strike any one who reads carefully the history of Christ is the immense importance He attached, not merely to His mission, but to Himself. Every great teacher, with this single exception, in exact proportion to his greatness, has been willing to be cast into the shade by the glory of the doctrine which he wished to teach. Socrates declared that his only wisdom was a consciousness of ignorance, and he constantly confessed to his hearers that he was merely a fellow-seeker with them after truth and goodness. The Nazarene maintained, on the contrary, that He was the light of the world, the shepherd of the souls of men, the way to eternal life, the vine or the life-tree of humanity. It is this which distinguishes Christ from all the rest of the world's teachers. "It is common in human history," says the author of 'Ecce Homo,' "to meet with men who assert some superiority over their fellows, but they dream of nothing greater than some partial control over the actions of others for the short space of a lifetime. To a few indeed it is given to influence future ages. Some have appeared who have been as levers to uplift the earth and roll it in another course. Homer by creating literature, Socrates by creating science, Cæsar by carrying civilisation inland from the shores of the Mediterranean, Newton by starting science in a steady career of progress, may be said to have attained this eminence. But these men gave a single impact, like that which is considered to have first set planets in motion. Christ claims to be a perpetual attracting power, like the sun which determines their orbits. They contributed to men some discovery and passed away: Christ's discovery is Himself. To humanity, struggling with its passions and its destiny, He says, 'Cling to me—cling ever closer to me.' He commanded men to leave everything and attach themselves to Him; He declared Himself King, Master, and Judge of men; He promised to give rest to all the weary and heavy laden; He instructed His followers to hope for eternal life from feeding on His body and blood. Further, these enormous pretensions were advanced by One whose special peculiarity, not only among His contemporaries, but among the remarkable men that have appeared before and since, was an almost feminine tenderness and humility. The 'Lamb of God' He had been called by the Baptist. Yet so clear to Him was His own dignity and importance to the race, that in the very same breath in which He asserts it in the most unmeasured language, He alludes also to His humility. 'Take my yoke upon you and learn of me; for I am meek and lowly in heart.' Meek and lowly He was; naturally content with obscurity; wanting the restless desire for distinction and eminence which is common in great men; fond of what was simple and homely, of children and poor people; occupying Himself so much with the concerns of others, with the relief of sickness and want, that the temptation to exaggerate the importance of His own thoughts and plans was not likely to master Him. And yet we find that He laid claim persistently, with the calmness of entire conviction, in opposition to the whole religious world, in spite of the offence which His own followers conceived, to a dominion more transcendent, more universal, more complete than the most delirious votary of glory ever aspired to in his dreams."

The explanation of all this Christ Himself gave when He said, "If ye love me, ye will keep my commandments." The charm of His own personality, His own essential lovableness, was the new motive which Christ introduced into the world.

He knew that we could not begin with a universal love, and so He endeavoured to create in us an enthusiasm for the race by first creating in us an enthusiasm for Himself.

We must inevitably grow like one whom we supremely love. Now Christ's most remarkable characteristic was self-forgetfulness. It never left Him, even in the darkest hours of His sad tragic life. He was the very impersonation of self-sacrifice, the very embodiment of love. From the beginning of His ministry until the end, He gave Himself unreservedly to the world. It is impossible to discover a single selfish action in the whole career of the Redeemer. He never gave a thought to His own physical comfort, and yet was always mindful of the wants of those who were about Him. He would not use His extraordinary powers for His own advancement, but was never tired of employing them for the good of others. The great Teacher of the ages was not self-absorbed, but could spare time to be kind and genial even to little children. He who found it His meat and drink to do His Father's will, was no gloomy egotist, but was fond of showing His sympathy for men by joining them at the social board or at the marriage-feast. He who was so strong as never to yield to the fiercest temptation, was yet so gentle as to make allowance for sinners whom society would have hounded to destruction. He who had been all His life homeless, knowing not where to lay His head, was careful to provide a home for His mother, even when He was in the very agony of death. He who was in an altogether unique sense the Son of God, delighted to call Himself the Son of man; went about continually doing good; sought not to be ministered unto, but to minister; and declared that He was ready, like a good shepherd, to lay down His life for the sheep. To love Christ, therefore, is to love Love. There have been not a few who have found it possible to conceive for Christ an attachment, the closeness of which no words can express — an attachment so absorbing that they have said, " I live no more, but Christ liveth in me." " Now such a feeling carries with it of necessity the feeling of love for all human beings. They have been made sacred by a reflected glory. It matters no longer what quality men may exhibit, amiable or unamiable; as the brothers of Christ, as the objects of His love in life and death, they must be dear to all to whom He is dear. The true disciple of Christ must think of the whole race, and of every member of it, with awful reverence and hope. If some human beings are abject and contemptible, if it be incredible to us that they have any high dignity or destiny, do we regard them from so great a height as Christ? Are we likely to be more pained by their faults and deficiencies than He was? Is our standard higher than His? And yet He associated with the meanest of the race. No contempt for them did He ever express; no suspicion that they might be less dear to the common Father; no doubt that they were capable of becoming perfect even as He was perfect." And whoever loves Christ will feel Christ's enthusiasm for humanity. Affection for the Saviour, once implanted in the individual heart, will in time impel its possessor to universal love.

I pointed out to you last Sunday that Christ's doctrine of righteousness was absolute and final. It is impossible that it can ever be superseded. The same may be said of His new motive. Eighteen hundred years have passed away, and it still remains the strongest of all moral influences. We cannot conceive of a stronger. With sublime assurance the Saviour declared, "Heaven and earth shall pass away, but my words shall not pass away." I know there are some educated, and many uneducated, persons who think that He was wrong. They imagine Christianity is exploded. They regard Jesus Himself as a well-meaning but ignorant fanatic. I must point out to you, however, that this is not the opinion of any critic of culture and acumen, who has really taken pains to study the Saviour's life.

For instance. Napoleon said, "Alexander, Cæsar, Charlemagne, and myself founded great empires, but the creation of our genius rested upon force." Jesus alone has founded an empire upon love, and to this day millions would die for Him. Matthew Arnold says, "As the course of the world is for ever establishing the pre-eminence of righteousness, so too the course of the world is for ever establishing what righteousness really is—that is to say, true Christianity."

John Stuart Mill says: "The new commandment to love one another; the recognition that the greatest are those who serve, not those who are served, by others; the reverence for the weak and humble, which is the foundation of chivalry, they and not the strong being pointed out as having the first place in God's regard and the first claim on their fellow-men; the lesson of the parable of the good Samaritan; that of 'he that is without sin, let him cast the first stone;' the precept of doing as we would be done by; and such other noble moralities . . . as are to be found in the authentic sayings of Jesus of Nazareth: these are surely in sufficient harmony with the intellect and feelings of every good man and woman to be in no danger of being let go, after having been once acknowledged as the creed of the best and foremost portion of our species. There will be, as there have been, shortcomings enough for a long time in acting on them; but that they should be forgotten, or cease to be operative on the human conscience, while human beings remain cultivated or civilised, may be pronounced once for all impossible. . . . The most valuable part of the effect on the character which Christianity has produced, by holding up in a Divine Person a standard of excellence and a model for imitation, is available even to the absolute unbeliever, and can never more be lost to humanity. For it is Christ, rather than God, whom Christianity has held up as a pattern of perfection. It is the God incarnate, more than the God of the Jews or of nature, who has taken so great and salutary a hold on the modern mind. And whatever else may be taken away from us by rational criticism, Christ is still left; a unique figure, not more unlike all His predecessors than all His followers, even those who had the direct benefit of His personal teaching. It is of no use to say that Christ, as represented in the gospels, is not historical, and that we know not how much of what is admirable has been superadded by His disciples. . . . Who among His disciples or among their proselytes was capable of inventing the sayings ascribed to Jesus, or of imagining the life and character revealed in the Gospels? Certainly not the fishermen of Galilee; as certainly not St Paul, whose character and idiosyncrasies were of a totally different sort; still less the early Christian writers, in whom nothing is more evident than that the good which was in them was all derived, as they always professed that it was derived, from a higher source. . . . About the life and sayings of Jesus there is a stamp of personal originality, combined with profundity of insight, which must place the Prophet of Nazareth, even in the estimation of those who have no belief in His inspiration, in the very first rank of the men of sublime genius whom our species can boast. When this pre-eminent genius is combined with the qualities of probably the greatest moral reformer and martyr who ever existed upon earth, religion cannot be said to have made a bad choice in selecting this man as the ideal representative and guide of humanity; nor even now would it be easy, even for an unbeliever, to find a better translation of the rule of virtue from the abstract into the concrete, than to endeavour so to live that Christ would approve our life."

Carlyle says: "We understand ourselves to be

risking no new assertion, but simply repeating what is already the conviction of the greatest in our age, when we say that cheerfully recognising, gratefully appropriating, whatever Voltaire has proved, or any other man has proved or shall prove, the Christian religion, once here, cannot again pass away; that in one form or other it will endure through all time. . . . Were the memory of this faith never so obscured, as indeed in every age the coarse passions and perceptions of the world do all but obliterate it in the hearts of most, yet in every pure soul, in every poet and wise man, it finds a new missionary, a new martyr, till the great volume of universal history is finally closed, and man's destinies are fulfilled on this earth. It is a height to which the human species were fated and enabled to attain, from which, having once attained it, they can never retrograde."

Rénan says: "To tear the name of Jesus from this world would be to shake it to its very foundations. Pure Christianity still presents itself at the end of eighteen centuries in the character of a universal and eternal religion. The religion of Jesus is in some respects the final religion. . . . After Him there is nothing more but to fructify and develop. All that may be done outside of the Christian tradition will be sterile. . . . Jesus remains to humanity an inexhaustible source of moral regeneration." And finally, Emerson says: "Love will accomplish what force could never achieve. Love would put a new face on this weary old world, in which we dwell too long as pagans and enemies. An acceptance of the sentiment of love throughout Christendom for a season would bring the felon and the outcast to our side in tears, with the devotion of their faculties to our service. This great overgrown dead Christendom of ours still keeps alive at least the name of one lover of mankind. But some day all men will be lovers, and every calamity will be dissolved in universal sunshine."

I might give you many more illustrations to show that this is the kind of estimate formed of Christ and of Christianity by the ablest and wisest of mankind. I must confess however that for the majority of men, who are incapable of critical analysis, of original thought, or even of wide reading, it is not so easy to arrive at such conclusions. Ordinary men get their opinions of Christianity from theologians, who have converted the religion of love into a religion of metaphysics. The doctrine and motive of Christianity have been obscured in clouds of meaningless verbiage. The sweet simple teaching of the Nazarene has been forgotten, and in its place men have been offered elaborate definitions and formulæ and creeds. But, believe me, the reign of theology is almost over. When the din and jargon of its controversies have died away, the voice of Jesus will once more be heard, saying what He said eighteen centuries ago, "These things I command you, that ye love one another. If you love me ye will keep my commandments." And the time will come when all men will respond, as some have even now responded,—"The love of Christ constraineth us." Then, and not till then, we shall have "the new earth wherein dwelleth righteousness." Then, and not till then, we shall discover all that we owe to Christ. " I heard the voice of many angels round about the throne, and the number of them was ten thousand times ten thousand, and thousands of thousands, saying with a loud voice, Worthy is the Lamb that was slain. And every creature which is in heaven and on the earth heard I saying, Blessing and honour and glory and power be unto Him that sitteth upon the throne, *and unto the Lamb*, for ever."

Inspiration.

VI.

THE PERSONALITY OF GOD.

YOU remember I told you that the real value of the Bible had been best explained by Matthew Arnold. His argument may be summed up under four heads: (1) Conduct is three-fourths of life. (2) It will be well with a man in proportion as his conduct is right, or in Scriptural phraseology righteous. (3) Conduct can only be righteous when it is in harmony with the Power not ourselves which makes for righteousness. (4) The Bible, more than any other book in the world, tends to bring about this harmony. These four propositions are, as he justly observes, matters of experience; they can be tested and verified by every man. Let me quote again Matthew Arnold's words. "It may be asked—why, even if there is an enduring

Power not ourselves that makes for righteousness, should we study the Bible that we may learn to obey Him? Will not other teachers and books do as well? The answer is, because this Power is *revealed* in Israel and the Bible, and not by other teachers and books — that is, there is infinitely more of Him there, He is plainer and easier to come at, and incomparably more impressive. If you want to know plastic art, you go to the Greeks; if you want to know science, you go to the Aryan genius. And why? Because they have the specialty for these things, for making us feel what they are and giving us an enthusiasm for them. Well, and so have Israel and the Bible a specialty for righteousness, for making us feel what it is and giving us an enthusiasm for it. And here again it is experience we invoke—try it. Having convinced yourself that there is an enduring Power not ourselves that makes for righteousness, set yourself next to try and learn more about the Power, and to feel an enthusiasm for it. And to this end take a course of the Bible, and then a course of Benjamin Franklin, Horace Greeley, Jeremy Bentham, and Mr Herbert Spencer, and see which has most effect, which satisfies you most, which gives most moral force."

This argument of Matthew Arnold's is quite

unanswerable; and I think that 'Literature and Dogma,' the book in which it is developed, is a most valuable contribution to the cause of real religion.

But there is one subordinate argument in the book with which I do not at all agree, which seems to me to involve considerable confusion of thought, and which, if it were really valid, would detract considerably from the glory of the Bible,—I allude to Arnold's doctrine of the impersonality of God. He maintains, in the first place, that we have no reason for regarding the Power not ourselves that makes for righteousness as a personal Power; and in the second place that the Jews in fact did not so regard it,—that it was to them merely the stream of tendency by which things fulfil the law of their being.

Now as to the first contention that we have no reason for regarding the Power not ourselves as personal, I reply that Matthew Arnold was mistaken. We have the most cogent reason. He knew little or nothing of metaphysics, or he would have known that the personality of God had been once and for ever proved by Hegel. Of the proof you will find a comparatively simple exposition in the last chapter of my 'Belief in God.' To-day I shall confine myself to Matthew Arnold's second contention, and I shall endeavour to show you that the Jews did believe in a personal God.

His argument in regard to the Jewish views of God involves two curious mistakes. (1) He confuses the idea of the personality of God with the orthodox doctrine of the Trinity. (2) He confuses metaphysical facts with metaphysical reasonings.

I. He does not distinguish between personality and tri-personality. Because he finds no trace of the one in the Bible, he asserts there is no trace of the other. It is of course quite evident to those who have intelligently read both, that there is nothing in the Bible answering to the so-called Athanasian Creed, still less to the bungling mistranslation of that Creed which we have in our Prayer-books. But Matthew Arnold proceeds to deduce from this fact the conclusion that the Jews regarded God as a mere stream of tendency. This argument is what, in logical language, is called a *non sequitur*; it is a fallacy, in which the conclusion does not follow from the premisses—has, in fact, nothing to do with it.

There is, as Matthew Arnold well points out, a great and striking contrast between the complicated theology of St Augustine and the simple theology of the psalmists. In his Soliloquies Augustine prays thus: "Come to my help, Thou one God, one eternal true substance, where is no discrepancy, no confusion, no transience, no indigence, no death; where is supreme concord, supreme constancy, supreme plenitude, supreme life; where nothing is lacking, nothing over and above; where He who begets and He who is begotten of Him are one; God, above whom is nothing, outside of whom is nothing, without whom is nothing; God, beneath whom is the whole, in whom is the whole, for whom is the whole; Holy Trinity, superadmirable Trinity, superinscrutable, superinaccessible, superincomprehensible, superintelligible, superessential, superessentially surpassing all sense, all reason, all intellect, all intelligence, all essence, of supercelestial minds. Oh, three coequal and coeternal Persons, the one true God, who by Thyself inhabitest eternity and light inaccessible; one God, three Persons; one essence, power, wisdom, goodness; one and undivided Trinity; open unto me the gates of righteousness." Compare with this the superb simplicity of, say Psalm cxliii.: "Teach me to do the thing that pleaseth Thee, for Thou art my God. Let Thy loving spirit lead me forth into the land of righteousness." The difference is enormous, and it is most important that we bear it in mind. There is no suggestion in the latter case of tri-personality.

But surely it must be evident that personality and tri-personality are different things, and that men may have believed in the former without believing in the latter. There is a doctrine of the Trinity which is at once Scriptural and rational. I have explained it to you in a sermon which has been printed by itself, and which is also contained in my 'Defects of Modern Christianity.' It is not necessary for me now to allude to it any further than to say that the true doctrine of the Trinity is perfectly compatible with the simplicity of the old Jewish conception of God. All I want you now to notice is this—the absence of any reference to the tri-personality of God in the Bible is not, as Matthew Arnold seems to think, tantamount to the denial of His personality.

II. Matthew Arnold makes a second mistake. He confuses metaphysical facts with metaphysical reasonings. He tells us that the Jews could not have known or written about personality, because they had no turn for metaphysics. Now let me try and explain to you the meaning of the word metaphysical, which Mr Arnold does not seem to have understood. You know what is meant by physical: that stands for everything which can be seen or touched, including the human body and brain, and it is very often used to include sensations, thoughts and emotions, which, though they cannot be seen or touched, are yet the correlates, so to speak, of the material changes in the brain. Now the metaphysical is that which lies beyond or beneath all this. In addition to your body, in addition to your brain, in addition to the molecular changes in your brain, in addition to the thoughts and sensations which correspond to these changes—there is also you yourself. But this self, or soul, or mind, or personality, or whatever you please to call it, though metaphysical, is nevertheless real; just as much a fact as the sensations or the thoughts which it experiences. It must exist in order to have experiences, and still more to bring the variety of experiences into the unity of an individual life. Its existence, though occasionally denied, is generally admitted by acute thinkers of all schools. Even Mr Herbert Spencer, who dislikes metaphysics quite as much as Matthew Arnold, nevertheless says, "Personality is a fact of which each one is conscious, a fact beyond all others the most certain."

So that we must not allow ourselves to be frightened by the term metaphysics. We must not allow ourselves to suppose that the Jews were incapable of believing in a personal God, because they were not apt at metaphysical speculation. A fact is one thing, reasoning about it is another. This is just as true in the metaphysical as in the physical sphere. Every man who is aware of his own existence is brought thereby face to face with a metaphysical fact. He may not know that it is metaphysical, but his ignorance does not alter the nature of the fact. I daresay there are persons in the world who do not know the meaning of the word physical—the average agricultural labourer, *e.g.*, whose vocabulary consists of only about 300 words. But he is acquainted with many physical things, whether he *calls* them physical or not. And similarly, though he may never have heard the terms metaphysics or personality, he is nevertheless vaguely aware of himself as a person. It is for him, no less than for the philosopher, "a fact beyond all others the most certain." Of course he cannot reason and speculate elaborately about this metaphysical fact; but neither can he reason and speculate elaborately about physical facts. And so the Jews—though they were incapable of producing the Soliloquies of Augustine or the Logic of Hegel, though they were incapable of any involved metaphysical speculations—were well enough acquainted with one metaphysical fact, with the fact viz., of personality; for to every one of them this was a fact of consciousness. There was nothing then to prevent the Jews from believing in a personal God. Such a belief would be suggested by their own individual experience.

And when we turn to the Bible we find it full of expressions that are quite incompatible with Matthew Arnold's view. The God of the Hebrews was a God who could be *loved.* Listen: "Oh taste and see how gracious the Lord is; blessed is the man that trusteth in Him. Thou art my hiding-place; Thou shalt preserve me from trouble. Like as a father pitieth his children, so the Lord pitieth them that fear Him. Can a woman forget her child, that she should not have compassion on the son of her womb? Yea, she may forget, yet will I not forget thee. The Lord is my shepherd, I shall not want. He maketh me to lie down in green pastures; He leadeth me beside the still waters. Yea, though I walk through the valley of the shadow of death, I will fear no evil, for Thou art with me. As the hart panteth after the water-brooks, so panteth my soul after Thee, O God. Your Father knoweth what things ye have need of. In everything let your requests be made known unto God; casting all your care upon Him, for He careth for you. The hour cometh that ye shall be scattered, and shall leave me alone; and yet I am not alone, for the Father is with me. As the Father hath loved me, *so* have I loved you." Men could never have loved, still less imagined themselves loved by, a stream of tendency. Matthew Arnold bids us remember that in all such passages we have the language of poetry rather than of science, of emotion rather than of thought. But the same might be said of a lover's ode. That is the language of poetry and emotion, and yet there is an objective reality corresponding to it. The reality and the worth of the object are to some extent guaranteed by the strength of the emotion and the beauty of the poem. And so we may feel quite sure that the religious emotion of the Hebrews would never have been evoked by any mere logical abstraction, by any inanimate, impersonal force, such as the " stream of tendency by which things fulfil the law of their being."

Besides, this is a conception which the Jews were quite incapable of forming. The Athanasian Creed in the Bible would be less of an anachronism. The Jews were not aware that things did fulfil the law of their being. They knew nothing about law in the scientific sense of the term. They did not believe in the uniformity of nature. So far from things fulfilling the law of their being by an inner necessity, the Jews imagined constant interference from without. The divine personality, to the Hebrew mind, was too much like the human. They sometimes credited their God with changeableness and caprice. It was an instance of inspiration, as remarkable as it was rare, when the Deity was described as "the same yesterday, to-day and for ever, without variableness or shadow of turning." Such a conception was never common among the Jews; never could have been common before the scientific discoveries of the present century; and indeed it is not yet common amongst ourselves. To credit the Jews, therefore, with a conception which is even now quite opposed to the ordinary man's way of thinking, is a curious instance of inconsistency on the part of a writer who wishes to free the Bible from anachronisms.

Finally let me say, the conception of a tendency by which things fulfil the law of their being, though scientifically in advance of anything to which the Jews had attained, is a very poor substitute for a personal God. In itself the conception is good and true. The course of nature is uniform; things do fulfil the law of their being with the most inviolable regularity. Science has proved this, and in so doing has helped to purify our idea of the

Deity. It has shown that changeableness, though an attribute of finite personality, does not belong to the Infinite. But it is absurd to argue that God is not a Person simply because He is not a capricious Person. We do not restrict the term personality to madmen, and yet their actions are pre-eminently chaotic, irregular, disorderly, meaningless and unpredictable. And to say that the regularity of nature does away with the necessity for a personal God, is to say the very opposite of the truth. Regularity, order, progress, are the distinctive evidences of mind. There is a far stronger logical necessity for *us* to believe in the personality of God than there was for the ancient Hebrews. Men sometimes shrink from applying this term to the Deity, from a sort of spurious feeling of reverence. They say it is dragging Him down to the level of a man. But to call Him a stream of tendency, is to drag Him down to a much lower level. The most poorly endowed individual that ever lived on earth is of infinitely more value, stands infinitely higher in the scale of being, than any stream of tendency, however vast, however powerful. "It is not a question," says Herbert Spencer, "whether we should apply the term personality or something lower to the Deity, the question is between personality and something higher." But we have no higher term. If He is less than personal we cannot reverence Him as a superior, we cannot even love Him as an equal; we are greater than He. He may be to us a matter of curiosity or of wonder; but as for worship,—we might as well worship the molecular forces or the law of gravitation. And any vainglorious sense of satisfaction we might feel at having nothing above us in the universe, would soon be dissipated by the thought, that having nothing above us means having nothing upon which we can rely. If we have been brought into existence by an involuntary stream of tendency, our life can have no purpose and no guarantee. The forces which have thoughtlessly given us being may as thoughtlessly annihilate us. By accident to-day we are here, by accident to-morrow we may be nowhere.

So I claim for the ancient Hebrews undying honour, because in the infancy of the race they discovered and taught the fact—without which life would have neither meaning nor hope, without which the universe would be devoid of all stability and beauty—the fact that the world and we have come from a Being who thinks and wills and loves, a Being who maketh the winds His angels, and flaming fires his ministers, a Being whose tender mercies are over all His works.

The Canon.

THE word canon signifies a line, rule, or standard; and anything which conforms to a rule or standard may be therefore called canonical. The old Alexandrian grammarians used the term canonical in the sense of classical; they applied it and restricted it to the best Greek authors, whose writings they regarded as models of excellence. Theologians have used the term canonical in the sense of inspired; and by the canon of Scripture is meant the authorised catalogue of inspired books.

The early history of the Hebrew canon is unfortunately veiled in obscurity. Something was probably done by Ezra, and still more by Nehemiah, in the way of collecting the religious writings of the Jews. Tradition asserts that Ezra got together the books of the Pentateuch under the title of the Law of Moses, and that Nehemiah added to this collection some of the historical books, some of the Psalms, and some of the prophets. But the first definite mention of a recognised collection of sacred writings is found about two hundred years before Christ in the writings of Jesus, the son of Sirach, who speaks of the law, the prophets, and the other books of the Fathers. We have no means of discovering, however, exactly which books were included in this collection. It is not till the time of Josephus, near the end of the first century, A.D., that we find a complete enumeration of the books which were regarded by the Jews as canonical. The list which Josephus gives corresponds with that which we have in our own Old Testament.

Of the three divisions mentioned by Jesus Sirach, the Jews long continued to venerate the first most highly. This division contained the Pentateuch, and was called the law. According to Philo, it was inspired in a way peculiar to itself. The second division, called the prophets, comprised, in the time of Josephus, Joshua, Judges, Samuel, Kings, which were designated the former prophets, as well as Isaiah, Jeremiah, Ezekiel, and the twelve minor prophets. Ruth originally formed part of Judges, and Lamentations part of Jeremiah. The books in this second division—probably because they were of later origin—were much less esteemed than those in the first; but they were nevertheless read in the public services along with the law. The third division, which Sirach simply calls the rest of the books, afterwards received a title of its own —viz., Chethubim in Hebrew, and Hagiographa in Greek. This division contained the Psalms, Proverbs, Job, Canticles, Ezra, Nehemiah, Chronicles, Esther and Daniel. The books in the third class were regarded by the Jews much as the Apocrypha is now regarded in the Church of England. They were considered of very inferior merit and authority, and with the exception of Esther none of them were read in public.

This canon, though generally recognised, was not considered irrevocably settled till quite the end of the first century. Up to that time the claims of several of the books were hotly discussed. Even Ezekiel, though belonging to the intermediate division, gave offence because some of its statements seemed to contradict the law. Esther was impugned, on the ground that the name of God was never once mentioned in it, and that therefore it could have nothing to do with religion. Some objected to the book of Proverbs because of its inconsistencies; others considered Ecclesiastes heretical; and others again declared that Canticles was sensual. Owing to this critical and sceptical spirit on the part of the Jewish rabbis, the suspected works were in danger of being altogether excluded from the canon. However, in A.D. 90, at a synod or council—these, you know, are the ecclesiastical terms for a committee—at a synod held in Jamnia, it was decided by a majority of votes that the books which had given offence should be formally sanctioned as canonical. We should like to know, but of course we cannot, the qualifications of each member of this synod. We do know, however, that one of the majority—R. Akibee—spoke of the Song of Songs as follows: "No day in the whole history of the world is of so much worth as the one in which the Canticles was given to Israel; for all the scriptures are holy, but the Song of Songs is most holy!"

The decision of the synod of Jamnia was never publicly challenged. A few individual critics continued to be sceptical, but their scepticism had little or no effect upon the current opinion. The third division of the canon was still for a while regarded as relatively inferior; but by degrees all the books that had been declared canonical came to be regarded as equally sacred. The canon adopted at Jamnia—the Palestinian canon, as it is called—has never since been altered.

But there is another canon—viz., the Alexandrian—which was made by the Jews of the dispersion, and which contains the Apocrypha. This word means concealed; and the books were so called because, like those contained in the third division of the Palestinian canon, they were not read in the public services. These apocryphal books are first found in a collected form in the Septuagint. This is a Greek version of the Hebrew Scriptures, which was made in Alexandria in the reign of Ptolemy Philadelphus; and it receives its name from the fact that seventy scholars were engaged in its production. This version, besides translations of the books recognised in the Palestinian canon, contains also a number of more recent writings, many of which were composed originally in Greek, others in Chaldee or Syriac, but few if any in Hebrew. These later productions were never accepted as canonical by the Palestinian Jews, partly from their aversion to Greek literature, and partly because they supposed the prophetic spirit to have ceased with the last of their own prophets.

The apocryphal books, however, were adopted in the early Christian Church. The Fathers for the first three centuries knew nothing of Hebrew. They used the Greek version of the Old Testament therefore; and from this version the translation into Latin called the Vulgate was afterwards made.

The early Fathers constantly quote the Apocrypha with the same respect as the rest of the Bible. The Council of Carthage, at which St Augustine was present and which was held at the end of the fourth century, mentions the apocryphal writings in its enumeration of the canonical Scriptures. And this decision was afterwards confirmed in 1546 by the Council of Trent, which added an anathema against those who did not receive as canonical all the specified books. According to this council, recognising the canonicity of the Apocrypha is part of what we must do to be saved. The Church of England, since its secession from the Church of Rome, refuses to admit the authority of the Council of Trent. In fact it only recognises the authority of four councils, in the decisions of which its own doctrines find support, those viz. of Nicea, Constantinople, Ephesus, and Chalcedon. In regard to the apocryphal books our Church, like the Lutheran, allows them to form part of the Bible, but denies their inspiration and therefore excludes them from the canon. In other words the English Church has adopted the Palestinian canon and not the Alexandrian. According to the sixth article, the apocryphal books are to be read for example of life and instruction of manners, but are not to be applied to establish any doctrine. The Reformed

Churches of the Continent advocate a strict separation of the two classes of books, and maintain that the Apocrypha should be excluded from the Bible altogether. The British and Foreign Bible Society has adopted for about forty years the practice of circulating the canonical books alone. They were led to take this course chiefly, I believe, through the clamour of their Scotch subscribers.

It is, however, quite impossible to draw any definite line of demarcation between the apocryphal books and the rest of the Old Testament. We are justified in the attempt neither by the authority of the early Church nor by common-sense. Perhaps no man did so much in ancient times as Jerome to make a wide distinction between the canonical and apocryphal books. Hence he is reckoned the bulwark of orthodoxy by writers who maintain the absolute validity of the Hebrew canon. Yet Jerome himself uses the apocryphal books in the same way as the canonical. In one passage he quotes Sirach between Matthew and Luke; and he generally introduces quotations from the Apocrypha with the words—"as the Scripture saith." No doubt some of the apocryphal writings are vastly inferior to some of the canonical, but others again are in some respects superior. Compare, for example, the Book of Wisdom with the Book of Ecclesiastes. The latter, as I have explained to you,[1] was written by a voluptuary and a cynic, who denies immortality and maintains that pleasure is the chief end of life. Ecclesiastes stands morally upon a lower level than Lord Chesterfield's Letters. The Book of Wisdom was written evidently with the purpose of refuting the immoral teaching of Ecclesiastes. The author of the Book of Wisdom puts all Koheleth's favourite doctrines into the mouths of those whom he calls "the wicked" or "the scoffers." In the Book of Wisdom it is the wicked who describe human life as short and miserable; it is they who call it madness. It is the wicked who assert that we shall be hereafter as though we had never been; that death and life are determined by chance; that our body will finally be turned into ashes and our spirit vanish into soft air; and that beyond the grave there is nothing but oblivion awaiting us. It is the wicked who say, "Let us enjoy the good things that are present; let us fill ourselves with costly wine and ointment." In the Book of Wisdom Koheleth is over and over again contradicted point-blank. For example, in reply to his assertion that he never succeeded in finding a single good woman, the writer of the Book of Wisdom observes sarcastically that those who despise wisdom must expect

[1] See my 'Agnosticism.'

to have foolish wives. And in reply to the assertion that the wise man dieth as the fool, the writer of the Book of Wisdom remarks that it is only in the sight of the unwise that he seems to die.

But notwithstanding all this it appears to me that Ecclesiastes is really the more valuable of the two. It is true the author of the Book of Wisdom assumes immortality, but I venture to say no man's faith in another existence was ever strengthened by a perusal of his treatise. It is true that Ecclesiastes denies immortality; but the author deduces for us, acutely and consistently, the corollaries of the denial. His philosophy of life is so mean, so ghastly, so repellent, that we are startled into reflection. We involuntarily say to ourselves—If the denial of immortality leads to such conclusions as Koheleth's, may not, must not, that denial be erroneous? So that, if by inspired you mean orthodox, then it is the Book of Wisdom which is inspired; if you mean clever, then it is Ecclesiastes. And when you talk of "establishing a doctrine," you must remember that there are two classes of people in the world who get their doctrines established in two totally different ways. For one class—by far the most numerous—the doctrine is established when it is stated upon authority; and this authority the Book of Wisdom lacks, because it is excluded from the canon. But there is another class, small and select, for whom the doctrine is only established when they have worked their way to it for themselves. And for this class the Book of Ecclesiastes would have been of the greatest assistance, even if it had been relegated to the Apocrypha. I am very glad however that, in spite of all opposition, it found its way into the canon, because this ensures its being more widely known and read. If it had not been canonical, it would take a brave man to preach upon it!

We come now to the New Testament. The idea of a canon of Christian writings had not been conceived in the time of the apostles, nor even in that of the apostolic fathers. For them the Old Testament alone was inspired and sacred. Justin Martyr, in the middle of the second century, thought very little of the Pauline Epistles, though he esteemed highly 1 Peter, 1 John, and the Apocrypha. But even those which he regarded as most valuable he never calls Scripture. Of the Apocalypse he says, "A man among us named John wrote it." In course of time, however, the apostolic writings, or those considered apostolic, were canonised, that is to say, raised to equal authority with the books of the Old Testament. It was probably considered necessary to have a code of Christian writings, divine and perfect like the Old Testament, to which appeal might be made against the heretics, and which would prevent the original tradition being lost by the multiplication of spurious and forged documents. And so we find, towards the end of the second century, a recognised canon of the New Testament, consisting of two parts, called respectively the Gospel and the Apostles. The first part contained our four Gospels; the second contained the Acts of the Apostles, thirteen Epistles of Paul, 1 John, 1 Peter, and the Book of Revelation. At this time 2 Peter, 2 and 3 John, the Epistle to the Hebrews, and the Epistles of St Jude and St James, were all regarded as non-apostolical, and therefore non-canonical; they were put on a level with the Shepherd of Hermas and the Epistle of Barnabas. In the middle of the third century Origen, while recognising the sanctity of those books which had been already canonised as apostolic, maintains that he was still in considerable doubt as to the worth of the rest. In the middle of the fourth century Eusebius was intrusted by the Emperor Constantine with a commission to make out a complete collection of the Christian writings which should be considered sacred. His list agrees with our own, except that he omits the Apocalypse which he regarded as spurious. But the books which he admits he divides into two classes—viz., the homologoumena, or those which were generally received; and the antilegomena, or those which had been controverted. In the second class he places the Epistles of James, Jude, 1 Peter, and 2 and 3 John. The canon of Eusebius was adopted by Athanasius. The latter however added the Apocalypse, and regarded all the books as having equal claims to be regarded as apostolic and inspired.

I have only two remarks to make in conclusion. You will notice that there is a serious historical inaccuracy in the sixth article of ours which, after giving the orthodox enumeration of the canonical books, declares that "of their authority there was never any doubt in the Church." Some of them, both in the Old and New Testaments, were doubted and disputed for centuries. My second remark is this, there are at least three important omissions in our canon. I allude to the book of Enoch which is quoted by Jude, the Teaching of the Twelve Apostles, and the Testament of the Twelve Patriarchs. Those books contain much that is of very great value, but they were not admitted into the canon, and never seem to have been regarded as having much claim to admission. I suppose this was because they were not written by apostles. But the same reason should have excluded, in the opinion of all competent modern critics, the Epistle to the Hebrews. The exclusion of the Teaching of the Twelve Apostles, which has only recently been rediscovered, is deeply to be regretted. It would have served to emphasise the importance of conduct, on which Christ laid so much stress. I shall speak to you about this book some other time. But for the present I will only say that, if it had been included in the Bible, and so recognised as authoritative, the whole history of Christendom would have been different. We should have had less ecclesiastical theology, and infinitely more practical religion.

True and False Discontent.

I.

IN REGARD TO PERSONAL CIRCUMSTANCES.

"Thou shalt not covet."—EXOD. xx. 17.
"Covet earnestly the best gifts."—1 COR. xii. 13.

A GOOD many persons who profess to be guided by the teaching of the Bible seem to have misread these passages. Judging by their conduct, they appear to take the reverse principle for their rule of life—do not covet at all the best gifts, but covet earnestly the worst. There is a strange perversity in human nature, which inclines us always to do exactly the opposite of what we ought. This is strikingly exemplified in the case of covetousness and discontent. Most men are eager for more money, more pleasure, more admiration; but they care little, if anything, about possessing a more enlightened mind, a more sympathetic heart, a more noble character. They feel far more jealous at the superior wealth of a rich neighbour, than at the superior virtue of a good neighbour. Circumstances often displease them, but their own conduct never. They are discontented where they ought to be contented; they are contented where they ought to be discontented. They are dissatisfied with Providence, but perfectly pleased with themselves.

Let us look to-day at true and false discontent in regard to personal circumstances.

And here we must distinguish between circumstances which are unalterable, and circumstances which are capable of being modified and changed. In matters of the first kind all discontent is bad and foolish. It not only does no good, but it does actual harm; it positively increases the evil at which we grumble. The more we think and speak about the weather, *c.g.*, the more detestable it appears—at least in England, where weather generally means bad weather; while if we had been thinking and speaking of something else we should probably have forgotten all about our atmospheric surroundings.

"Things without remedy should be without regard."

No doubt discontent may be in some degree constitutional, a matter of *physique*, proceeding rather from a diseased state of nerves than from the mind or heart. But even in these cases there is a good deal that we may accomplish for ourselves by voluntary effort. The mind may exert almost as great an influence upon the body as the body exerts upon the mind. A temperament which is naturally inclined to melancholy may by voluntary effort be considerably modified, if not indeed made altogether sanguine. We should persistently cultivate the habit—unless we have it by nature—of forcing ourselves to dwell on the agreeable side of things rather than on the disagreeable, of forcing ourselves to think rather of the pleasures which we have than of those which we have not. There is so much pleasantness in life which the most of us lose through want of thought. It is pleasant to exist, to breathe, to move, to talk, to think, to read. But a pleasure must be attended to in order to be felt. And therefore it often happens that pleasures, of which we are actually in possession and which we might be enjoying, are practically lost to us because our attention is all fixed on other pleasures, of which we are not in possession and of which therefore we can only feel the absence. We are like the dog who dropped the real piece of meat, in order to seize upon its shadow which seemed larger.

Happiness often lies so close to our feet that we overlook it; we discover its existence only when it has vanished and cannot be recalled. There is scarcely a faculty more worthy of being cultivated, and there is no faculty so much neglected by most of us, as the faculty for enjoyment, the faculty for perceiving and making the most of the pleasures which are actually ours. If I were the chancellor of a university, I think I should do my best to secure the founding of a new chair, a chair of Life. I don't mean the science of life—biology—there are plenty of chairs for that; but I mean the art of life, the theory of living well, of living the best possible life, of making the very most of our existence physically, mentally, morally, and spiritually. I daresay, if the thing was to be done properly, we should require several chairs and several professors. But they would all, I am sure, insist upon the importance of cultivating the faculty of enjoyment. It may be cultivated. It is cultivated, as a rule, in the highest degree amongst the really wise. The cleverest men and women generally find the greatest pleasure in little things. Indeed, to my mind, this is one of the tests of greatness.

> " Endow the fool with sun and moon,
>   Being his, he holds them mean and low;
> But to the wise a little boon
>   Is great, because the giver's so."

One thing that tends to make people discontented is, that they expect too much happiness, especially of an ecstatic and extraordinary kind. We take an exaggerated view of our right to happiness. We think we deserve it, we think we ought to have it, and that we are hardly dealt with if it is denied us. "The whim we have of happiness is somewhat thus. By certain valuations and averages of our own striking, we come upon some sort of average terrestrial lot; this we fancy belongs to us by nature and of indefeasible right. It is simple payment of our wages, of our deserts; requires neither thanks nor complaint; only such *overplus* as there may be do we account happiness; any *deficit*, again, is misery. Now consider that we make the valuation of our own deserts and ourselves, and what a fund of self-conceit there is in each of us, do you wonder that the balance should so often dip the wrong way, and many a blockhead cry, See, there, what a payment! was ever worthy gentleman so used? I tell thee, blockhead, it all comes of thy vanity, of what thou fanciest those same deserts of thine to be. Fancy that thou deservest to be hanged, as is most likely, thou wilt feel it happiness to be only shot; fancy that thou deservest to be hanged in a hair-halter, and it will be luxury to die in hemp. So true is it that the fraction of life can be increased in value, not so much by increasing your numerator as by lessening your denominator; nay, unless my algebra deceives me, unity itself divided by zero will give infinity. Make thy claim of wages a zero then, and thou hast the world under thy feet. Well did the wisest of our time write, it is only with renunciation that life, properly speaking, can be said to begin."

O. W. Holmes has less quaintly but very forcibly expressed the same truth. "When one of us, who has been led by native vanity or senseless flattery to think himself or herself possessed of talent, arrives at the full and final conclusion that he or she is really dull, it is one of the most tranquillising and blessed convictions that can enter a mortal's mind. All our failures, our shortcomings, our strange disappointments in the effect of our efforts, are lifted from our bruised shoulders, like Christian's pack, at the feet of that Omnipotence which has seen fit to deny us the pleasant gift of high intelligence, with which one look may overflow us in a wider sphere of being."

Another thing that tends to make us discontented is that we overestimate the importance of happiness. We hold an erroneous view as to the desirability of being *always* happy. Happiness is a good thing, a very good thing; and we should always—

pace the ascetics—take it most thankfully when we can get it. But it is not the only good thing in the universe. Unhappiness may sometimes be a good, may be even better and more useful than happiness. Some amount of misery is without doubt essential for the development of the individual and the race. " I asked myself — what is this that, ever since earliest years, thou hast been fretting and fuming, and lamenting, and self-tormenting, on account of? Say, in a word, is it not because thou art not happy? Because the Thou, sweet gentleman, is not sufficiently honoured, nourished, soft-bedded, and lovingly cared for? Foolish soul! What act of legislation was there that thou shouldst be happy? A little while ago thou hadst no right to be at all. What if thou wert born and predestined not to be happy, but to be unhappy? Art thou nothing other than a vulture then, that fliest through the universe seeking after something to eat, and shrieking dolefully because carrion enough is not given to thee? Close thy Byron, open thy Goethe. There is in man a higher than the love of happiness; he can do without happiness, and instead thereof find blessedness! Was it not to preach forth this same higher, that sages and martyrs, the poet and the priest in all times, have spoken and suffered; bearing testimony through life and through death of the God-like that is in man, and how in the God-like only has he strength and freedom? Which God-inspired doctrine thou also art honoured to be taught, and broken with manifold afflictions, even till thou become contrite and learn it! Thank destiny for these; thankfully bear what yet remains, thou hadst need of them; the Self in thee needed to be annihilated. By benignant fever-paroxysms is life rooting out the deep-seated chronic disease and triumphs over death. On the roaring billows of time thou art not engulfed, but borne aloft into the azure of eternity. Love not pleasure, love God. This is the everlasting yea, wherein all contradictions are solved, wherein whoso walks and works it is well with him."

Close thy Byron, open thy Goethe! One does not like to say anything against the dead, and I feel specially loath to say anything against Byron to-day, when his centenary is being celebrated. He no doubt did a great work politically for Greece; he was no doubt a poet of the highest rank; he could ill be spared from our national literature; but notwithstanding all this it must be said, for it is true, that his theory of life was rotten to the core. He seems to have held that he had a right to an infinite amount of happiness, and that he was at liberty to whine and howl if he did not get it, even though his own conduct must have inevitably made him wretched in any rational universe of which it is possible to conceive.

There is another reason why we are much less happy, and therefore much less contented, than we might be. It is this. We have not learnt to take enough pleasure in the pleasure of other people. The professors of life to whom I have before referred would, I am quite sure, not only insist upon the importance of cultivating the faculty of enjoyment with a view to making the most of our own pleasures, but would also urge its cultivation with a view to making the most of the pleasures of others. "The heart," says a Japanese proverb, "makes the world." What we find the world will depend very much upon what the world finds us. Doing our duty as Christians, learning to live in the lives of others, is one of the surest means towards living a happy life of our own. In this way our pleasures will be increased and our pains diminished ten thousand fold. This is finely illustrated in one of Adelaide Proctor's poems, where an old man is relating the story of his life to his little niece :—

> "Hark! the wind among the cedars
> Waves their white arms to and fro;
> I remember how I watched them
> Sixty Christmas days ago;

> Then I dreamt a glorious vision
>   Of great deeds to crown each year;
> Sixty Christmas days have found me
>   Useless, helpless, blind—and here!"

He goes on to relate to her how his soldier-brother had won the fame and renown which he himself had failed to win. And then he says—

> "Since the crown on him had fallen,
>   Victor in a noble strife,
> I could live and die contented
>   With my poor ignoble life.
> I am proud to be his brother,
>   Proud to think that hope was true;
> Though I longed and strove so vainly,
>   What I failed in he could do."

The secret of contentment is, as I before intimated, the secret of happiness. You remember the conversation between the keeper and King Henry VI.:—

> "*Keeper.* Ay, but thou talkest as if thou wert a king.
> *King Henry.* Why, so I am, in mind; and that's enough.
> *Keeper.* But, if thou be a king, where is thy crown?
> *King Henry.* My crown is in my heart, not on my head;
> Not deck'd with diamonds and Indian stones,
> Nor to be seen: my crown is call'd content;
> A crown it is, that seldom kings enjoy."

But there is another side to this question. Though it is very undesirable to fret and grumble over circumstances which cannot be changed, yet it is most desirable, in so far as our condition is capable of being improved, that we should be sufficiently discontented with it to effect this improvement. The morbid discontent enervates and paralyses. The healthy discontent stimulates and encourages. Instead of lamenting that our circumstances are not made better for us by accident or by Providence, we should set about endeavouring to make them better for ourselves. We should always be trying to improve them. No one who is capable of earning £200 a-year should be content with earning £100. No one who can make £10,000 a-year should be satisfied with £5000. No one who is worth £100,000 should be willing to take £50,000. And so with regard to position. Every one who is capable of rising to the top of the tree in his profession should be discontented—with a healthy, manly discontent—so long as he finds himself only in the middle.

"The present is enough for common souls"—and for common souls only. This rivalry, this desire to get on, this determination to outstrip if possible our neighbours, is in reality good for the world at large no less than for the individual whom it inspires. Landor truly says: "Those who are satisfied sit still and do nothing; those who are not satisfied are the sole benefactors of the world." If you would like to see this proved, you had better read Mallock's 'Social Equality.' "The human character," as he remarks, " is so constituted that, without the desire of inequality as a motive, the higher forms of skill or even of application are unproducible. In spite of the modest life characteristic of the scientific student, in spite of the absence in it of struggle for wealth, or perhaps more properly I may say, because of this absence, we can clearly detect in it marks of a tendency, in proportion as exceptional power is felt, not only to use this power, but to claim a position corresponding to it. Let a man of science who has made some great discovery have this discovery claimed for an inferior and later rival, and his indignation will afford a singular revelation to us. He will feel, and very rightly, that he has been defrauded of an honour that was due to him; and though he may not have thought of it until he finds it to be withheld, the value he has unconsciously put upon it will be revealed to us by his anger at its loss." This desire for inequality, or in other words a healthy discontent, is not a tendency to be crushed. It is an impulse given us from above. It has been at the root of all the great achievements of the human race, achievements which not only benefited the individual by whom they were originated, but indirectly benefited the world through them. But for discontent men would never have emerged from primeval barbarism.

And it seems to me very important that this should be borne in mind in our dealings with the lower classes. The first thing we have to do is to make them discontented,—discontented with themselves and their surroundings. What! you say, do they not grumble enough, and too much? They may grumble perhaps at times about some comparatively unimportant grievances, but upon the whole the worst phase of their degradation consists in their being too contented. They are, to use Lewis Morris's words, "sunk in a fathomless slough of content." I am not at all sure that this is sufficiently understood by some of the university workers in the East End at Toynbee Hall and similar institutions. I am inclined to think there is rather too much of the "hail fellow well met" in their deportment towards the lower classes. It is the most cruel kindness. Endeavouring to persuade these people that they are already as good as their betters, is the most infallible method of preventing them from ever becoming so. If you want really to benefit them, you must begin, kindly but firmly, to make them conscious of their inferiority. The one thing you have to do is to inspire them with a healthy discontent. But there is always a danger that people with socialistic tendencies, in their efforts to produce equality, will be content with levelling down instead of levelling up.

For one and all of us that amount of discontent is necessary—neither more nor less—which will incite us, nay compel us, to make continual progress, physical, mental, moral, spiritual,

"From well to better, daily self-surpast."

True and False Discontent.

II.

FALSE DISCONTENT IN REGARD TO KNOWLEDGE.

IT is not uncommon, I think, to meet with a false, morbid and hurtful discontent in regard to the limitations of human knowledge. Why, it is sometimes asked, have we not been told distinctly and unmistakably whence we came and whither we are going? Why has it not been explained to us how the world was made? Why have we been left to discover the mysteries of nature for ourselves, instead of having them divinely revealed? Why does the acquisition of knowledge require so much effort? Why is the attainment of certainty difficult, almost impossible? And in particular, why have not the fundamental doctrines of religion been miraculously unfolded to us, in such a way as to preclude all possibility of mistake? Why, if there be a God, does He not reveal His existence and His character, so that all men may know and believe? Why, if immortality be a fact, are we not allowed to communicate with those who have gone before? Why have we not received some definite information as to the life that awaits us hereafter?

Now I suppose you and I have at times asked some of these questions. We may perhaps scarcely see the presumptuousness of asking them. And yet, taken together, they amount to the modest inquiry—Why do I not know all about everything? why am I not omniscient? why am I not God?

The limitation of human knowledge is largely, at any rate, due to the finitude of the human mind. And surely nothing can be more foolish than to grumble at this finitude. God Himself could not have made us infinite. And the finitude of the human mind carries with it, not only the present, but the eternal limitation of human knowledge. The limits may be always receding, but they can never be completely removed. The wisest finite being will not to the end of eternity know the full history of any single particle of matter; for every such particle is related to an infinite number of other particles, and by them it is conditioned and made to be what it is. The history of an atom, therefore, would require infinite time to study and infinite faculties to comprehend. And if this be true of every tiniest fragment of the material of the universe which we can touch and weigh and analyse and experiment upon, how much more profoundly true must it be of the infinite and eternal Mind, whom no man hath seen or can see, who can never be fully comprehended except by Himself alone?

"If you will think of it," says Mr Savage in his 'Belief in God,' "it is almost impossible in the nature of things for an infinite, boundless, absolute Being to reveal Himself as infinite, as boundless, to a finite and limited nature. It is not a question as to whether God would like to reveal Himself to man as He is and all He is; it is a question of possibility. The Omnipotent cannot commit that which is absurd. Omnipotence itself cannot make a square without four sides to it. Omnipotence itself cannot make a stick without two ends. Omnipotence cannot achieve that which is essentially and inherently impossible. And so the infinite, as infinite, cannot be revealed to the finite. Suppose a man attempts to reveal to me, while I am in the centre of the continent, the Atlantic ocean,—what will he do? He will try perhaps a verbal description. But unless I have seen the ocean, the words cannot mean to me what they mean to the speaker. Suppose he brings me a bucketful of water from the Atlantic, has he revealed to me the ocean? It is only a bucketful of water, no matter where it came from. He is confined by the limits of the method he uses in which to reveal it to me. So the infinite cannot possibly reveal itself as infinite to the finite. It can only manifest itself in limited, confined ways, with broken lights and fragmentary utterances."

But you would have the revelation very distinct and unmistakable so far as it goes? Well, there is no possibility of an unmistakable revelation. "Suppose that God by an interposition of miraculous power should write His name across the sky in letters of stars, should thus declare that God is, that He loves men, that He desires them to do so-and-so. This would be in some one specific language of the world; and it would then have to be translated and interpreted to all the rest of the nations. Or if it were written in all the different languages of the world, the meanings of words change from age to age; languages become obsolete and die; and so in a few hundreds or thousands of years the starry message would have become meaningless. Besides, it would all along be open to any man to question whether this particular arrangement of stars did not take place under the influence of natural law. If their arrangement into systems and galaxies is no proof of Deity, neither would their arrangement into words and sentences be a proof. "If they hear not Moses and the prophets, neither will they be persuaded though one rose from the dead."

But it may be said, granting the impossibility of an absolute, infallible, unmistakable, complete revelation of the Infinite — granting this, surely we might know more than we do; the occasional discoveries of genius might have been taught to the race at the beginning; men might have been prevented from wandering century after century in error and delusion; or at any rate we might have been endowed with faculties that would make the acquisition of knowledge as easy and as pleasant and as quick, as it is now difficult and painful and slow. Surely this was within the scope of Omnipotence.

I reply—how do you know? Perhaps not. You are accustomed to speak of the adaptation which is observable in nature, and I agree with you that there is adaptation. But are you aware what adaptation implies? Adaptation is the employment of means for the accomplishment of ends; and of course if the ends could have been accomplished without the means, the means would not have been employed. Adaptation is the overcoming of difficulties which are in the way of the adapter, and which, if not overcome, would preclude the accomplishment of his purposes. Everything combines to show that in the case of creation these difficulties were gigantic, and that they are only being gradually conquered during the slow progress of evolution. And besides these initial difficulties, there are others which would inevitably arise from the necessary solidarity or oneness of the universe. Worlds, races, individuals, are not, and could not be, isolated. They are parts of a single whole. Everything in the universe affects, and is in turn affected by, everything else. The development of what we call mind, for example, is no doubt to some extent conditioned by the possibilities and impossibilities of what we call matter. The development of the individual is conditioned by his circumstances and surroundings; and these circumstances and surroundings are conditioned again by an infinite number of events which have been taking place in infinite space throughout infinite time. If any one of these events had been different, the entire character of the universe would have been changed; perhaps, in that case, there could have been no rational, coherent universe at all. And so it is nonsense to assume that we might have known more, might have been more highly endowed, more miraculously instructed, more favourably circumstanced. The problem of creation was a problem of infinite complexity, and how can any finite being dare to say that it could have been more skilfully solved? It may be absolutely impossible for the Almighty to reveal Himself one whit more clearly or more quickly to one single human being than He has already done. It may be absolutely impossible that the circumstances of a single individual should be changed for the better, in any manner that would not involve a change in the entire system of the universe for the worse.

And even if it had been possible for the Deity to give us miraculously more knowledge than we possess, it might not have been expedient. The keynote of the universe is progress. We see this in physical evolution; we see it in the development of the human race. And what higher endowment could have been bestowed on us than the capacity for progress? You say, why were we not made perfect at the first, and then there would have been no need for progress? I reply, an intelligent being cannot be made perfect. He can be put into the way of becoming perfect, and that is the very most that can be done for him. If you think happiness—no, I will not say happiness, but a certain low form of physical comfort—if you think that is the most desirable life, then, I grant, you may logically regret the necessity for acquiring knowledge. But surely comfort is not enough to make an ideal life. If you want to become anything worth becoming, you must do more than enjoy pleasure. I know of one way only, I can conceive of one way only, in which you can become great or good, and that is through conflict, effort, pain. We need not grumble, therefore, at the difficulty of acquiring knowledge. That difficulty is its own reward. It braces and develops the mind just as athletic exercises brace and develop the body. We need not grumble that much must always remain unknown; it is a matter for thanksgiving. If nothing were left for us to learn, life would become stagnant and monotonous, and, for the best of us at any rate, would lose its chief charm. We need not grumble at the painful consciousness of ignorance which sometimes afflicts us. It serves many important purposes. Darkness has its uses as well as light. We develop the roots of our hyacinths by keeping them in the shade. And similarly it is only after we have realised the disadvantages of ignorance, that we have gained the strongest incentive to knowledge.

These are just a few out of many considerations that might be offered, all of which tend to show that grumbling at the limits of human knowledge is a most foolish not to say wicked waste of time. This limitation may be inevitable, may even be eminently desirable. The universe as a whole, and our own personal environment and circumstances in particular, may be in all respects the very best which Omnipotence could devise, nay the very best which Omniscience could conceive.

And even if the limitation of knowledge were proved to be an evil,—there it is, it cannot be helped; grumbling at it does no good, but on the contrary does much harm. We saw last Sunday that the more we grumbled at what we did not like, the more sensible we became of its unpleasantness, and that thus our discontent actually increased the evils of which we were complaining. We saw too that while we were thinking of what was painful in our circumstances, we were losing, through want of attention, many pleasures which we should otherwise have enjoyed. There are few of us whose circumstances are *all* painful. There are few of us for whom life does not contain many pleasures, though they may be of a simple and unobtrusive kind. It is scarcely too much to say that it will depend upon the balance of attention whether we find life to be agreeable or the reverse. If we will persist in dwelling on its painful elements, we shall lose altogether its brightness and its joy. We saw too last Sunday that the false and grumbling kind of discontent had a depressing, paralysing effect, and prevented us from making any efforts for such improvement of our circumstances and surroundings as would otherwise have been within our power. The time we spend, for example, in lamenting a failure, might have been employed in achieving a success. So here in regard to knowledge. There are morbid agnostics who are for ever whining about the limitation of human knowledge; and the more they lament the more they increase the evil of which they complain. They dwell so much upon what is unknowable, that they lose sight altogether of what is knowable. Because they cannot have a physical and a tangible revelation, therefore they will pay no heed to any revelation whatsoever. Because God cannot be painted on the retina, therefore they will not look for Him with the mind. Because they cannot know everything about the supersensible world, they give themselves up to despair and refuse to know anything.

I believe[1] that God has spoken to man, that He

[1] I quote again, with certain verbal alterations, from Savage's 'Belief in God.'

is speaking to-day, and that in the very nature of things, being the living and working God, He must speak to every intelligence that is competent to understand. God has given man a revelation, a revelation in two volumes—volume first, the physical laws and life of the universe; and volume second, the nature and history and aspirations and hopes and struggles of man. Physical nature and man are the perpetual, the living, the progressive, the ever-unfolding revelation of God. God has revealed Himself as existing, as the one, as the infinite, as the eternal,[1] as intelligent, as conscious, as personal, as good, as the father and friend of man. Look over the leaves for a moment of this magnificent revelation, and see some of the things therein contained. The greatness of God, His grandeur, is manifest in the stars, the depths, the infinite depths of the heavens over our head; and even in this world the might and majesty of the mountains, the grandeur of the oceans, the perilous magnificence of avalanches, the precipitous heights and mountainous valleys like the Yosemite; the thunderous grandeur of cataracts like Niagara; the overpowering greatness that thrusts itself upon us at every turn, and awes us with the fulness of the majesty of the Being of which even those

---

[1] So far Herbert Spencer would go.

things afford but the faintest suggestion. In the placid brightness of the moon passing across the silvery night sky; the sheen of the waters under the glancing rays of the sun; the beautiful tinting of the unfolding rose; the more beautiful tinting of a maiden's cheek; the deep unfathomable beauty of a child's eye; the instinct of beauty in man that forms wonderful statues of stone and covers canvas with the creations of his thought; all the infinite beauty of the world; the music of bird-songs; the beauty of the plumage of the bird of paradise; the wondrous finish of the humming-bird's wing; the beauty in the heavens above and in the earth beneath; — and all these things are but glints and flashes of the infinite beauty of God. And then the love of God, manifested in the infinite bounty of the universe on every hand; welling up in the feelings of friendship; incarnate in the mother bending over the cradle of her child, or watching through hours of silent agony day after day, night after night; the love that binds husband and wife together, and creates all the best happiness of the world; the devotion witnessed to by martyr fires, by the heroic struggles and toils and travels and battles for humanity and for right; the pity, the tenderness, the charity of men like Wilberforce, of men like Howard, men that cared and suffered for those whom they had never seen and would never see,—all these things, simply whisperings of what can never be completely uttered, of the unspeakable reserve that is behind.

If all this does not teach us to believe in God, nothing would suffice to do so. It has been enough for many ordinary men and women; it has been enough for all extraordinary thinkers of the first rank. It was enough for the greatest philosopher of this century, Charles Darwin. "No man," he said, "can stand in the tropic forests without feeling that they are temples filled with the varied productions of the God of nature, and that there is more in man than the breath of his body." And again: "The chief argument for the existence of God is the impossibility of conceiving that this grand and wondrous universe, with our conscious selves, arose by chance."

Finally in one word, let me say to believe in God—really and fully to believe in God—is to be freed from every remnant of morbid discontent. It is to believe that whatever is, is best.

> "Yes, in the maddening maze of things,
> And tossed by storm and flood,
> To one fixed stake my spirit clings,—
> I know that God is good."

True and False Discontent.

III.

TRUE DISCONTENT IN REGARD TO KNOWLEDGE.

THE subject with which we were engaged last Sunday was false discontent or morbid grumbling at the limitation of human faculties. Some limitation, as I pointed out to you, necessarily followed from the fact that we were finite; our knowledge is and will always be inevitably limited. And even supposing it had been theoretically possible for the Deity to teach us more quickly and easily and surely than we are at present able to learn, such a kind of education might have been pre-eminently undesirable. But in any case, all abstract considerations apart, the limitations of knowledge which actually exist will not be removed by grumbling. Morbid discontent makes us only more conscious than ever of that which we dislike. We may become so depressed and paralysed by thinking perpetually of what cannot be known, that we shall lack the necessary energy to make ourselves acquainted with what can be known. Morbid discontent is always an unmixed curse.

There is however another kind of discontent, which is not depressing, but on the contrary essentially inspiring. This is discontent not with the inevitable, but with that which is capable of improvement; not with the possibilities of knowledge in general, but with our own attainments in particular; discontent, not that so much must always remain unknown for every finite intelligence, but that we know so little in comparison with what others know, in comparison with what we might have known, in comparison with what we may yet know. All the vast stores of knowledge which are now in the possession of the race owe their existence in the last resort to this healthy discontent.

There is something very pathetic, is there not? about the helplessness and ignorance of the primitive man. He knew neither the meanings nor causes of any of the phenomena of nature. He could not guess which of them were recurrent, nor when they would recur. It seemed as if the earth were the playground of capricious spirits, who made things pleasant or unpleasant for him just as the fancy seized them. At the first eclipse he thought the sun had been swallowed up for ever: during a thunderstorm he imagined that the world was coming to an end; and at all times he felt himself surrounded by a chaos of lawless forces, which were likely at any moment to combine for his destruction. How surprised he must be now if he knows the achievements of his descendants! We have analysed the material world into a few component elements, and discovered that earth and sea and air, trees and mountains, the bodies of animals and of men, sun, moon and stars, are nothing more than these simple elements in disguise. We have marked out precisely the course which the earth and the planets pursue; we know exactly the whereabouts of a comet which has not been visible for generations; we have discovered the law—the law of gravitation, viz.,—which binds all the parts of the universe into a whole. We have estimated with the minutest accuracy the velocity of light and sound and nervous energy; and we have discovered the correlation of physical forces, so that we are able to change one into another at our will. The old chaotic universe has been reduced to order; its phenomena have been arranged and classified;

we can guess pretty accurately what Nature has done in the past; we can predict infallibly most of what she will do in the future; we understand her as well—nay, better—than ourselves.

Now all these treasures of science are, as I said, the result of discontent. Men soon became conscious of their ignorance, soon began to chafe under it, soon tried to conquer it. They were not content to remain the playthings of nature; and so they watched and thought and conjectured and puzzled and reasoned; and the result is that thousands and tens of thousands of problems which presented difficulties apparently insuperable have been completely and for ever solved. These magnificent results have been achieved through the efforts of a few—a comparatively few—inquiring minds. The average man does not inquire. He is not discontented. He is perfectly satisfied with what he actually knows—or with what he actually does not know. "Mankind," says Johnson, "have a great aversion to intellectual labour. Even if knowledge were easily attained, more people would be content to be ignorant than would take even a little trouble to acquire it." The truly discontented man, the man of scientific spirit, will devote his life, if needs be, "to read the secret of a weed's plain heart." The falsely contented man would not take the same amount of trouble, though he knew it would make him master of universal knowledge.

The true discontent is, I am afraid, much rarer in the mental than in the physical sphere. Most people want to get on—as it is called—in the latter. But most people—I think I may almost venture to say most people—do *not* want to get on in the former. Dr Johnson, in his Dictionary, has wittily defined enough to be " a little more than you've got." We all realise the truthfulness of this definition in regard to physical matters—in regard to money, for example, and pleasure, and popularity. But in regard to knowledge, Dr Johnson's definition would often be quite inapplicable. Enough knowledge with a vast number of people, is just as much as they've got. If they know grammar, they rather look down upon those who do not. But if they know only the grammar of one language, they have not the slightest desire to know the grammar of two. People like this, of course, never know anything about science; and they do not want to. They look upon scientific pursuits as a waste of time. What is the good of it? What can it matter whether gravity acts directly as the mass and inversely as the square of the distance, or inversely as the mass and directly as the square of the distance? The scientific spirit they regard as a sort of monomania, or at any rate as an amiable foible. In the East End there are people degraded in body, living in the midst of degrading physical associations, and they are nevertheless contented. And there are people in the West End, degraded in mind, living in the midst of degrading mental associations, passing day after day, week after week, month after month, without ever receiving or exchanging an idea; reading nothing but the fashionable intelligence in the 'Morning Post'; talking nothing but small-talk; eating, drinking, sleeping; fishing, shooting, hunting; riding, driving, yachting; dancing, flirting, sight-seeing—but thinking, never. And they are satisfied with their mental condition. In fact, satisfied is scarcely the word to express their strong degree of contentment. They are proud of themselves. They take a special pride in what they call their opinions—I suppose for the reason that they are specially worthless. Where their opinions come from they would find it impossible to say; but they have got them, and that is enough. They will neither change nor add to them on any consideration whatever. If by chance they hear anything that sounds like a new idea, they shudder and are dismayed. They do not, they naively tell us, want their opinions disturbed. Their poor little stock of notions they regard as a complete system of philosophy, and they pity or despise every one who does not possess the same intellectual treasures.

It is a strange thing that you always find most humility where there is least apparent need for it. I am constantly meeting with fresh illustrations of this fact. I have, you must know, a very large correspondence. Scores, in the course of the year hundreds of persons write to me about my sermons, my lectures and my books. To the great majority of these writers I feel myself largely indebted. Sometimes they point out blunders into which I have fallen; sometimes they draw my attention to omissions, the importance of which I had overlooked; sometimes they give me completely new ideas. Now, without a single exception, all the letters which have taught me anything have been written in a modest and diffident manner. The writers address me apologetically. Though they are really conferring a favour, they seem afraid lest they should be taking a liberty. And the modesty of the letter is almost always in exact proportion to its value. I remember one, for example, the writer of which seemed more than usually self-distrustful, in which it was suggested that most of the topics I discussed in a certain sermon would have been better omitted, and that a good many topics which I omitted would have been better discussed. The suggestion was a good one; my correspondent was quite right.[1] On the other hand, self-complacency and ignorance, impertinence and stupidity, always go together. I sometimes—very rarely however I am happy to say—receive a rude letter, generally anonymous, written in a high and mighty style, simply informing me of the fact that the writer does not approve of me, and drawing explicitly or implicitly the inference that *therefore* I must be a fool. Now I am never quite able to see that the conclusion follows from the premisses. So that letters of this description teach me nothing, leave me exactly where they found me; and I should be inclined to regard them as altogether wasted, but for the satisfaction which the writers themselves undoubtedly experience.

Every human being ought to cultivate a noble discontent. We should be discontented with the present state of the world's knowledge and try to add to it; and especially we should be discontented with the small proportion of existing knowledge which we have at present mastered, and determine that we will continually master more. To add to the world's knowledge, to make fresh discoveries, may be beyond the reach of most of us; though I think we are far too apt to assume this. If you

---

[1] A sermon on the Culture of the Body.

read the lives of discoverers, what will strike you most is not their genius but their patience. You will be surprised not at the quickness but at the slowness with which their discoveries were made. In fact genius itself has been defined as an infinite capacity for taking pains. I suspect that most of us have brains enough to discover something in some department of human knowledge: what we really lack is the perseverance and the will.

But setting aside, if you like, the possibility of our adding to the stores of human knowledge, it is within the power of the simplest and the busiest of us to make ourselves every day somewhat better acquainted with the results of the labours of others. There was a time when books were only within the reach of the wealthiest, and when scarcely any one but a clergyman could read. There was a time when literature was heavy in all senses of the word, and when it took half a life to wade through a dozen folios, from which after all there was little to be learnt. But now for a shilling — in fact for ninepence — we can buy a science primer as it is called, which will give us in an hour or two a rough idea of the scope and contents of a science. These books are written by the most eminent experts, in the most simple and interesting style, and they will quickly put us in possession of knowledge which it took centuries of labour to discover. Make yourselves acquainted with these little books, if you have not done so already. You might perhaps begin with the one on astronomy by Lockyer, or that on geology by Geikie. Then there are other books, a little more expensive but equally simple and even more interesting, which will carry you further in your scientific studies, such as Professor Tyndall's 'Fragments of Science,' or Professor Huxley's 'Lay Sermons.' And with regard to religious knowledge, you have such books as 'Ecce Homo' and Caird's 'Philosophy of Religion,' containing more thought and more inspiration than whole libraries-full of bygone theology. I commend these last-mentioned books especially to your notice, if you want to make progress in religious knowledge. And I hope you do. I hope you do not think you know all that can be known, all that needs to be known, about the Deity. I told you last week that a finite mind could never completely fathom the mysteries involved in a single particle of matter. How much more difficult must it be to understand the mind and heart of God! But there is one thing which may encourage us. Though personality is the greatest mystery in the universe, yet it is easier to know a person than a thing, because here sympathy and communion may come to our aid. In religion, living and learning are identical. To live a really religious life, is to grow in religious knowledge. "He that will do His will," said Christ, "shall know of the doctrine." To think of God, to pray to God, to love God, to do the work of God,—all this is helping us to know God.

> "For meek obedience, that is light,
> And following that is finding Him."

Once more let me urge upon you to cultivate discontent. Remember what Carlyle says, "That a man should die ignorant who had the capacity for knowledge, this I call a tragedy, even if it happens twenty times in a minute." Think of what there is to learn, think of how little you at present know, think of the value and the glory of knowledge, till you become discontented and inspired, discontented with the present and inspired for the future. You will need all the inspiration you can get.

> "The heights, by great men won and kept,
> Were not attained by sudden flight;
> But they, while their companions slept,
> Were toiling upwards in the night."

True and False Discontent.

IV.

FALSE DISCONTENT WITH THE WORLD AS A WHOLE —PESSIMISM.

A.—THE PLEASURES OF LIFE.

DISCONTENT, so far as it regards personal circumstances and the limitations of knowledge, we have already considered. Let us now proceed to look at it in relation to the world as a whole. There is a false discontent, we have seen, which will lead one man to grumble at his circumstances, even at those which are unalterable; and there is a true discontent which will prompt another to struggle for the improvement of his circumstances, so far as they are capable of being changed. Similarly in regard to knowledge, some men are always repining that they do not know everything; while with others the consciousness of ignorance serves only as a stimulus, making them the more determined to know all they can. And the same difference may be noticed in men's attitude towards the world as a whole. Some distinguish themselves chiefly by calling attention to the wretchedness of life; while others are remarkable for their successful endeavours to increase its happiness. There is a right and a wrong way of being discontented with the world. Let us begin with the wrong, with that false discontent at the limitation of human happiness, which in its extreme and dogmatic form is called pessimism. This doctrine of despair asserts that life even at the best is not worth living; that upon the whole pain predominates over pleasure; and that it would have been better for the world and for men never to have been called out of nothingness.

Now I should like you to notice that pessimism is a state of mind which can only exist in thoughtful, and indeed in somewhat sympathetic, persons. Sully says: "From the point of view of what is called a healthy common-sense, all inquiries into the worth of human life doubtless seem unnecessary and even ridiculous. The bulk of mankind pursue their various ends as a matter of course, and never raise the question whether the result will compensate for the toil. . . . The object of pursuit shines afar, drawing to itself fond regard, and inspiring them with the assurance of an attainable good. The world presents itself to very many as fair and rich in treasure, and they rejoice in the fancied security of permanent sources of gladness. They do not care to measure the exact range of the golden rays of happiness. They are only conscious that the earth abounds in well-springs of delight, that beauty and love make the air about them sunny and warm." It is seldom, however, that this feeling lasts uninterruptedly, even with the most sanguine. "The intrusion of unsuspected pain, of a sense of weariness in pursuit, of sharp blows of disappointment, sooner or later disturbs the happy dreamer with a rude shock, and forces on him the impression of discordant evil." But most men recover from the shock, and go on again hoping, as they say, for better luck next time. And even when they feel supremely wretched, they are not tempted to generalise about the wretchedness of the race; they are too busy thinking of their own trouble. So far from believing that others are equally miserable, they are as a rule inclined to suppose that they themselves are exceptionally unfortunate. But in some cases, owing to temperament and environment, men become so morbidly

I

sensitive to their own sufferings and to the sufferings of the race, that they grow quite incapable of appreciating any of the compensatory joys and pleasures. Evil becomes to them the one impressive fact of existence. They dwell upon it and brood over it, till they can think of nothing else.

The literatures of the world abound with illustrations of this despondent view of life. "All our days pass away in Thy wrath: we spend our years as a tale that is told. The days of our years are threescore years and ten; and if by reason of strength they be fourscore years, yet is their strength labour and sorrow; for it is soon cut off, and we fly away." "Vanity of vanities, all is vanity. What profit hath a man of all his labour which he taketh under the sun? I have seen all the works that are done under the sun, and behold, all is vanity and vexation of spirit." We find the same feeling amongst the Greeks. Theognis and the Sophists say in almost the same words—"The best thing is not to be born; the next best thing is to die as soon as possible." Menander says, "The gods take to themselves early in life the one they love." So too amongst the Romans Seneca speaks of death as the best invention of nature, and in this he is followed by many of the Stoics. The Persian poet, Omar Khayyam, gives the following gloomy description of life :—

> " We are no better than a moving row
> Of tragic shadow-shapes, that come and go
> Round with the sun-illumined lantern, held
> At midnight by the master of the show;
> Impotent pieces of the game he plays
> Upon his chequer-board of nights and days;
> Hither and thither moves, and checks and slays,
> And one by one back in the cupboard lays."

In the East pessimism has been particularly prevalent. It forms the essence of the religions of Brahmanism and Buddhism. All Hindu philosophers are possessed by the conviction that life is a burden; and their gospel is always the same—viz., that true wisdom consists in a perception of the nothingness of all things, and in a desire to become nothing, to be extinguished. And we find the same spirit in modern times. Diderot, in his letter to Sophie Voland, says : " To be amid pain and weeping the plaything of uncertainty, of error, of want, of sickness, of wickedness, of passion, every step from the moment when we learn to lisp to the time of departure when our voice falters; to dwell among rogues and charlatans of every kind; not to know whence we come, why we are come, whither we go; this is called the most important gift of our parents and of nature—life." And in England we have had our Shelley and our Byron.

> " The flower that smiles to day
>   To-morrow dies;
> All that we wish to stay
>   Tempts, and then flies.
> What is this world's delight?
> Lightning that mocks the night,
>   Brief even as bright."

> " Count o'er the joys thine hours have seen,
> Count o'er thy days from anguish free,
> And know, whatever thou hast been,
> 'Tis something better not to be."

Leopardi has put it, perhaps, as strongly as it can be put. "One thing only is certain—viz., that pain persists."

Moreover, several systems of philosophy have been produced in Europe, notably those of Schopenhauer and Hartmann, the fundamental purpose of which is to show that pain and wretchedness are everywhere in excess of pleasure and joy; and that this overplus of misery follows inevitably from the very constitution of nature and of man. Schopenhauer tries to prove that the world is as bad as it can possibly be, if it is to continue to exist at all. Suppose, he says, that any of the perturbations of the planets, instead of being gradually balanced by others, continued to increase, the world would soon reach its end. The earthquake of Lisbon, the destruction of Pompeii, are only playful hints of what might then take place. A small alteration of the atmosphere, which cannot even be chemically detected, causes cholera, yellow fever, black death, &c., which carry off millions of men; a somewhat greater alteration would extinguish all life. A very moderate increase of heat would dry up all rivers and springs. The brutes have received just barely so much in the way of organs and powers as enables them to procure, with the greatest exertion, sustenance for themselves and their offspring. Even of the human race, powerful as are the weapons it possesses in understanding and reason, nine-tenths live in constant conflict and want, always balancing themselves with difficulty and effort upon the brink of destruction. Thus throughout, as for the continuation of the whole, so also for that of each individual being, the conditions are barely and scantily given, but nothing over. The individual life is a ceaseless battle for existence, while at every step it is threatened by extinction. The world, therefore, if it were a little worse than it is, would be destroyed. A worse world could not exist.

And further, he asserts, it follows from our constitution that suffering must be the very essence of our life. The things for which we are ever craving will never yield us real satisfaction. Our ardent pursuit of happiness springs out of blind instinct, not out of rational choice. Men do not seek to live because they know they can be happy; but they think they can be happy because an irresistible pressure urges them to live. But all life involves desires, cravings, wants—in a single word, striving; and this striving arises from a sense of defect, which is the only persistent element of our being. Every momentary pleasure is followed by a new sense of pain. Our life is one insatiable thirst.

Hartmann, too, though he differs metaphysically on many points from Schopenhauer, yet agrees with him in maintaining that there is in human life a decided preponderance of misery. According to Hartmann the world is the result of an act of blind folly on the part of what he calls the Unconscious.

Now I want to show you that pessimism, whether it be that of the ordinary man, of the poet, or of the philosopher, is radically false.

In the first place, here as everywhere else, discontent exaggerates the evil with which it finds fault. Pessimists overestimate the pains, and underestimate the pleasures, of life. The theoretical pessimists, Schopenhauer especially, have asserted that pleasure is always preceded by pain. This assertion is flagrantly contradicted by everyday facts. " Where is the want, the longing, the striving, the dissatisfaction, the pain, preceding the innumerable sensations of pleasure which are excited in us during a walk on a bright spring morning? Whether we should enjoy pleasure as much without some previous experience of pain is another question. But we can all probably recall some happy experience, consisting of a long chain of quiet gratifications, from which pain was wholly absent: days of pleasant sojourn among interesting scenes abroad, days of harmonious intercourse with friends in some lovely retreat, afford examples of such experiences."

Pessimists not unfrequently reject all testimony but their own. Hartmann says the opinion of the generality of men on this subject is untrustworthy, because they are inclined to magnify the value of life. But manifestly happiness is a personal matter; and the individual alone can tell whether he is happy or not. The vast majority of mankind, at any rate, find at least so much pleasure in existence that they are glad to be alive. Even those who believe in the superior enjoyments of the next world, seldom evince any eagerness to leave the inferior enjoyments of this—except perhaps when they are singing hymns in church. Now it is of no use for the philosopher to tell them that, according to his theory, they ought to be miserable. It is his theory which is at fault, and not their feelings; about them there can be no mistake, for feelings are what they are felt to be.

Furthermore, many of the commonest and the most valuable pleasures of life are completely ignored by the pessimists. For example, Hartmann makes no mention of the pleasures of work or of laughter. Work he deals with in its painful aspect, where an excessive degree of it is necessary for the maintenance of life. But he does not speak of the agreeable kinds of muscular activity, such as walking or rowing or climbing; nor does he say anything of the keen enjoyment which the student finds in his intellectual labours. No; he quietly classifies work amongst the miseries of human existence. And of laughter he does not say a word. Yet "laughter serves to transform all the lighter evils of existence into sources of after gaiety; it may even throw a glamour of light over some of the gloomiest experiences." One need hardly wonder that a pessimist should be a little shy in talking about it.

"Life seems to include," says Mr Greg, "the amplest conceivable provision for a being of the most capacious and various desires. The surface of the earth is strewed with flowers, the path of years is paved and planted with enjoyments.

Every sort of beauty has been lavished on our allotted home; beauties to enrapture every sense; beauties to satisfy every taste; forms the noblest and the loveliest; colours the most gorgeous and the most delicate; odours the sweetest and the subtlest; harmonies the most soothing and the most stirring; the sunny glories of the day, the pale Elysian grace of moonlight; the lake, the mountain, the primeval forest, and the boundless ocean; the silent pinnacles of aged snow in one hemisphere, the marvels of tropical luxuriance in another; the serenity of sunsets; the sublimity of storms;—everything is bestowed in boundless profusion on the scene of our existence; we can conceive or desire nothing more exquisite or perfect than what is around us every hour. And our faculties are so framed as to be consciously alive to it all. The provision made for our sensuous enjoyment is in overflowing abundance; and so is that for the other elements of our complex nature. Who that has revelled in the marvels of the world of thought, does not confess that the intelligence has been dowered with at least as profuse a beneficence as the senses? Who that has truly tasted and fathomed human love in its dawning and its crowning joys, has not thanked God for a felicity that passeth understanding? If we had set our fancy to picture a Creator occupied solely in devising delight for the children whom He loved, we could not conceive one single element of bliss which is not here. We might retrench casualties; we might superadd duration and extension; we might wish that which is partial, occasional and transient to be universal and enduring; but we need not, and we could not, introduce one new ingredient of joy." Of all this pessimists say nothing.

> "Why wilt thou make bright music
>   Give forth a sound of pain?
> Why wilt thou weave fair flowers
>   Into a weary chain?
>
> Why turn each cool grey shadow
>   Into a world of fears?
> Why say the winds are wailing?
>   Why call the dewdrops tears?
>
> The voices of happy nature,
>   And the heaven's sunny gleam,
> Reprove thy sick heart's fancies,
>   Upbraid thy foolish dream.
>
> Listen, and I will tell thee
>   The song creation sings,
> From the humming of bees in the heather
>   To the flutter of angel's wings.
>
> An echo rings for ever,
>   The sound can never cease;
> It speaks to God of glory,
>   It speaks to earth of peace.

Above thy peevish wailing
  Rises that holy song,—
Above earth's foolish clamour,
  Above the voice of wrong.

So leave thy heart's sick fancies,
  And lend thy willing voice
To the sweet, sweet song of glory
  That bids the world rejoice."

True and False Discontent.

V.

PESSIMISM (*continued*).

B.—THE NECESSITY FOR PAIN.

ANOTHER German Emperor has passed away, after a short and tragic reign. But short and tragic though it was, it possessed a glory all its own. Succeeding in a dying state to the Empire, experiencing every day the terrific progress of his ghastly disease, the Emperor Frederick nevertheless won, in the short space of three months, the admiration and the love of the whole civilised world,—a kingly, imperial achievement unique in the history of the race. No man ever had a heavier burden, but he bore it patiently, even cheerfully, to the end. No man ever had more temptation, no man could ever have more excuse, to shirk

responsibility; but he devoted himself unsparingly
to his duty till he died. You may not perhaps
altogether agree with his policy. You may think
—as I am inclined to think—that he was too much
of a Radical, that his views were too utopian; but
we all feel sure that he did most earnestly desire
the wellbeing of his subjects, and that in all his
public acts he was instigated by this motive alone.
To those who knew him he was very lovable;
kind and considerate, with a keen sense of humour
and a boyish love of fun. He was a brave soldier
and a skilful general. He united in a rare degree
the courtesy of a gentleman with the dignity of an
emperor. But more than all, he was a good man—
one of the best of men; perhaps if we take everything into account, we shall not be far wrong if
we say he was quite the best man this century has
produced.

We have seen (*A*) that the pessimists take an
exaggerated view of the miseries of life. I pass
on to notice (*B*) that they overlook the necessity
for pain.

Some pain is manifestly needed as a warning to
preserve us from greater pain—to keep us from
destruction. If pain had not been attached to injurious actions and habits, animals and men would

long ago have passed out of existence. Suppose, for example, that fire did not hurt, we might easily be burnt to death before we knew that we were in danger. Suppose the loss of health were not attended with discomfort, we should lack the strongest motive for preserving it. And the same is true of the pangs of remorse which follow what we call sin. In point of fact all injurious deeds may be regarded as sins, and the pain which accompanies them may always be looked upon as a punishment. When a man injures himself directly, he really at the same time injures others indirectly, for his own power of usefulness has been diminished. And conversely, when he injures others directly, he really at the same time injures himself indirectly, for his own character has been deteriorated. The actions and habits to which pain, physical or moral, has been attached are bad apart from the pain. And since that pain tends to prevent us from doing ourselves harm, it may be regarded as a token of the wisdom and beneficence of God, as a proof that we live not in the worst possible, but rather in the best possible, world.

Further, pain is necessary for the development of character, especially in its higher phases. I have pointed out to you before[1] that in some way

[1] See my 'Origin of Evil.'

or other, though we cannot exactly tell how, pain acts as an intellectual and spiritual stimulus. This is a fact of experience. The world's greatest teachers have often, if not generally, been men who have suffered much, *e.g.*, Dante, Shakespeare, Darwin. Shelley has said—

> "Most wretched men are cradled into poetry by wrong;
> They learn in suffering what they teach in song."

I have pointed out to you that suffering develops in us pity, mercy and the spirit of self-sacrifice, and that as a general rule the noblest men and the sweetest women are those who have suffered most. I have pointed out to you that suffering develops in us self-respect, self-reliance, and all that is implied in the expression strength of character. Our very pleasures are actually increased by pain; because we enjoy our good fortune all the more for having struggled up to it through hardship, conflict and effort. The kind of suffering then which leads to the perfecting of our character, may be regarded as a still further proof of the wisdom and beneficence of God, and of the fact that we are living in the best possible world.

There is another reason why some amount of pain is inevitable, and to this I shall call your attention in the next sermon.

In the meantime I want to answer one or two objections which may be raised against all arguments of this description. In the first place, it may be said that, however many reasons we may find for part of the misery of existence, we can never account for all. That is quite true. Only, don't you see? if we can discover reasons for some suffering, we may not illogically believe, or at any rate hope, that there *are* reasons, good and sufficient reasons, which will account for all suffering, though at present we have not discovered them.

Further, it may be objected, in the second place, that it is idle to talk of the necessity of suffering, for with Omnipotence there is no necessity. Omnipotence could keep us from injurious conduct without the infliction of pain. Omnipotence could create us perfect to start with, and then there would be no need for the discipline of pain. This objection was very well put in a letter I received last week. "Perhaps finite minds can only learn goodness by means of suffering; but in that case whence came this necessity? If from God—if He made the necessity, so to speak—then He has given us all this pain and unhappiness; if not, then the necessity overrules Him, and takes our fate out of His hands. I should like to believe, not that God cannot help our suffering, but that He means us to go through it all for some as yet undiscovered reason. I should like to believe that there is misery in the world, not in spite of, but because of His love."

Well, now, let us look this question boldly in the face. It is to be approached with all modesty and reverence, for it is the question as to the possible probable limitations of Omnipotence. But it is a question which we cannot shirk. It is a question to which we must find some sort of answer—tentative answer at any rate—if we would vindicate the ways of God.

At the outset let me warn you against being misled by words. When we use the abstract term omnipotence, we mean a concrete person who is omnipotent, and we generally mean God, who is not only powerful but also wise and good. Well now bearing this in mind, let us see whether there are not some limitations which we must ascribe to the Deity, if we would not be guilty of blasphemy. And first of moral limitations. Those who say that absolutely nothing is impossible with God, must be prepared of course to admit the truth of their assertion in the moral sphere. And some eminent thinkers have even gone as far as this. For God, they say, there is no right and no wrong, except what He chooses arbitrarily to consider such. One moment He may like a thing, and then it is right. The next moment He may dislike it, and then it becomes wrong. In other worlds and at other times He may have commanded what here and now He forbids; elsewhere in the future He may forbid what here and now He commands. He might have told us—for anything we know to the contrary He may yet tell us—to hate Himself and to murder one another. With those who hold this view I cannot argue; we have no common ground on which to stand. Suffice it to say that such an impersonation of irrational caprice I for one will never worship. My God, though theoretically He may have the power to do something unkind, yet practically He can never exercise this power. He is eternally prevented by His love. The being, if such there were, who had no moral restraint within, who recognised no moral restraint without, I should for ever hate and resist. He is *too omnipotent* to be adored.

Now to say that the Deity cannot do wrong is only to say, in other words, that He is not absolutely free from limitations and restraint. I think moreover there is another kind of necessity—viz., mathematical, by which even the Infinite is bound. This kind of necessity is so called because it finds its best illustrations in mathematical science. There are, it would seem, other truths besides those in the moral sphere, which Omnipotence itself cannot alter and by which Omnipotence itself must abide. Do you suppose that the Deity could make a square with only three sides or a line with only one end? Admitting for the sake of argument that theoretically He had the power, do you suppose that under any conceivable circumstances He would use it? Surely not. It would be prostitution. It would be the employment of infinite power for the production of what was essentially irrational and absurd. It would be the same kind of folly as if some one, who was capable of writing a sensible book, were deliberately to produce a volume with the words so arranged as to convey no meaning whatsoever. The same kind of folly, but infinitely worse in degree; for the guilt of foolishness increases in proportion to capacity for wisdom. A Being therefore who attempted to reverse the truths of mathematics would not be divine. A really divine Being must be restrained by wisdom in the exercise of His power. There is then, I think we may feel assured, a mathematical as well as a moral necessity, to which Deity itself must yield.

Similarly it seems to me, though we cannot in the present state of knowledge prove it, there may be restraints in the physical sphere equally necessary and equally unalterable. For example, when it is asked, Why were we not made susceptible to pleasure and insusceptible to pain? I reply, because most probably it was impossible. If we knew what pleasure and pain really were, we should very likely see that the question was absurd. It is probable that susceptibility to pleasure can no more exist without susceptibility to pain than a line can exist with only one end. And even supposing it were theoretically possible to separate the two susceptibilities, it might be pre-eminently undesirable that they should be separated; and therefore this separation would be practically impossible for a Being who was not only powerful but also wise and good. Would you like to have been made of cast-iron instead of flesh and blood? Such a metallic frame might have been guaranteed incapable of suffering; and yet, I fancy, you would rather be what you are.

It appears to me then that there may be an infinite number of things which are practically impossible for a Being who deserves to be called God. We are so accustomed to look upon restraints as bad. It is the greatest possible mistake. Restraint may be an excellence as well as a defect. The necessity by which the Deity is, to use my correspondent's expression, overridden, may arise from the supreme perfectness of His own essential nature. Why is poetry so much more beautiful than prose? Because of the restraints of rhythm. Why is a good man's life so much more beautiful than a bad man's? Because of the restraints of conscience. Many things are possible for a prose writer which are impossible for the poet; many things are possible for a villain which are impossible for a man of honour. And therefore infinite wisdom and goodness can involve nothing less than infinite restraint.

But it may be argued, surely Omniscience could conceive of many means by which to accomplish a definite result; and therefore, though we cannot see how the discipline of intelligent creatures could be effected apart from the instrumentality of pain, Omniscience might have devised a plan. Perhaps. But though Omniscience may conceive of many *good* methods, it can only conceive of one *best* method. And God, just because he is God, is necessarily restricted to the last. The alternatives therefore which my correspondent suggests may not be contradictory but complementary. Instead of being opposed, the one may actually involve the other. God may be unable to help our suffering, and yet He may intend us and cause us to suffer. He may be unable to help it for the same reason that He causes it, because it is necessary for our development. The misery of the world may exist in spite of *and* because of His love. We can see that the method which has been adopted for our discipline in life is sometimes good. Does it then require such a very great effort to believe that it is always best?

True and False Discontent.

VI.

PESSIMISM (*continued*).

B.—THE NECESSITY FOR PAIN (*continued*).

SOME amount of pain, we have seen, is necessary to preserve us from greater pain, to warn us when we are in danger; and pain is also requisite for the development of the higher phases of human character. I mentioned last Sunday, and we have seen more fully on previous occasions, the important part played by suffering in the development of self-reliance and self-respect, of pity, mercy and the spirit of self-sacrifice. There is also a further necessity for pain arising from the reign of law. To this point I will call your attention to-day.

At the outset I will frankly admit that, in regard to the laws of nature in general and the laws of life in particular, there is one great difficulty which theists have never been able to remove. The difficulty is this. After due allowance has been made for all the suffering which is useful, either directly or indirectly, in the development of individuals and of races, there still remains an enormous amount of agony, for the existence of which it is impossible even to imagine any sufficient reason. Why then, it is asked, are the laws of sentient existence what they are? There might have been, it is said, other and better biological laws, that would not have entailed such an awful amount of apparently wasted suffering, that would not have involved such an enormous number of lives which come prematurely to an end. The prodigal waste of life in nature is used by Lange, the historian of materialism, as an argument against the existence of God, or at least against the existence of a Creator who made the world according to an intelligible plan. "If a man, in order to shoot a hare, were to discharge a thousand guns on a great moor in all possible directions; if, in order to get into a locked-up room, he were to buy ten thousand casual keys and try them all; if, in order to have a house, he were to build a town and leave all other houses to wind and weather,—assuredly no one would call such proceedings purposeful.

The Necessity for Pain.   153

But whoever will study the modern scientific laws of the propagation of species will find everywhere the same kind of waste. The perishing of vital germs, the abortion of the process begun, is the rule; the natural development is a special case, one amongst thousands." "We behold the face of nature," says Darwin, "bright with gladness; we do not see, or we forget, that the birds which are idly singing round us mostly live on insects or seeds, and are thus constantly destroying life; we forget how largely these songsters or their eggs or their nestlings are destroyed by other birds or by beasts of prey." No satisfactory explanation of this can be given.

It used to be said that everything discordant and repulsive in nature resulted from "the Fall." But that is a doctrine which would be ridiculous, if it were not immoral. It has been asserted by theologians that the suffering of animals is intended by the Deity as a punishment for the guilt of man. Those who make this assertion practically identify God with the devil. Only a degraded being, destitute of the most elementary respect for justice, could possibly be guided by the contemptible motives which were formerly attributed to the Almighty. We have now learned that a vindictive Deity is a contradiction in terms, and that therefore no such being can possibly exist. But though we have got rid of the old-fashioned explanation, we have not found any other to supply its place. We are obliged to confess that we do not know of any rational purpose which can be answered by nature's seemingly ruthless waste of suffering and of life.

The wastefulness of nature is legitimately regarded by the pessimists as an argument in favour of their views. It seems to me the only argument they have which is worth much. But this argument, I must confess, is a powerful one. It does present a very serious difficulty to those who would believe in the existence of a God, who is at once powerful and wise and good.

A serious difficulty—but not quite insuperable. Because, as I pointed out to you, if we can sometimes see that some suffering is useful and indeed necessary, we have then a logical basis for the hope that there may be satisfactory reasons—though as yet undiscovered — for all the suffering of the sentient world.

Now it seems to me that pain is to some extent a necessity, not only for the reasons which I have before mentioned, but also because it is inevitably involved in the reign of law. Let us see.

You all know what is meant by a law in the

scientific sense. It is the way in which nature does things. A law of nature is the connection which we find established between certain causes and certain effects. Gravitation is a law of nature: any piece of matter will attract any other piece of matter with a force which for twice the distance is a quarter as great. The first law of motion is a law of nature: any material body, after being once set in motion, will keep on moving, unless interfered with, in a straight line with uniform velocity. By the reign of law is meant the uniformity of nature. She always does things in the same way. The same causes are always connected with the same effects. Her methods of procedure never vary. Each one of her laws is absolutely unalterable. Of course the laws of nature, as we have expressed them, are only generalisations from our experience, and the doctrine of the reign of law is merely a still wider generalisation. But there is nothing, and never has been anything, in our experience to impugn them; every fresh experience affords new confirmation of them; and they are therefore as certain as experience itself. There is no doctrine confirmed by such overwhelming evidence as the doctrine of the uniformity of nature.

Now there is, no doubt, something awesome in the thought of the absolute inviolability of law; in the thought that nature goes on her way quite regardless of your wishes and of mine. She is so strong and so indifferent! But I want you to look at the bright side of this. I want you to see that a world dominated by law is the only world in which it is possible to live a rational life.

Once men did not believe in the reign of law. They always recognised, of course, a certain amount of order and regularity in the phenomena of nature. A very little experience taught them that fire burnt, that food nourished, that poison killed. And they looked with confidence for the repetition of ordinary phenomena under ordinary circumstances. But extraordinary phenomena, they thought, knew no law: these were determined by accident, or by the ever-changing caprices of the gods. One never knew what those old gods would be at. They sent storms, eclipses, pestilences, whenever they happened to be in a rage. They killed men or restored them to life, worked all sorts of miracles either pleasant or unpleasant, without any warning or reason or rule. They were always doing something which it was impossible to foresee. Now, do you not perceive that, so far as men believed this, life was reduced to an absurdity? There was nothing firm, fixed, steadfast, on which they could rely. They had no ground of assurance or security. They might do their best, and be thwarted by a bad-tempered god; they might do their worst, and be rewarded by the equally irrational caprice of a good-tempered god. Life became a pure matter of chance. There was no inducement to act wisely; a man might just as well—so far as good or bad fortune were concerned—be a fool.

The modern universe, then, with its reign of law, is an infinitely more desirable place to live in than the chaotic, haphazard world in which the ancients believed. It would be a more desirable place, even though the old gods had only interfered for the purpose of warding off pain and suffering. Any such interference, though it might at first sight appear beneficent, would in reality be cruel; for it would destroy the rationality of life. The reign of law no doubt often entails on individuals the direst suffering, and the fact that such suffering is not miraculously prevented, is often regarded as an argument against the existence of God. But it is not conceivable that a Being worthy of the name of God should ever interfere with nature in this arbitrary way; for to do so would at once convert the universe into chaos. The first requisite for a rational life is the certain knowledge that the same effects will always follow, and will only follow, from the same causes; that they will never be miraculously averted; that they will never be miraculously produced. It seems hard no doubt, it is hard, that a mother should lose her darling child by accident or disease, and that she cannot by any agony of prayer recall the child to life. But it would be harder for the world if she could. The child has died through a violation of some of nature's laws, and if such violation were ever unattended with death, men would lose all inducement to discover and obey them. It seems hard no doubt, that girls, young and innocent, like Kate and Lily whom Walter Besant so graphically describes in 'Katherine Regina,'—it is hard that they should be destitute and wretched. Lily says to her friend, "We have done no harm to anybody; why are we so horribly punished? There are thousands of wicked women who have plenty of food and no anxiety. I have prayed, I have prayed for hours in the night; I have torn out my heart with prayer; I have prayed till I felt my words echoed back from the senseless rocks." It is hard for the individual that such prayers are not answered; but it would be harder for the world if they were. The miraculous providing of food and comfort for one person would lead all others to expect a similar miraculous provision. It seems hard, it is hard, that the man who has taken poison by accident dies, as surely as if he had taken it on purpose. But it would be harder for the world if he did not. If one act of carelessness were ever overruled, the race would cease to feel any necessity for care. It seems hard, it is hard, that children are made to suffer for their fathers' crimes. But it would be harder for the world if they were not. If the penalties of wrong-doing were averted from the children, the fathers would lose the strongest motive to do right. Vicarious suffering has a great part to play in the moral development of mankind.

Each individual is apt to think that an exception might be made in his favour. But of course that could not be. If the laws of nature were broken for one person, justice would require that they should be broken for thousands, for all. And if only one law of nature could be proved to have been even but once violated, our faith in law would be at an end; we should feel that we were living in a disorderly universe; we should lose the sense of the paramount importance of conduct; we should know that we were the sport of chance.

In spite of all the suffering it involves, I maintain that the world is a better world with the reign of law than it could be without. I maintain that the suffering which follows from the uniformity of nature is no disproof, but on the contrary part of the proof, of the existence of a wise and beneficient God, part of the proof that we are living, not in the worst, but rather in the best possible world. The uniformity of nature makes us feel that there is at the heart of things neither chance nor caprice but Reason, Reason in which there is neither variableness nor shadow of turning, Reason which is the same yesterday, to-day and for ever. Nature by her uniformity assures us that in so far as we discover and obey her laws it will be well with us, well with us precisely in proportion to our knowledge and obedience. To law we owe all we are, all we have, all we can ever hope for. "Of law," says Hooker, "there can be no less acknowledged than that her seat is the bosom of God, her voice the harmony of the world. All things in heaven and earth do her homage, the very least as not beneath her care and the greatest as not exempted from her power; both angels and men and all creatures of what condition soever, though each in different sort and manner yet all with uniform consent, admiring her as the mother of their peace and joy.

True and False Discontent.

VII.

PESSIMISM (*continued*).

C.—ITS FALSE IDEAL.

WE have seen (*A*) that the pessimists underestimate human pleasures. Hartmann, *e.g.*, quietly puts down work amongst the miseries of existence, ignoring altogether the enjoyment which frequently attends it. And, on the other hand, he does not make any mention of laughter in his short list of what he considers the good things of life; yet to laughter we owe a very large proportion of the brightness of existence. This is just an example of what we find constantly in pessimistic books,—they grossly overestimate the misery and underestimate the joy of life.

We have seen (*B*) that they overlook the necessity for pain. I have tried to show you that pain forms an essential part of a rational universe. Some amount of suffering follows inevitably from what is called the reign of law—that is, from the unchangeableness of the laws of nature. Any world in which it is possible to live a rational life, must be governed by invariable laws. We must know for certain that our welfare will depend upon obedience to these laws; we must be quite sure that the same causes will always produce the same effects; we must be able to rely on the reign of law with full assurance of faith. Sometimes the normal working of these laws will bring disaster—unmerited disaster—upon the individual. But interference with the laws in order to save the individual is impossible, for such interference would amount to the abrogation of the laws altogether, and would at once convert the universe into chaos. We have also seen that there was a still further necessity for pain, partly to serve as a warning and to keep us from greater pain, and partly to develop the higher phases of character, such as self-reliance, self-respect, pity, mercy and the spirit of self-sacrifice. I admitted however that there was far more pain in the world, especially amongst the lower animals, than could be accounted for on these grounds. But, I said, if we could sometimes find a sufficient reason for some pain, we might not illogically hope that there were sufficient reasons for all pain, though as yet we had been unable to discover them. The point we have reached then is this, some amount of pain—there may be differences of opinion as to how much—but some amount of pain is absolutely inevitable for a rational life of moral development.

(*C.*) I come to-day to my third argument against the pessimists. They do not seem to approve of a rational life of moral development. They have another, and what appears to me an unworthy, ideal.

Now it is only fair to state the arguments of one's opponents in the clearest and most forcible way; and I have never seen the pessimistic doctrine as to the essential unsatisfactoriness of life more powerfully expounded, than in a paper which I received the other day from a member of the congregation. I will therefore read you some extracts from it. The writer begins by drawing a distinction between happiness and satisfaction; and, while admitting that there is much happiness in the world, maintains that there is little or no satisfaction. She says: "There may be far more happiness in the world than is generally recognised. I think there is. Probably every life has some happiness: a few lives have little else. But happiness is not enough,—is not satisfactory. With it there is always a want, a longing; and the greater one's happiness becomes, the greater is this feeling of unsatisfaction. I do not think that many human beings have ever experienced satisfaction at all; and even those who have experienced it, have kept it but a few moments, which formed a sharp contrast to the rest of their life. It is generally known only by the want of it. There is a great unsatisfaction in life; and that is the only reason for dreams of satisfaction." The writer then goes on to give illustrations of the various circumstances which specially call forth in us this feeling of unsatisfaction. "The effect of scenery," she says, "is more than half pain, especially if it is the sea; sunset or distance of any kind soon becomes unbearable. But perhaps the sense of unsatisfaction is never so strong as under the influence of music. The longing and the hoplessness are never more keenly felt, than when music is making us happy with new ideas and hopes."

She then proceeds to show that this feeling is no accident; that it is, and must ever be, inseparable from human life; that it is in fact a law of nature. "Repose must be impossible unless by a deliberate blinding of all one's perceptions and numbing of all one's energies. Progress is the law of the universe; one would be unwilling not to progress; but how can one ever be satisfied while one is struggling towards the unattained? As we are hemmed in on all sides by limits and restraints we can never hope for satisfaction. There is nothing for it but to face the idea of an unsatisfied eternity,—an idea which almost makes one long to *dis*believe in immortality. The weariness of always striving and never attaining, of always longing and never getting, would lead, if one allowed one's self to dwell on it, to a despair in which extinction would be our fondest hope, not only for ourselves but for humanity. One can only turn one's attention steadily to the grandeur of eternal progress, and dwell on the attainable, carefully avoiding the thought of the unattainable. But the feeling of unsatisfaction nevertheless remains."

"The old theological view gave some hope of satisfaction in the end. One could wait millions of years if only one had the prospect of getting it some day. It is impossible to return to the heaven of one's childhood. But there was less unsatisfaction then. The God of one's childhood was at rest; but now the idea of progress forms a necessary part of our conception of the Deity. How can there be satisfaction, even for God, while there is an unattained? And how can there ever be any satisfaction for man, when not only an unattained, but an unattainable, must lie for ever beyond his reach? God and man alike are working on, progressing; so far it is bright, all the brighter and nobler for showing us more in common between the two than we had at first supposed. But both alike are hemmed in by limitations, both alike are confronted by the great Impossible; and in face of this I see no prospect of satisfaction for God or man now or ever. It seems as if there ought to be something to correspond to our longing. If there be in all conscious intelligences an endless desire, impossible in the nature of things ever to be gratified, the universe must be at heart irrational. And belief in the rationality of the universe is the last stronghold of our faith. If that goes, nothing remains. Unless there is a Supreme Reason pervading all things, we are practically without a God. There may exist a Being greater than ourselves, perhaps greater even than we can ever conceive. But impossibility is greater still; reason and love are comparatively helpless; God and man alike are ultimately powerless."

Now that is brilliant writing; but I venture to think it contains a lurking fallacy.

There are two ideals of life diametrically opposed—the ideal of rest and the ideal of progress. These are mutually exclusive. You cannot move on and stand still in the same indivisible moment of time. It is evident that so far as you are at rest, you cannot be progressing; in so far as you are progressing, you cannot be at rest. The pessimists generally assume that the best kind of world would be one in which all sentient creatures, from the beginning of their lives to the end, were in possession of everything which they were capable of desiring. But this is an assumption which fills me with amazement, especially when I find it made, as I so often do, by persons of refinement and culture, whose own experience should teach them that there is something far better than sensuous repose. If an uninterrupted state of complete satisfaction be the highest life, then assuredly this earth of ours is the worst possible world. We ought to have been kept, miraculously if need be, from everything that could be even momentarily unpleasant. We should have been taught, by instinct or revelation or in some other fashion, everything we ever required to know. But the whole genius of our existence is different. We have to find things out for ourselves, if we want to know them; we have to learn what is called "experience" by failure and mistakes; we have to live—if we live at all—by effort, conflict, pain. The key-note of our life is discipline, and the end of our life is progress. The pessimists generally seem to take it for granted that discipline is a nuisance and progress a bore. But my correspondent holds a somewhat different position. She is wiser, but less consistent. She speaks of the grandeur of eternal progress. But she complains that there does not go along with this the apathy of eternal repose. It is like the demand for a line with only one end. How can I ever be satisfied, she asks, while struggling towards the unattained? How could you ever be satisfied, I reply, unless there were an unattained to struggle towards? The existence of the unattained is the *sine quâ non* of progress.

The consciousness of unsatisfaction seems to me nothing else than the consciousness of our powers. My correspondent has told us that scenery, music and happiness make us most sensible of the fact that we are not satisfied. I think she is right. For scenery, music and happiness make us most sensible of the infinite possibilities of our nature. And if this consciousness of unsatisfaction is to be called pain,—remember it is pain which we prefer to any inferior pleasure, it is pain which we endeavour and delight to feel, it is the pain of ecstasy.

Progress no doubt involves effort and work; but effort and work are in themselves agreeable. It is all very well to talk of the pleasures of rest; and rest is certainly pleasant enough when we are fatigued. But the pleasures of exercise are infinitely greater. Who would be asleep when he might be hunting or rowing or playing tennis? And I do not at all agree with my correspondent in thinking that our changed views about heaven are a loss. On the contrary I think they are a decided gain. According to the old-fashioned theology, heaven was a place of eternal idleness, where even the Deity had nothing to do. There was repose, no doubt, but it was the repose of death. All the noblest natures recoiled from the thought of spending eternity in such a place, and in such a way. They felt that the life of earth was far diviner in spite of the pain which it sometimes involved. They were right. To my mind the saddest world in which there was progress would be infinitely more suggestive of reason than the happiest world in which there was none.

Of course if progress were impossible, the desire for it would be a curse; if the unattained were always to be unattainable, the longing for it would be hell. But the bitterest pessimist must admit that we are constantly attaining the unattained, ay that we are constantly attaining the unattainable. How many things are to-day commonplaces in science and art, for the discovery of which our ancestors would have thought it ridiculous to hope even in their wildest dreams! And the impossible itself need no longer be regarded as a bugbear. In spite of the hindrances and difficulties and limits which may have been in the path of the Creator at the beginning, the world has been created and progress is being achieved. The impossible has not prevented happiness, does not prevent an ever-increasing happiness, and there is no reason to suppose that in the end it will prevent anything except that which is contradictory, irrational and absurd.

Who then, I ask, can wish for a world of sensuous repose? Is not satisfaction that degraded and degrading form of contentment which only a low nature can feel? Is not unsatisfaction that true and inspiring form of discontent which no noble nature can ever be without? Is not the possibility of endless progress the highest endowment which an intelligent being can possess? And does not the fact that we realise this power in ourselves go far to prove that we are living, not in the worst, but rather in the best possible, world.

> "Nothing resting in its own completeness
> Can have worth or beauty; but alone
> Because it tends and leads to further sweetness,
> Fuller, higher, deeper than its own.

Spring's real glory dwells not in the meaning,
Gracious though it be, of her blue hours;
But is hidden in her tender leaning
To the summer's richer wealth of flowers.

Life is only bright when it proceedeth
Towards a truer, deeper Life above;
Human love is sweetest when it leadeth
To a more divine and perfect Love.

Dare not to blame God's gifts for incompleteness:
In that want their value lies; they leave
The promise of a far diviner sweetness
Than any which as yet we can conceive."

True and False Discontent.

VIII.

PESSIMISM (*continued*).

D.—THE EVOLUTION OF LOVE.

I POINTED out in the last sermon (*C*) that the pessimistic ideal of life is an ideal of reform rather than of progress. But not only so. They assert (*D*) that during the course of evolution no progress has been made, or only a progress in pain. They represent to us the history of the universe pretty much as follows. In the beginning, millions of millions of years ago, matter existed as a diffused mass of incandescent vapour, which was in a state of rotatory motion. As it revolved portions of it became detached. Every such portion broken off from the primitive nebula was the beginning of a sidereal system, from which again other masses became detached and formed planets; and from these in like manner during their rotation there were still further disruptions, which led to the formation of moons. The whole of our solar system therefore once existed as a single mass of vapour, and the earth was formed, like the other planets, by disruption from a central mass. Even when it had become detached the earth was for a long time in a state of incandescence; but after myriads of years of radiation the surface cooled into the solid state, and the vapours that surrounded it condensed into the primeval ocean. After another long lapse of time there was formed at the bottom of the ocean that curious compound of carbon called protoplasm, which is the physical basis of life. And with life came waste. At first there was only vegetable life. The beds of the oceans and the surface of the earth teemed with it; but the luxuriance and grandeur of the primeval flora was all thrown away; there was no eye to see it, no sentient creature to derive the slightest benefit from it. By-and-by however, after still further changes in the atmosphere and the temperature, animal life began, and with it came pain. The old waste continued. Thousands of germs perished for every living creature that came into existence; those who did actually come to life were liable to accident and to disease; and if they were specially weak, they were as a rule devoured by the strong. With every rise in the zoological scale, organisms become more delicate, and the capacity for pain increases till it reaches its climax in man. The whole creation groans.

And so the pessimists sometimes turn round upon us and inquire, How about your old argument from design ? We admit, they say, that the world cannot be altogether the work of chance; there is too much definite, awful, relentless regularity about it for that. But whatever design there may be in it, is an evil design; if any intelligence has been at work upon nature, it is a devilish intelligence; if the Creator had a purpose in creation it was none other than the evolution of pain.

Now you see the pessimists here assume that nothing has emerged in the course of evolution but pain, or at any rate nothing worth speaking of in comparison with pain, nothing certainly which is of sufficient value at all to compensate for pain. A strange assumption for men of education and refinement. *Have they never heard of Love?* We can trace its dim beginning as far back as the dawn of sentient life. At first it was but a blind instinct; but by degrees it was carried, even amongst what we are accustomed to call brutes, to the point of virtue, to the point of heroism; as when a bird voluntarily gives up its life for its offspring, or a dog begs off from punishment the child that has been torturing him. In the human race, at the lowest end of the scale I doubt if you could find a person so degraded as never to have denied himself for any one; at the other end of the scale you find —Christ; and of Christ it is expressly declared by St Paul that he was but "the first-born of many brethren."

"The worst possible world," say the pessimists, and yet it is already permeated through and through with love. In the course of evolution love has emerged along with pain, and as I have tried to show you partly by means of pain. Would not this result have been worth, if necessary, ten thousand times the cost? Would any one barter away for a little more enjoyment the highest gift of evolution? Surely, even now, the end justifies the means—any means. Even now there is enough to compensate for millenniums of what we call waste. Waste! As if anything could be waste which formed part of the steady onward move of circumstances that was to culminate in the birth of love! The Author of the universe, who to the jaundiced vision of the pessimists appears occupied solely in devising pain, has been all along creating love. If this is the result of His bad things—and of course waste, pain, conflict, taken separately, are bad things—what must be the unsearchable riches of His good things? The evolution of love is now going on with amazing rapidity. Positive philosophers and Christian thinkers, all cultivated persons —except pessimists— recognise its value and its beauty. The number of self-sacrificing men and women, the number of those who have merged their own life and wellbeing in the life and wellbeing of the race, is continually on the increase. And assuredly the time is coming when there will be a reign of love in humanity, as invariable and as universal as the present reign of law in nature. That is

> "The one, far-off, divine event
> Towards which the whole creation moves."

And where is the man who would begrudge his own contribution of suffering towards a consummation so devoutly to be wished?

Pessimism, as a system of dogmatic belief, seems to me the meanest and the silliest creed with which ever the earth was cursed. It is mean; for it assumes that there is nothing valuable but pleasure, it assumes that the goodness or badness of the world may be determined by that criterion alone. It is silly; for its fundamental assertion, that life is not worth living, is flatly contradicted by the vast majority of the human race. Professor Huxley, in the 'Nineteenth Century,' though taking a much less optimistic view of life than I have endeavoured to give you, is yet very severe with the pessimists. He says, " If the optimism of Leibnitz is a foolish though pleasant dream, the pessimism of Schopenhauer is a nightmare, the more foolish because of its hideousness. Error which is not pleasant is surely the worst form of wrong. This may not be the best of all possible worlds, but to say that it is the worst is mere petulant nonsense. A worn-out voluptuary may find nothing good under the sun; a vain and inexperienced youth, who cannot get the moon he cries for, may vent his irritation in pessimistic moanings; but there can be no doubt in the mind of any reasonable person that mankind could get on fairly well with vastly less happiness and far more misery, than find their way into the lives of nine persons out of ten. Men with any manhood in them would find life worth living under far worse conditions than the present."

But though pessimism as a systematic creed is essentially mean and silly, pessimism as a passing mood of feeling may come to the wisest and the best of us. It may be forced on us by a great historic crisis; it may be forced on us by some overwhelming personal calamity; nay, if we are a little out of health, if we are over-fatigued, if the weather be disagreeable, we may all of us find that we are for the time inclined to be pessimists. In one of the many valuable letters I have received on this subject, the writer points out very acutely how the same circumstances will at one time depress us, which at other times would make us hopeful and glad. By way of illustration she refers to a celebrated passage in Professor Tyndall's 'Musings on the Matterhorn': "Hacked and hurt by time, the aspect of the mountain from its higher crags saddened me. Hitherto the impression it made was that of savage strength, here we had inexorable decay. But this notion of decay implied a reference to a period when the Matterhorn was in the full strength of mountainhood. Thought naturally ran back to its remoter origin and sculpture. Nor did thought halt there, but wandered on through molten worlds to that nebulous haze, which philosophers have regarded as the source of all material things. I tried to look at this universal cloud as containing within itself the prediction of all that has since occurred. I tried to imagine it as the seat of those forces whose action was to arise in solar and stellar systems and all that they involve. Did that formless fog contain potentially the sadness with which I regarded the Matterhorn?" Now, says the writer, that feeling of sadness which invaded his spirit at the top of the mountain, was probably due more to the exhaustion of his nervous system than to any change in the mountain itself. The thoughts of decay were his, not nature's. At another time, with his body restored to the normal condition, those very rocks might have made him glad; they might have given him an assurance of infinite progress, of order brought out of disorder, of life wrung from death; and seeing how in the natural world strife had given birth to beauty, he might have learnt to hope that it would perhaps be so in the moral sphere, and that all the sufferings which had been involved in the progress of evolution were not worthy to be compared with the infinite and eternal glory for which they were the necessary preparation.

But though various causes over which we have no control may lead to our experiencing at times the pessimistic mood, let us take care that we do our best as quickly as possible to shake it off. You remember the high priest of æstheticism—before he was married, he is wiser now—rather prided himself on his melancholy. And there are others who do the same. Just as some people think agnosticism a proof of cleverness, so others think pessimism a proof of culture. Your youthful agnostic, fresh from school, feels his mind to be of such a superior order, that he considers quite beneath his notice arguments which were powerful enough to convince the mind of Hegel. Similarly there are pessimists who feel themselves possessed of an organism so highly strung, that they are compelled to regard as coarse and commonplace pleasures which were pure enough and keen enough to fill with ecstasy the heart of Wordsworth. They assiduously cultivate their melancholy. They revel in the poetry of despair. They are positively glad to find the universe out of joint. All this puts them, they fancy, on a higher platform than that occupied by the vulgar herd. They glory in their pessimism as a proof of their superior refinement! They might as well glory in their toothache as a proof of the superior delicacy of their nerves. There is no delicacy about it. There is nothing but disease. The most delicate nerves in their normal state will never give pain. And so with the pessimistic mood. It is abnormal. It is not the sign of a cultivated ear to hear nothing in the world but discords; it is not the sign of a cultivated eye to see nothing in the world but ugliness; nor is it the sign of a cultivated heart to discover nothing in life but its worthlessness. The pessimistic mood is an unhealthy mood. It is a sign that something is wrong with him who feels it. Cultivate it! Foster it! As well might you cultivate delirium or fever. I tell you it is a disease, and it must be cured. And if you ask me how—I reply, by forcing yourself to dwell on the bright, rather than on the dark, side of things. Instead of brooding over waste and pain and disease and disappointment and death, think of pleasure, happiness, beauty, love, life—life with its infinite power and promise. Cultivate cheerfulness!

"O wonder of Cosmical Order! O Maker and Ruler of all,
Before whose infinite greatness in silence we worship and fall!

Could I doubt that the will which keeps this great universe
    steadfast and sure,
Can be less than His creatures thought, full of goodness, pitiful,
    pure?

Could I dream that the Power which keeps those great suns
    circling around,
Takes no thought for the humblest life which flutters and falls to
    the ground?

O Faith! thou art higher than all.—Then I turned from the
    glories above,
And from every casement new-lit there shone a soft radiance of
    love:

Young mothers were teaching their children to fold little hands
    in prayer;
Strong fathers were resting from toil, 'mid the hush of the Sab-
    bath air;

Peasant lovers strolled through the lanes, shy and diffident each
    with each,
Yet knit by some subtle union too fine for their halting speech :

Humble lives, to low thought, and low ; but linked, to the
    thinker's eye,
By a bond that is stronger than death, with the lights of the
    farthest sky :

Here as there, the great drama of life rolled on, and a jubilant
    voice
Thrilled through me ineffable, vast, and bade me exult and
    rejoice."

True and False Discontent.

IX.

TRUE DISCONTENT WITH THE WORLD.

WE have been engaged for about two months in the consideration of true and false discontent. We first of all noticed discontent in relation to personal conditions and environment. Those who are falsely—*i.e.*, unwisely—discontented, grumble at all their circumstances, even at those which cannot possibly be altered; while the truly—*i.e.*, the wisely—discontented, are just so far dissatisfied that they feel stimulated to improve such of their circumstances as are capable of being changed. Similarly in regard to knowledge, some people are always repining that they cannot know everything all at once: while others spend their time in patiently learning to know more and more. And the same difference may be noticed in the mental attitude, which people assume towards the world as a whole. Some grumble at its being so wretched; others make it happier. With the former class we have been engaged for several Sundays. We have seen that the world after all is not nearly so miserable as they would have us believe. Even judged by the criterion of pleasure, life for most men is decidedly worth living. But this, as I pointed out, is a low criterion. The real purpose of life is progress and development. And looked at from this point of view, we saw that pain itself, about which the pessimists make such a fuss, was often useful and indeed inevitable.

But just because the purpose of life is progress, just because the environment of human beings and the human beings themselves are capable of improvement, it follows that we should not be satisfied with the world as it is. In other words, there is a true, a wise, an honourable discontent, quite different from pessimism, giving us inspiration instead of despair. A certain sense of unsatisfaction, as we have seen, is the key-note of every noble life. We ought to feel discontented with the present condition of this world, for it is in our power to make it better; and if we were not discontented with it we should never try.

But this feeling of discontent is often conspicuous by its absence. Instead of it we frequently find, especially in commonplace people, a most ignoble contentment. They are quite satisfied with this world, simply because they are having a good time themselves. They make no effort, they have no desire, to improve the condition of those less favourably circumstanced. I remember hearing an amusing description of a sermon delivered in Westminster Abbey some years ago. The description was given me by a professor of political economy,—a man who was naturally very interested in all economical problems. He never went to church if he could help it, but on this occasion he was obliged to escort some ladies, and so there he was. He told me that for the first five minutes he almost thought he was going to like the sermon. The preacher began by drawing a graphic picture of the miseries of the poor in an overcrowded city: and the professor expected that some suggestions would follow as to how these miseries might be alleviated and diminished. But no. The preacher contented himself with saying that they would receive compensation, at least some of them *might* receive compensation—he was not sure that they all would—but some of them might receive compensation, or at any rate have a better time, in the next world. And therefore the practical conclusion of the sermon was that their sufferings did not matter, that everything was all right. But the sufferings do matter; everything is not all right. The sermon was the outcome of a false and mean contentment.

There can, I think, be no doubt that in the past the Church has to some extent fostered such a spirit. The Church has sometimes maintained, or appeared to maintain, the doctrine that our only duty in the world was to prepare to get out of it, that we had nothing of any importance to do upon earth except to make ready for heaven. Wherever this doctrine came from, it never came from Christ. He denounced in the most unmeasured terms the Pharisees and Scribes and all of His contemporaries who professed it. Our conduct *here* towards our fellows was, He always maintained, the first and all-important consideration. It would depend entirely on this conduct whether we were saved or lost. Kindliness is salvation, both for this world and the next. That is Christ's teaching. Some people do not like it: they would rather be saved in some other way—in any other way. That I can understand. But why, when they have discarded all that is most essential in the teaching of Christ, they should persist in calling themselves Christians—that I cannot understand. It is this false assumption of the name of Christian that makes the religion of Christ, which is really the most beautiful religion in the world, so often appear to be the most contemptible.

In every one who sincerely desires the well-being of his fellow-creatures, there must inevitably be a keen feeling of discontent with the present conditions of this world—(1) as regards pleasure, (2) as regards knowledge, and (3) as regards character.

And, first, of pleasure. Though, as I have argued, the world as a whole is not a bad place; though upon the whole there is more happiness in it than misery; though upon the whole life for nearly all human beings is worth living; nevertheless it must be admitted that there is vastly more pain in the world and vastly less pleasure than there ought to be—than there might be. I have said that pain is not altogether a useless thing, that it subserves many important purposes. Now one of the most important of the purposes which pain subserves is this: it affords us a strong stimulus to try to get rid of it. Pain is abnormal and unnatural. Though it is often necessary, it is never intended to be permanent. It is at best merely a means to an end; and, paradoxical as it may sound, the sooner the means is removed the sooner the end will be accomplished. There are people called ascetics, who think that there is not enough pain in the world, and who are always trying to increase it. By fastings, flagellations and penances, by inducing people to give up amusements and everything really enjoyable, they do their best to make this world what it was never intended to be—the worst of all possible worlds. But, as I have often told you, Christ was no ascetic. The very Man of Sorrows refused to join in the irrational worship of pain. He never refused pleasure merely because it was pleasant; never chose pain merely because it was painful. He understood the Father too well for that. As one of my correspondents has ingeniously pointed out, the very way we resent it shows that pain is not one of the laws of our nature, but that on the contrary it arises from a violation of those laws. I believe that in all cases where pain is voluntarily endured for its own sake, the individual is morally as well as physically injured. And I am sure that whenever others are allowed to suffer pain from which they might be rescued, those who allow it are guilty of a great moral wrong.

Now there is an enormous amount of disease and poverty and wretchedness in our midst, which a wise legislature and a Christian Church might remove. I do not know exactly how. Certainly not in the way which the mob orators of Trafalgar Square would recommend : they want to steal the property of the most deserving,—of those who by themselves or their ancestors have made England what it is,— they would like to confiscate all this property and distribute it among the dregs of the community. Nobody but a demagogue inebriated with his own verbosity could ever advocate such a plan as that. But though it is easy to see how *not* to improve matters, how the condition of the world might be made worse than it is at present,—it is by no means easy to discover the right way to go to work. But this undertaking, difficult though it be, is one of the first duties of the legislature,—is, I believe, *the* first duty of the Church. It is an undertaking which requires great learning and great wisdom, as well as great enthusiasm. Without the learning and the wisdom the enthusiasm may do more harm than good. It will be a happy day for the Church, and a still happier day for the world, when clergymen read less of St Augustine and more of Adam Smith, and when the bishops require all candidates for holy orders to pass an examination in political economy. And even as private individuals each of us is under a solemn obligation to increase pleasure and diminish pain as far as in us lies ; to read and to reflect and to work, with a view to the brightening and gladdening of the lives of our relations and friends and dependants, and of any members of the destitute classes with whom we are, or may become, acquainted. That is the first and simplest and most evident duty of every Christian man and woman.

Secondly. Let me say a word about the healthy discontent as regards the present state of the world's knowledge. I do not mean in regard to that which is known at first hand by experts. There is no room for anything but gratitude and admiration in regard to what scientific men have already discovered; and there is no fear but that they will continue to make fresh discoveries up to the furthest limit of human patience and ingenuity. I am referring to knowledge at second hand of what is already known to some one. There is a vast amount of unnecessary ignorance in our midst, both amongst the upper and lower classes. And this ignorance, in addition to the physical sufferings which follow from it, involves mental and moral degradation. An enormous amount of physical misery, especially amongst the very poor, might be easily prevented if they had but the most elementary knowledge of the laws of health, of the properties of food, of the way to make the best of their small earnings. And this knowledge might by the State or by the Church, or better still by the united action of both, be brought within the reach of all. By adopting a more sensible and practical system of education, by means of popular lectures and useful tracts, instead of the wretched things called tracts on which so much money is annually wasted,—in a great variety of ways, if the State and the Church only could make up their minds to it, the poorest classes might not only be made familiar with the elements of useful knowledge, but might also begin to experience some of the *pleasures* of reading, on which Mr Balfour so eloquently discoursed at St Andrews. As he truly said, reading for pleasure is a good thing. If you can get people to enjoy books, you at once raise them morally as well as mentally. This alone will save them from the most degrading kinds of physical temptations.

I admit, of course, that it is a duty of the Church to teach men to read for other purposes than mere pleasure, that it is a duty of the Church to offer men profound instruction upon moral and spiritual subjects. But the Church has too often begun its work at the wrong end. It has gone to men who were not fit for earth, and tried by doctrine or ritual to make them immediately fit for heaven. It has bluntly offered the consolations of religion to those who have hitherto only experienced the consolations of beer. How absurd! It is like trying to build a house from the roof downwards!

"That is not first which is spiritual, but that which is natural; and afterwards that which is spiritual." Christ knew this. He treated men's bodies first, and their souls afterwards. You remember the poor man who couldn't get into the pool. Christ did not preach to him till after he was cured, and then He said, "Go and sin no more." It is no wonder, when the ministers of Christ are ignorant of human nature and destitute of common-sense, that all their efforts to what they call "save" the poor, should be absolutely futile.

Thirdly. But though it is necessary to attend—and, I think, to attend first—to the bodies and minds of men, that is not all which is required of us. We ought also to be discontented with the present condition of human character. I should like you to read the chapter on the Law of Edification in 'Ecce Homo.' Though philanthropy is an essential part of Christianity, it is by no means the whole.

"Christ described in one of His parables a man such as philanthropy might produce, if it were perfectly successful—a man enjoying every physical comfort and determining to give himself up to enjoyment—but He describes him with horror rather than satisfaction." And yet Christ was always so eager to relieve physical distress and to promote physical comfort. But if you reflect you will discover that the paradox is not very difficult to explain. "A good parent will be careful of the physical condition of his child, will tend him assiduously in sickness, relieve his wants, and endeavour in every way to make him happy. But the good parent will not rest content with seeing his child comfortable and secure from pain. He will consider that other and greater things than physical comfort are to be procured for him, and for the sake of these greater things he will even sacrifice some of his comforts, and see with satisfaction that the child suffers a certain amount of pain and goes without certain pleasures. The affection which pets and pampers its object is not excessive, as it is sometimes described, but a feeble affection, or rather the affection of a feeble nature. Now the love of Christ for humanity was no such feeble love. It was not an exceedingly keen sensibility, which made Him feel more painfully than other men the sufferings of which the world is full. It was a powerful, calm, contemplative love. It was a love of men for what they might be, a love of the ideal man in each, or as Christ Himself might have said, a love of the image of God in each man. Accordingly, the enthusiasm of humanity in Him did not propose to itself principally to procure gratification and enjoyment for the senses of men, but to make the divine image more glorious in them, and to purge it as far as possible from impurities."

And it is our bounden duty as Christians to use every means to raise men to the moral elevation of Christ. It is our duty, as the apostle expresses it, to "provoke others to love." And how is this to be effected? "The enthusiasm of humanity can hardly be kindled except by a personal influence, acting through example or impassioned exhortation. When Christ would kindle it in His disciples, He breathed on them and said, 'Receive the Holy Ghost;' intimating by this great symbolic act that life passes into the soul of a man, as it were, by contagion with another living soul. Contrivance, however, and organisation may do much in marshalling this personal influence, in bringing it to bear upon the greatest number in the most effective way; it may also do much in preventing man's natural susceptibility to the enthusiasm being dulled by adverse circumstances, and in giving fuel to the enthusiasm where it already burns." As it is the duty of Christians to study human wellbeing systematically with a view to philanthropy, so is it their duty, with a view to edification, to consider at large the conditions most favourable to goodness, and by what social arrangements temptations to vice may be reduced to the lowest point, and goodness have the most numerous and the most powerful motives. Here is a whole field of investigation upon which Christians are bound to enter, and which is a principal part of the work belonging properly to the Church.

And if in any degree we are to do our duty in these matters, either as private individuals or as members of the Church, we must be inspired with a noble discontent, we must be determined to leave the world better than we found it.

> "Do not crouch to-day, and worship
>   The old Past, whose life is fled;
> Hush your voice in tender reverence—
>   Crowned he lies, but cold and dead.
>
> For the Present reigns our monarch,
>   With an added weight of hours;
> Honour her, for she is mighty;
>   Honour her, for she is ours.
>
> Noble things the great Past promised,
>   Holy dreams both strange and new;
> But the Present shall fulfil them,
>   What he promised she shall do."

Christmas Day.

TO-DAY is Christ's birthday,—at least it has been set apart throughout Christendom as the day on which the birth of Jesus should be celebrated. From our earliest infancy we have been accustomed to associate the 25th of December with the manger in the inn of Bethlehem, where the new-born Christ was laid. That event, seemingly so trivial and insignificant, will be celebrated all over the world to-day. There is always a curious contrast, in the case of every man of genius, between the helplessness of his birth and the magic power of his name after he is dead and gone. In the case of Christ this contrast is pre-eminently remarkable. Who could have thought on Christmas Day eighteen hundred and eighty-seven years ago, that the infant lying in that lowly cradle was destined to become the most illustrious personage in the world's history, that to the end of time the day would be called His day and be regarded as the central point of civilised chronology?

Who could have guessed that that helpless child was to become the acknowledged God of all the most advanced nations upon earth? Yet so it is.

A marvellous triumph no doubt, and a triumph with which any one who cared for glory might well be satisfied. But with such a triumph we may be sure Christ would not be satisfied. For all this is perfectly compatible with failure, or comparative failure, in regard to the real purpose of His life, perfectly compatible with the corruption and degradation of his religion into something no better than the superstitions which he intended His own religion to replace. And the fact is the outward and visible triumph of Christianity has been attended all along with an inward and less noticeable defeat. The profession of Christianity is respectable, so men are ready enough to call Christ Lord; and His so-called disciples may be reckoned by hundreds of millions. But in regard to the practice of Christianity—the only thing for which Christ cared—it is quite different. Christianity is practised only by a very small proportion of those who profess it. In fact the great majority of its professors do not seem aware that there is anything practical in it. They regard it as a system of forms and observances and creeds, though for such things Christ cared nothing. This emasculated and degraded form of Christianity is constantly presented to the world as the religion of Christ. And the more such a spurious Christianity progresses, the more is the real Christianity of Christ thrown into the shade.

All religions may be divided into two classes which are diametrically opposed. Christianity, as Christ founded it, belongs to the one class; Christianity, as since corrupted, belongs to the second. We have, on the one hand, religions which aim at saving men from divine vengeance; and, on the other, religions which aim at saving men from their own sins. All barbarous religions belong to the first class; Buddhism and Christ's Christianity to the second.

Barbarous religions, I say, belong to the first class. These are the religions which come earliest in the world's history, and which men ought to outgrow. Savages are taught by their priests that the gods are spiteful and revengeful beings, but that they may be propitiated by offerings of barley, wine, or blood; and there—with these propitiations —the religion of savages begins and ends. The gods do not trouble themselves, thinks the savage, about my conduct; I may please myself about that so long only as I offer them their favourite bribes. Christianity, on the contrary — that is to say,

Christ's Christianity—belongs to a totally different class of religions. Christ taught that God was not vindictive, that there was no need to buy His forbearance, that He was full of fatherly love, more willing to give than we to receive, but that His best gifts could only be received by those whose conduct was itself good.

In the time of Christ the Pharisees were the representatives of the old barbarous religions, and they were continually finding fault with Christ, who made it evident enough, while He lived, that He believed in a religion of a totally different character to theirs. "There came together certain of the Pharisees and Scribes. And when they saw some of His disciples eat bread with defiled, that is to say with unwashen hands, they found fault. For the Pharisees and all the Jews, except they wash their hands oft, eat not, holding the tradition of the elders. And when they come from the market, except they wash, they eat not. And many other things there be, which they have received to hold, as the washing of cups and pots and brazen vessels and of tables. Then the Pharisees and Scribes asked Him, Why walk not Thy disciples according to the tradition of the elders, but eat bread with unwashen hands? He answered and said unto them, Well hath Esaias prophesied of you, you hypocrites, as it is written, This people honoureth me with their lips but their heart is far from me. Howbeit in vain do they worship me, teaching for doctrines the commandments of men. For, laying aside the commandment of God, ye hold the tradition of men, as the washing of pots and cups: and many other suchlike things ye do. And he said unto them, Full well ye reject the commandment of God, that ye may keep your own tradition. . . . There is nothing from without a man that can defile a man. . . . That which cometh out of a man, that defileth him. For from within, out of the heart of men, proceed evil thoughts, adulteries, fornications, murders, thefts, lasciviousness, an evil eye, blasphemy, pride, foolishness. All these evil things come from within, and defile the man."

Now, notwithstanding the plainness of Christ's teaching during His lifetime, notwithstanding the plainness of the account of that teaching which we find in the evangelists, the religion of Christ has been for the most part misrepresented by those who call themselves, and believe themselves to be, His disciples. Much of what passes current as Christianity in Europe to-day is not Christianity at all, bears no resemblance to Christianity, is indeed, in every respect opposed to Christianity. If Christ were in the world now, He would attack Christianity—the commonplace Christianity of Christendom—as violently as He ever attacked Pharisaism. For His religion has been transformed and corrupted past all recognition. Broadly speaking it is scarcely too much to say, that the Christianity of Christendom *is not* the Christianity of Christ. From being a religion of conduct it has been made into a religion of ceremony and of creed. From being the highest of all religions, it seems in danger of becoming one of the lowest.

This is a strong statement; but you will find it remarkably confirmed in the various attacks which are made upon Christianity from time to time by hostile critics. They do not see that the Christianity of Christ and the Christianity of Christendom are two distinct things, so distinct as to be often antagonistic and contradictory. They fancy that they are attacking the Christianity of Christ, but they are not. They are attacking only a caricature, which Christ Himself would denounce just as strongly. We may admit all that they say as against the Christianity of Christendom, and our faith in the beauty and value of Christ's Christianity may be at the same time confirmed. Look, for example, at Mr Cotter Morison's 'Service of Man.' It is written to prove that Christianity is a failure, that men will be happier, and at the same time more moral, when we have got rid of it altogether. Mr Morison asserts that Christianity, by its doctrine of justification by faith, by its insisting on repentance for the past rather than good conduct in the present, by its exaggerated emphasis of belief and its comparative disregard of morality, tends to foster immorality and to make the world more wretched than it need be. Mr Morison, therefore, bids us shake off Christianity. He urges us to substitute for the ceremonial service of God the practical service of man.

Now, if the distinction I have so often insisted upon between the Christianity of Christ and the Christianity of Christendom were commonly recognised, Mr Morison's book would never have been written. It never occurs to him that the two things are not identical. Yet so different are they, that in attacking the one he does not touch the other; nay, his condemnation of the religion which he regards as Christianity is a tacit but powerful tribute to the real religion of Christ.

Christ never taught the doctrine of justification by faith in the Lutheran sense—that is, in the sense of something different from and opposed to works. "He that believeth on me, the works that I do shall he do also, and greater works than these shall he do." "He that heareth my words and doeth them not, shall be likened unto a foolish man who built his house upon the sand; and the rain descended and the floods came, and the wind blew and beat upon that house, and it fell, and great was the fall of it." Christ never taught that repentance would save a man, apart from the conduct to which a sincere repentance leads. "Not every one that saith unto me, Lord, Lord, shall enter into the kingdom of heaven; but he that doeth the will of my Father." As for putting creed above conduct, Christ did nothing of the kind. No teacher since the world began ever laid so little stress upon creed, and so much upon conduct, as Jesus of Nazareth. He promulgated no dogmas, He insisted on no articles, He enunciated no definitions. His only creed was the golden rule, and that was not so much a doctrine to be believed as a precept to be obeyed.

Christianity is generally attacked as a system of creed or of ceremony, seldom as a system of morals. It is admitted by all that Christ's moral teaching was good, if not the best. But it is assumed by the opponents of the Christian religion that morality is only a detail—something of comparative insignificance in the Christian system. And this is true of Christianity as it has so often been misrepresented in Christendom. But it is not true of

Christianity as understood and unfolded by Christ. He regarded morality as of paramount importance; in fact He identified it with religion. Duty and salvation, according to Him, were synonymous terms; but so strangely has Christianity been transformed, that things which Christ ignored have come to be regarded as its very essence, and what Christ asserted to be the one thing needful has come to be altogether ignored. How many persons do you suppose there are in Christendom to-day who, if they were asked to give in a single sentence the pith and gist and essence of Christianity, would ever dream of mentioning the golden rule? And yet it was in the golden rule that Christ summed up His own religion. How many persons are there, do you suppose, in Christendom to-day who, if they were asked to state in a single word what was necessary for the salvation of the soul, would ever dream of mentioning the word *kindness?* Yet, according to Christ, it was this characteristic which determined whether a man was to go to heaven or to hell. "*Come.*" Why? Because you have been baptised and received the Communion. Because you have thought of the Trinity without dividing the substance or confounding the persons? "*Depart.*" Why? Because you have held yourself aloof from the Churches of Christendom? Because you have not believed rightly the doctrine of the incarnation? No! Saving the soul is learning to be kind. This may not be orthodox; but at any rate it is the teaching of the Bible.

The identification of religion with morality is especially remarkable, when we remember how much God was to Christ. There can be no doubt that Christ did identify the two. We must accept the fact, even if we do not find a reason for it. But we can. At first sight it seems strange that Christ should have reduced all sins to sin against one's neighbour — in one word, to selfishness; and that, where summarising His teaching, He should say nothing of sins against God, of sins against Himself, of sins which men may commit against their own nature. But if you think for a little you may see, on the one hand that selfishness implies and includes all forms of sin; and on the other hand that perfect unselfishness is really equivalent to perfect sinlessness. In the first place, I say, selfishness implies and includes all other forms of sin. For when we sin against our neighbour, we at the same time injure our own moral nature; we displease the heavenly Father, who cares for him no less than for us; and we crucify the Son of God afresh who, so far as we are concerned, seems to have lived and died in vain. And in the second place, perfect unselfishness is equivalent to perfect sinlessness. For he who would never sin against his neighbour must never sin against himself, nor against Christ, nor against God. The very idea of human brotherhood is based upon that of divine fatherhood. Men are brethren because they are the children of a common Father. And just in proportion as they believe in Him, will they realise and fulfil their obligations to each other. Again, personal devotedness to Christ is the best means of fostering a universal devotedness to the welfare of the race. "If ye love me," He Himself said, "ye will keep my words." And no other means will produce the same effect. A passionate enthusiasm for the welfare of humanity will be developed in us, just in proportion as we have learnt to admire and love the great example of self-sacrifice, who sought not to be ministered unto but to minister, and who died, as He had lived, to redeem the world from evil. And with regard to sins against ourselves, we acquire an additional motive against committing them, when we become imbued with a love for others. In injuring ourselves we injure our brethren, both by our example and by our diminished power of usefulness; and just in proportion as we love our neighbour, shall we listen to the voice which bids us do ourselves no harm.

I like Christmas Day. I think it is a more Christian day than any other in the Church's calendar. All the observances connected with the season serve to remind us of the morality, the sociality, the geniality of the religion of Christ, which at other seasons are forgotten or ignored. The Christmas cards which are sent us and which we send to others, the presents which we give and receive, the decorations in our houses and in our churches, the family gatherings, the dinner-parties, the games, the pantomimes, the dances—the very dances this time of year, you know, have quite a different character from the crowded and unsociable balls of the season—the way in which we wish a Merry Christmas to every one, and really feel as if we meant it,—all these things make one love the season of Christmas better than any other season in the year. And it is to-day at once my duty and my privilege as a minister of Christ, to remind you that the spirit of Christmas Day should be, for a Christian, the spirit of every day. Let us try to make it so.

It is said that about the time of the birth of Christ certain prophetic souls—shepherds they are called in the New Testament—heard an angelic song, foretelling peace on earth and goodwill towards men. For hundreds of years, however, peace and goodwill have been conspicuous throughout

Christendom by their absence. But there will come a time when the hollowness of orthodox Christianity will be discovered, and when the real Christianity of Christ will take its place. Then, and not till then, will the angel's song be fulfilled.

> " It came upon the midnight clear,—
> That glorious song of old,
> From angels bending near the earth
> To touch their harps of gold :
> ' Peace to the earth, goodwill to men,
> From heaven's all-gracious King.'
> The world in solemn stillness lay
> To hear the angels sing.
>
> Still through the cloven skies they come
> With peaceful wings unfurled ;
> And still their heavenly music floats
> O'er all the weary world.
> Above its sad and lowly plains
> They bend on heavenly wing ;
> And ever o'er its Babel sounds
> The blessed angels sing.
>
> Yet with the woes of sin and strife
> The world has suffered long ;
> Beneath the angel-strain have rolled
> Two thousand years of wrong ;
> And men at war with men hear not
> The love-song which they bring.
> Oh hush the noise, ye men of strife,
> And hear the angels sing !
>
> And ye beneath life's crushing load,
> Whose forms are bending low,
> Who toil along the climbing way
> With painful steps and slow,

Christmas Day.

Look now ! for glad and golden hours
    Come swiftly on the wing ;
Oh rest beside the weary road
    And hear the angels sing !

For lo ! the days are hastening on,
    By prophet bards foretold,
When with the ever-circling years
    Comes back the age of gold ;
When peace shall over all the earth
    Its blessed banner fling,
And the whole world SEND BACK the song
    Which now the angels sing."

New Year's Day.

"Thus saith the Lord, Consider your ways."—HAG. i. 5.
"My people will not consider."—ISA. i. 3.

STRANGE, passing strange! God's people—nay, His children, divine beings—will not consider. And yet, strange though it is, it is true. Instead of acting according to the dictates of reason, we act for the most part on impulse, especially the impulse of custom. We are creatures of habit. We go on day after day, week after week, year after year, feeling, thinking, living, as we have been accustomed to do, without stopping to reflect whether our thoughts are wise or foolish, whether our feelings are good or bad, whether our life is ideal or commonplace. We do not consider our ways. Our power of introspection and self-examination, our faculty of sitting in judgment on ourselves,—these are the highest faculties we possess, and we ought to be proud to use them. Yet often and often it may be truly said that we "do not consider."

It must be admitted there is a certain excuse for us. We really have very little time. The wear and tear of life — especially London life — is so great, that when we do have a chance of sitting down for a moment alone, we are far too tired for serious thought. We hurry from one engagement to another — engagements mostly which we are bound to fulfil — as fast as horses or steam can carry us. And when we get home at night, it is time—very often more than time—to go to bed. On the old-fashioned English Sunday, people had plenty of opportunity for reflection in the intervals of worship; but they generally went to sleep instead. And under the new fashion we are almost as much hurried as on week-days. We pay calls all the afternoon; we go out to dinner in the evening; and we are lucky if we have no engagement afterwards. The hour or two we spend in church on Sunday mornings might be conducive to reflection. But generally they are not. Most persons find that the prayers are too long, and involve too much repetition and monotony. Robert Hall used to say that there were persons who first prayed him into the spirit, and then prayed him out again. Such is the effect, I fear, of our own liturgy. And then the sermon;—well, that ought to conduce to reflection, but generally it does not help us much. Either the preacher tells us what we knew before, and then we return more the slaves of custom than ever; or he tells us what we did not know before, and then as a rule we go home and abuse him, wasting our few moments of leisure in discussing the motes that are in his eyes, which we might better have employed in attempting to take the motes, or perhaps the beams, out of our own eyes. A certain allowance, no doubt, is to be made for all men on account of the pressure of circumstances; and some are less thoughtless than others: but it may be said universally of all of us, that we do not consider our ways as we should,—as we might.

There is one day in the year when such consideration is almost forced upon us—viz., New Year's Day. The first of January, like Janus after whom the month is named, has two faces, one looking to the years that are past, the other to the time that lies before us. We can hardly help remembering to-day that another of our "threescore years and ten" has gone. And this is not a cheerful thought, especially if our past has been in any degree wasted. But never mind; let us look the thought in the face this morning; let us for a few moments consider our ways. Let us look behind and before.

And first behind. From our past experience, so

far as it was bad, we may learn warnings; so far as it was good, we may find suggestions for making it better still. Out of failures or comparative failures the wise man makes stepping-stones to success. Let us ask ourselves, therefore, were our ways last year wise ways? I don't mean—did we never do stupid things? Of course we did many. Pre-eminently stupid must we be if we are not aware of it; and, on the contrary, we are almost wise if we have sense enough always to discover when we have been stupid. I mean, was the set of our lives, the general tenor and tendency of our lives,—was that wise? Are we, in spite of the stupid things, upon the whole developing, progressing, making the best of ourselves. If not, why not? Is it all the fault of circumstances?

And first, regarding the culture of the body. It is scarcely necessary to say we ought to take care of our health. Injuring our health is suicide— slow perhaps, but suicide none the less. It is through the organism the soul receives its impressions and does its work. The wellbeing of the organism, therefore, should be our first concern. How was it with you in this respect last year? Did you live a healthy life? Or, if circumstances prevented that, did you do what you could to counteract them? How about your eating and drinking? Was that altogether satisfactory from the point of view of self-development? Did you eat too much to please yourself? or too little to please some ritualistic clergyman? How about your recreations? Did you have enough? Did you realise the importance of recreation for a healthy and vigorous life? Or did you keep on with your work when prudence told you you should stop? Did you always take care that your recreations were of the right sort—really re-creative? Did you go in for unwholesome amusements? or for wholesome amusements to an unwholesome extent? In one word, are you in as good health as you were last year? If not, why not? Is it all the fault of circumstances?

Secondly, regarding culture of the mind. It is our duty to try and become constantly more perfect, not only in body but in mind; and this of course involves the constant endeavour to know as much as we can about as many subjects as possible. Here our development will chiefly depend upon our reading.

There are people who read nothing but novels. Now I have nothing to say against works of fiction: I only want to remind you that they form but one department of literature. The old-fashioned condemnation of novels was absurd. Some no doubt are stupid; but so are some sermons—just a few. Some novels are bad; so is some meat. But you would not argue (unless you happen to be a vegetarian) that because some butchers sell diseased meat, therefore all meat must be unwholesome. Apart from the fact that we should sometimes read for amusement—the mind needs relaxation as much as the body—there are many works of fiction pregnant with instruction. Novels are the modern form of the drama: Shakespeare would have written them had he lived to-day.

But it is our duty, as far as possible, to read all kinds of books on all kinds of subjects. Did you do so last year? You may not have much time. You may be engaged in business all day long, and this leaves little energy for reading. But have you made the most of your opportunities, such as they are? Have you really tried to know as much as you can about the wonderful world you live in, and to make yourself acquainted with the thoughts of the great and wise and good of all ages? Are you conscious of your ignorance—comparative ignorance at any rate—in every department of human knowledge? Do you seriously wish to become less ignorant? Do you really try to discover magazines, books, persons, that will teach you something? Do you know more to-day than this time last year? Have all your mental faculties during the past year been strengthened by use? If not, why not? Was it all the fault of circumstances?

Then, thirdly, there is the culture of the heart—that faculty by which we sympathise with our fellow-men and wish to do them good. We are not doing the best for ourselves unless we are doing the best we can for humanity. Self-development includes living in and for the lives of others. Have you tried to cultivate your faculty of sympathy? What have you done for others during the past year? You may have given them some money, you could hardly avoid it, it would have looked so bad if you had not; but was that all? Have you made your wife happy? Do your children feel that there could not be so good and kind a father? Are your servants glad that they are in your service? Are the people you meet at dinners and dances the better or the worse for meeting you? Are you doing anything, by your words, by your example, by your personal efforts, for the amelioration of the race? Are you trying to improve the world or any part of it,—your country, for example, or your county, your town or your parish? If not, why not? Is it all the fault of circumstances?

And lastly, as to the culture of the spirit. Complete self-development includes not only living for others, but living with God. Nothing will so help us in doing our duty to others as the thought that we are brethren, that we are the children of one common Father. Besides, in our union with the Infinite lies our own real greatness. By ourselves we are weak, foolish, erring. It is only in communion with God we realise the fact that we are in a sense, that we may become in a higher sense, ourselves divine,—perfect as He is perfect.

Now what have you done during the past year for your spiritual culture? Have you sometimes retired into a secret spot, not for the purpose of saying your customary prayers and offering up your customary requests, but that you might be alone with God? Have you tried to find a church where the service is rendered in such a way as to help your devotion? Or have you dropped into any church that happened to be at hand, so as to get the thing over as quickly as possible? Have you sought out a preacher who would teach and stimulate and encourage you? Or have you persisted in hearing sermons, the only effect of which was to bore and annoy you? Are you really anxious that your own finite life should be suffused by the infinite life of God? If not, why not? Is it all the fault of circumstances?

And to-day we should look forward as well as

backward; we should consider our future ways. Have you any scheme or plan of life? If so, what is it? Will it bear serious examination? What do you intend to do this year? What are you going to make of yourself? Will you not to-day and now resolve to profit by the past and to be wiser in all time to come? Will you not to-day and now determine henceforth to do your very utmost to live a noble and progressive life?

In conclusion, I should like to wish you all a Happy New Year:—happy, if it may be so; but if sadness must come, may God give you speedily the interest of tears!

"*Thanksgiving Service*" *at the Foundling.*

I HAVE three things to do to-day. The first arises out of the fact that this is our Jubilee Service. I have to express for myself and you our humble but heart-felt congratulations to her Majesty our Queen, upon the completion of the fiftieth year of her reign, and upon the outburst of enthusiastic loyalty which that event has evoked from all classes of her subjects. Never has a monarch been more worthy of a people's love. If any proof of this were needed, it is to be found in the "complete and beautiful triumph" of Tuesday last. For, as the 'Times' truly said, "In bygone ages the English people were loyal with little reflection, being ready to cheer any wearer of the crown, and even to give their lives for the sovereign, simply because he occupied the throne. In the present age, the people have become too critical for this impulsive and unreasoning devotion; and their homage, being no longer a mere matter of form, possesses the greater value. The singular strength and warmth of attachment to the Queen, which all sorts and conditions of people delight to manifest, is chiefly due to the prevailing conviction that she cordially reciprocates all their good and kindly wishes." During fifty years she has associated herself with all the joys and sorrows of her people. Hundreds, if not thousands, of her afflicted subjects she has personally endeavoured to console. She has written to them, she has assisted them, she has sometimes gone and wept with them. They tell a pretty story in Scotland of a poor woman who had lost a child, and who received a visit of condolence from the Queen. The neighbours afterwards asked her what the Queen had said. The reply was, "She didna say onything; she jist sat and grat wi' me!" It is something—it is much—that for half a century she has governed her mighty empire with such unfailing wisdom. But it is more—infinitely more—that she has shown a genuine sympathy for every individual subject whom she knew to be in distress. She has been at once the best of queens and the most womanly of women. With all our hearts we say God bless her!

The second thing I have to do this morning is to

give you some little account of the history and objects of the Foundling Hospital. It was founded in 1739, and it owed its existence to Captain Coram. This philanthropic gentleman had, it seems, more than once stumbled over infants who had been left in the streets to die; and he conceived the idea of founding an institution where these poor little waifs might be received and nurtured. In most cases the infants had been deserted by their mothers in order to avoid disgrace. Captain Coram thought it was the duty of a Christian community, not only to prevent the destruction of every such innocent child, but also and specially to help its mother to recover her lost position, and to give her a fresh start in life. He endeavoured to enlist public opinion in favour of such a scheme; but public opinion was against him, and for seventeen years he laboured in vain to change it. At last, however, he succeeded, chiefly through the influence of some noble ladies — noble by birth and noble in character. Women have the reputation of being very hard upon one another's failings. And no doubt they sometimes are. But in this institution we have a proof that it is not always so. Had it not been for the assistance of ladies possessing great influence in the State, Captain Coram's scheme would never have been carried out. At last however a royal charter was granted for the foundation of a hospital which was "to maintain and educate exposed and deserted children."

For a time the hospital was badly managed and did more harm than good. Captain Coram had himself pointed out that great care would be needed for the proper working of such an undertaking. But for a long while no such care was shown. The first admission of children took place in 1741 under the following advertisement. "To-morrow at eight o'clock in the evening this house will be opened for the reception of twenty children, under the following regulations.—No child exceeding the age of two months will be taken in, nor such as have the evil, leprosy or disease of the like nature, whereby the health of the other children may be endangered; for the discovery whereof every child is to be inspected as soon as it is brought; and the person who brings it is to come in at the outward door and ring a bell at the inward door, and not go away until the child is returned or notice given of its reception; but no questions whatever will be asked of any person who brings a child, nor shall any servant of the house presume to endeavour to discover who such person is, on pain of being discharged." On such occasions the number of applications was greatly in excess of the number of children to be admitted. There were frequently a hundred women at the door, when only twenty children could be received. This gave rise to a good deal of scrambling, not to say fighting, which was eventually put a stop to by making the women ballot for the right of presenting their infants for inspection. Those who drew balls of a certain colour went up first, and if any of their children were rejected on the ground of health or age, ballots were again taken to fill up the vacancies. Of course it is manifest that very little good could come of a system of charity so unguardedly dispensed, especially as chance so often favours the least deserving. In fifteen years—viz., from 1741 to 1756—1384 children were received, or upon an average 92 annually. This was only a small proportion of those for whom admittance had been sought.

The managers however looked forward all along to the time when they should be able to open their hospital upon the most unrestricted plan. At last they applied to Parliament for help. The House of Commons agreed that it was desirable for the hospital to receive all the children offered to it, and grants of money sufficient for this purpose were guaranteed. A basket was accordingly hung outside of the gates of the hospital, and an advertisement publicly announced that all children under the age of two months tendered for admission would be received, in pursuance of which on the 2d June 1756, the first day of general reception, 117 children were admitted.

The new system was even worse than the old. The workhouses handed over all their infants to this convenient receptacle. It happened not unfrequently that a father who was unwilling to be at the expense of keeping his child, would take it by force from its mother and deposit it in the Foundling basket. The hospital was so useful, that from every part of England children were sent up to it by the score. In fact there arose a new trade. There were a considerable number of persons who undertook to convey children to the Foundling Hospital at so much a-head. These traders often found it the simplest and most agreeable plan to pocket the fee without doing the work. At Monmouth a person was tried for the murder of his child, which was found drowned with a stone about its neck; when the prisoner proved that he delivered it to a travelling tinker, who received a guinea from him to carry it to the hospital. Nay it was publicly asserted in the House of Commons that one man, who had the charge of five infants in baskets, happened in his journey to get intoxicated, lay all night asleep on a common, and in the morning he found three of the children dead! A man one day riding into London, being asked what he had in his panniers, answered, "I have two children in each; I brought them from Yorkshire for the Foundling Hospital. I used to have eight guineas for a trip, but lately another man has set up against me, which has lowered my price." Even in cases where children were really left at the hospital, the barbarous wretches who conveyed them, not content with the gratuity they received, stripped the poor infants of their clothing into the bargain, leaving them naked in the basket at the hospital gate.

In the four years during which this system lasted, 15,000 children were received into the hospital. The avowed object of the institution — viz., the saving of life—was frustrated by the magnitude of the scale on which it was attempted. Many of the infants received at the gates did not live to be taken into the wards; and altogether there was a mortality of over 70 per cent. It became evident therefore that the institution must be worked upon a different principle. The House of Commons decided that the indiscriminate admission of all children into the hospital had been attended with many evil consequences, and ordered it to be discontinued. For some time after this, owing to want of funds, children were received for payment, and no inquiries were made; but since 1801 no child has been received into the hospital, either directly or indirectly, with any sum of money large or small.

The present practice of the governors seems perfectly unexceptionable. Each application for admission is now decided on its own merits. Any illegitimate child less than twelve months old is eligible, provided its father cannot be found, and provided there are no other relations able or willing to maintain it. Each child must be brought by its mother, who is required to prove, to the satisfaction of the governors, that she had previously borne a good character, and that she is desirous of living in the future an honest and honourable life. In competing cases, where other things were equal, the child of that mother would be selected whose previous character had been the best, and who had the best prospect of retrieving the past through the aid of the institution. In the words of one of my illustrious predecessors, Sydney Smith, "No child drinks of our cup or eats of our bread whose reception, upon the whole, we are not certain to be more conducive than pernicious to the interests of religion and good morals. We help no mother whom it would not be merciless and shocking to turn away; we exercise the trust reposed in us with a trembling and sensitive conscience; we do not think it enough to say, This woman is wretched and betrayed and forsaken, but we calmly reflect if it be expedient that her tears should be dried up, her loneliness sheltered and her wants supplied." There is, I know, a prudish, hellish cruelty which would condemn every deserted mother to everlasting despair, and this cruelty is sometimes manifested by persons who dare to call themselves Christians. Christians? Why, when a woman was brought to Christ convicted of a far worse sin than that of the persons whose children we receive, what did Christ say? "Let him that is without sin cast the first stone at her. Woman, hath no man condemned thee? neither do I condemn thee." We are not concerned to show ourselves more righteous than Christ. I believe there is no institution in London which is more in harmony with the genius of Christianity and with the spirit of Christ than the Foundling Hospital. And if I may say without impertinence before their faces what I have sometimes said behind their backs, I believe there is no body of men who work more conscientiously and more assiduously for the good of others than the governors of this institution.

The third and last thing I have to do is to say a word or two to those of my young friends behind me who are to-day celebrating their majority. Let me begin by congratulating you on your coming of age. You have passed safely through infancy and childhood and are now grown up. You have received a good education; you have had a fair start in life; an honourable future is open to each of you. All this is matter for thankfulness. And you have done well to come here to-day to offer up your thanks to Almighty God.

But there is only one way of truly thanking God, and that is by our lives. The words of our lips are by themselves worthless. Unless they correspond to the general tenor of our conduct, they are mere breath—wasted breath—mockery. And therefore if you really feel grateful, as I am sure you do, you must resolve to show it. And you will never have a better opportunity than to-day for forming such a resolution. You all know what is meant by a red-letter day. In the almanac certain days—such as Sundays and saints' days—are printed in red ink. Just as these red-letter days stand out conspicuously in the almanac, so to-day stands out conspicuously in your lives. It is quite different from the ordinary everyday days. There is a peculiar solemnity and impressiveness attaching to it. A good resolution formed seriously to-day will not soon be forgotten. It will make all the rest of your lives better than they otherwise would have been. There is one simple resolution I want you to make. I want you to remember that you are grown up and resolve to act accordingly. Coming of age is called coming to years of discretion. It is not unfortunately always so in fact; but that is what it always should be. Discretion means discernment,—distinguishing between things that differ, between right and wrong, between the desirable and undesirable, between what is wise and what is foolish. It is this discretion or discernment which makes the real difference between a grown-up person and a child. The man or woman who lacks this faculty—or rather who neglects to use it, for we all have it—the man or the woman who does not use the faculty of discretion, is in reality only a baby, a large baby, but a baby for all that.

Now there are three things which make up your life, and to which this faculty of discretion or discernment is to be applied—thoughts, words, acts. Get into the way of asking yourself, Am I thinking wisely or foolishly? am I speaking kindly or unkindly? am I acting rightly or wrongly? The more you accustom yourselves to this kind of self-examination, the better and nobler will your lives become. If your lives are to be what they should be, you must make a hard fight for it. But realising clearly the difference between what you *are* thinking and saying and doing, and what you *ought* to be thinking and saying and doing, is more than half the battle. Evil is wrought by want of thought more than by want of heart. By far the larger proportion of the misery and wickedness in the world is due to the fact that people will not reflect, will not remember that they have come to years of discretion. Do you therefore remember it to-day, and resolve that you will remember it all the days of your life. Remember that you are grown up! That is text and sermon all in one; or if you would like it in Scriptural language,— there are some people, you know, who think that a text ought always to be taken out of the Bible, —well I can give you one even shorter than my own—" be men."

Science and Religion.

"*What God hath joined together, let not man put asunder.*"—
MATT. xix. 6.

I WISH to speak to you this morning about the so-called conflict between science and religion. I want to explain to you that what is thus erroneously described is really the conflict between science and a certain low form of theology. I want to show you that between true religion and genuine science there never has been, and never can be, any incompatibility.

I had better begin by explaining terms. Science, you know, means knowledge,—systematised, classified knowledge. Very frequently the word science is taken as standing for the physical sciences exclusively. It is so understood, of course, whenever it is regarded as something different from theology. For theology is itself a science; it is a classification of our knowledge, or supposed knowledge, of God.

Theology, therefore, is no more religion than any other science is religion. It is impossible to overestimate the mischief which has arisen from confounding theology with religion. There are no two things in the universe more different. Theology is a science, religion is an art. Theology is theory, religion is practice. Theology is concerned with the intellect, religion with the heart. Theology is formulated knowledge, religion is a mode of life. It has been commonly, almost universally, assumed that an eminent theologian must be an eminent example of piety. But we might just as well imagine that, because a man was an expert in physiology, he must have a fine *physique*. A theologian is not *as such* religious, is not necessarily religious, any more than an astronomer or a chemist. A theologian may be a worse man than an atheist. There is no more connection between the knowledge of theology and the practice of religion than between the knowledge of geography and the possession of a landed estate. So that even if *science and theology* were always and necessarily in conflict, it would not follow that there was any incompatibility between *science and religion*.

But further, I must point out to you that there are two kinds of theology, and it is only with one of these that physical science ever conflicts. There is, in the first place, a stagnant theology, which assumes that all is known which ever can be known regarding the nature of God and the methods of His working, and which objects to any discoveries not provided for in its own cut-and-dried little system. This was the theology which prevailed during the middle ages, and between which and physical science the conflict was very fierce. In fact the theologians, when they had the chance, were in the habit of literally roasting the scientists. There is however another theology, which is not stagnant but progressive, which is not opposed to science but which is itself strictly scientific. This rational, progressive, scientific theology recognises the fact that, as truth is infinite, it can never be at any given time more than partially known. This theology is always open to the reception of new ideas, and can therefore never come into conflict with any scientific truths. The rational theologian thankfully accepts the discoveries of the physicists, as valuable additions to the knowledge of God. For the physical scientist is concerned, though he may not himself realise the fact, with divine revelation. There could be no such thing as science at all unless nature were a revelation of mind. Consider. Science, according to Bacon's well-known phrase, is "the interpretation of nature."

To interpret is to explain, and nothing can be explained which is not in itself rational. Nature is interpretable, because she has an intelligent constitution; and to say that her constitution is intelligent, is to say that she is dominated and suffused by thought. Thought can only grasp what is the outcome of thought. Reason can only comprehend what is reasonable. You cannot explain the conduct of a fool; you cannot interpret the actions of a lunatic. They are chaotic, irregular, contradictory, meaningless, absurd. It is only in proportion to a man's intelligence that his actions bear an intelligible relation to one another. Similarly if nature were merely a fortuitous concurrence of atoms—an irrational system destitute of thought—there would be no possibility of knowledge; she would lack the coherency which only thought can supply. The atoms would be constantly rushing aimlessly about, we could never discover what they were after, we could never foresee what would happen next. Even supposing they had by chance produced such a world as this, no reliance could be placed on them. At any moment they might do something which they had never done before. At any moment the earth might vanish from beneath our feet, or in ten thousand other ways the prevailing arrangements might be suddenly reversed. There could be no course of nature, no laws of sequence, no possibility of scientific prediction, in the case of an irrational play of atoms. But, as it is, we know exactly how the forces of nature act, and how they will continue to act. We can express their mode of working in the most precise mathematical formulæ. All the parts of nature are bound together by intellectual, and therefore intelligible, relations. Progress in knowledge consists in discovering the order, the law, the system—in a word, the reason—which underlies material phenomena. Interpreting nature is neither more nor less than making our own the thoughts which nature implies. Scientific hypotheses consist in guessing at these thoughts; scientific verification in proving that we have guessed aright. When after many failures Kepler at last hit upon the laws of planetary motion, he exclaimed, "O God, I think again Thy thoughts after Thee!" Science, then, is but a partial copy of an intellectual system coextensive with the material universe. And the devotion to truth which characterises the scientific man is just the determination to give up his own individual fancies and predictions and prejudices, to lay aside his own private and erroneous views, and to adopt the thoughts which are higher than his — the thoughts, namely, of the Infinite thinker. Between the physical scientist and the *rational* theologian there can therefore be no possible conflict. Their aim is actually identical. They are both seeking to discover the mind of God.

And it is equally impossible that there could be any conflict between legitimate science and genuine religion. Just as science consists in the free surrender of the mind, so religion consists in the free surrender of the heart, to the Power which is not ourselves. Just as it is the aim of the scientist to get rid of his own erroneous opinions and to adopt the thoughts which are the thoughts of Nature, so we can only be religious by allowing our hearts to be possessed and ruled by a Love that is purer, by a Will which is holier, than our own. Religion does for the heart what science does for the intellect. To be scientific is to adopt the thoughts of God. To be religious is to adopt the feelings and sentiments and emotions and purposes of God. So that the genuinely religious man is not proceeding in a direction opposite to that which the man of science takes; he is only going further in the same direction.

Why is it, then, that so many eminent philosophers speak and write as if religion and science were necessarily opposed and contradictory? It is important for us to consider this question. A great name is constantly mistaken for a great argument. And it not unfrequently happens that a person naturally inclined to be religious grows ashamed of his inclination, when a few clever men tell him that religion is unscientific.

Now there is no doubt a strong bias against religion existing in the minds of many eminent modern scientists. And for this the theology of the middle ages is very mainly responsible. Century after century it did its best to discourage scientific pursuits; and when it failed in this despicable purpose, it avenged itself by the most cruel, not to say fiendish, persecutions. If you think of Copernicus, Galileo, Bruno; if you read the long, ghastly story of the treatment which for ages scientists received at the hands of theologians; if you remember that many of the opinions which were once defended by torture and by murder, are now known to be absurdly erroneous;—you will understand why those who devote their lives to the pursuit of physical science should have conceived a dislike for everything that has ever been connected with theology, not excluding even the ideas of the soul and of God —ideas which theology has so grossly caricatured and abused. The old medieval theologians thought themselves eminent examples of piety. The modern scientists take them at their word and say—not unjustly—if that is religion, the world would be better off without any.

But further, the hostility of many scientific men to religion may be partly accounted for by the one-sidedness which is very apt to characterise the specialist. Exclusive attention to any pursuit has a tendency to narrow a man's sympathies, and make him intellectually incapable of dealing with matters outside his accustomed sphere of thought. Bacon said, "A little natural philosophy, and the first entrance into it, doth dispose the opinion to atheism; but much natural philosophy, and wading deep into it, will bring about men's minds to religion." Now, judging by the modern scientists, this is not true. Men like Tyndall and Huxley are no tyros in natural philosophy; they have "waded deep into it"; and yet their minds are not brought about to religion. One cause of this, I think, may be found in the fact of their exclusive, or almost exclusive, devotion to physical studies. Men who spend their entire lives in investigating the properties of matter, are in danger of forgetting that there is anything else; and at last perhaps they become absolutely incapable of conceiving the possibility of immaterial existence. Men who enthusiastically cultivate the intellect are very apt to ignore and neglect the heart.

And this one-sidedness generally fosters a spirit of arrogance, which is incompatible with honest and unbiassed inquiry in the obnoxious spheres of thought. The self-complacent conceit of the older theologians has been transferred to some of the modern scientists. All truth is contained in our theology, said the former. All truth will be discovered by us physicists, say the latter. Away with your physical experimenters, said the old theologians. Away with your poets and philosophers and saints, say the new scientists.

We can hardly wonder, perhaps—though it is a pity—that they should have been intoxicated by their triumphs in the study of matter. Their spectroscopes have revealed the constituent elements of sun and stars. Their geological surveys have shown, written clearly on the rocks, the history of life from the eozoon up to man. Their telescopes have detected in the Milky Way planets in the very process of creation. Their microscopes have brought the invisible within the range of their vision. They have gone abroad throughout the physical universe weighing, measuring, analysing, foretelling; and they begin to feel as if nothing could be hid from their instruments of research. "I have swept the heavens with my telescope," said Lalande, "and have not found a God." "We have examined the brain with our microscopes," say the physiologists, "and have not found a soul." What we cannot discover, say all the materialists, with our physical instruments and by our physical methods, cannot possibly exist. The older theologians, foolish as they were, were never guilty of greater folly than this.

Now do not misunderstand me. Nothing could be further from my intention than to speak of the great masters in physical science without becoming respect. I have the highest possible admiration for them. But what I would most earnestly insist upon is this,—the magnificence of their achievements in physics does not give any authority whatsoever to their views upon other subjects. No one can be an expert in everything. And modern physicists, when they wander into the sphere of metaphysics, not unfrequently talk nonsense. Let me give you one striking illustration — viz., Professor Huxley's teaching in regard to the freedom of the will. His general opinion, as you know, is that we are not free agents, that we are mere machines worked by vital forces. And yet he says, without seeing the inconsistency, "A human being, though a machine, is capable within certain limits of self-adjustment." And again: "Our volition counts for something as a condition of the course of events." That a man of his enormous ability should not see the inconsistency, is a very remarkable illustration of the helplessness—the almost childish helplessness—of the physicists in alien spheres of thought. Since a machine is incapable of self-adjustment,[1] to say that I am capable of it is to say that I am not a machine. Since the desire of a being under absolute restraint does not count for anything as a condition of the course of events, to say that mine does is to say that I am so far free. Professor Huxley's views on this subject are self-contradictory and therefore absurd. Nor is this after all very surprising, since it is a subject which he has not studied.

We need experts, not only in one or two, but in all departments of investigation. You would not go to a psychologist if you wanted information as to the nature of life, and why should you go to a biologist if you want to be instructed as to the nature of the mind? To adopt Professor Huxley's opinions on questions relating to the soul, is like going to consult the senior wrangler when out of health, or seeking the advice of a bookworm in the purchase of a horse. The wrangler may have

---

[1] It is scarcely necessary to mention that the so-called self-adjusting machines must act, like all other machines, as they are made to act.

amused himself at odd moments by dabbling a little in medicine; the bookworm may have bestridden a horse or two in his day; still, we might be excused for feeling a little hesitation in accepting their judgment as infallible. Similarly, the physicist has a mission in the world which cannot be fulfilled by the metaphysical philosopher; and the metaphysical philosopher has a mission which cannot be fulfilled by the physicist. This was once recognised by Professor Tyndall. In the eloquent conclusion to the Belfast address he says, "The world embraces not only a Newton but a Shakespeare, not only a Boyle but a Raphael, not only a Kant but a Beethoven, not only a Darwin but a Carlyle. Not in each of these, but in all, is human nature whole. They are not opposed but supplementary; not mutually exclusive but reconcilable." That is true—though the agnostics, Tyndall himself among the number, are constantly forgetting it. They seem to imagine that human nature will be explained, so far as explanation is possible, by physical investigators alone. But there are other experts in other departments of human experience; and on what ground can we refuse to listen to them? Ignoring the arguments of the mental philosopher is as one-sided and unjustifiable as closing one's ears against the teaching

Science and Religion. 243

of the physical scientist. Finely has Walt Whitman said, "We will joyfully accept modern science, and loyally follow it; but there remains a still higher flight, a higher fact — the eternal soul of man. To me the crown of scientism will be to open the way for a more splendid theology, for ampler and diviner songs."

The ampler songs of which Whitman speaks may not come in your day or mine. Our race as yet is in its babyhood. The agnostics are not alone in their one-sidedness. All men are one-sided more or less. Our vision is blurred, our aims are petty, our sympathies are contracted. But it need not always be so. It will not always be so. There come to some of us now and again moments of prophetic inspiration, when the things of the present are as though they were not, when we live in the far-off future. In a moment such as that, I hear an anthem of surpassing indescribable beauty; I can distinguish the voices of scientists as they mingle harmoniously with the voices of poets, philosophers and saints. The anthem ascends to the eternal throne. It is the offering of perfected humanity to God.

The editor of the 'Whitehall Review' did me the honour to write a long article upon this sermon. But from the tenor of the article, I was afraid that I had not made the general drift of my argument quite clear. So I sent him the following letter, which he was good enough to insert :—

Sir,—In your kindly criticism of my sermon upon Science and Religion, you say that "Professor Huxley came in for his lashing." I am sorry I should have given you this impression. All that I wanted to insist upon was the fact that experts in physics had no claim to authority in metaphysics. I gave, as an illustration of the metaphysical weakness of the physicists, Professor Huxley's remarks upon the freedom of the will, which as I pointed out appeared to be contradictory and therefore absurd, just as the remarks of a mental philosopher would probably be if he attempted to dogmatise on biological subjects. Professor Huxley himself showed brilliantly a little while ago that the Prime Minister of England may be very ignorant of palæontology—so ignorant that an eighteenpenny manual would have made him comparatively well informed. And so we need not be surprised if a President of the Royal Society finds himself at sea, when he attempts to deal with such problems as the existence of the soul or the freedom of the will. Surely it is not "lashing" Professor Huxley to say that he is, and must be, subject to the laws of nature. And it is one of the laws of nature that no man can be an expert in everything.—I remain, sir, your obedient servant,

A. W. Momerie.

Patience.

"Let patience have her perfect work."—JAMES i. 4.

THERE is perhaps no quality which we so much need, and at the same time no quality in which most of us are so deficient, as that of patience. This word means, as you know, the capacity for bearing or enduring. And there are two things in human life which specially call for the exercise of patience—viz., work and trouble. Let me say a word or two about each.

And first, of work. Most people have to work in order to live at all. And those who would live worthily, successfully, greatly, must not only work, but work hard, work continuously, work till they die. There is a pathetic little verse—I forget whose—representing a conversation between Man and Destiny. It is as follows:—

> "Does the road wind up hill all the way?
>   Yes, to the very end.
> Will the day's journey take the whole long day?
>   From morn to night, my friend."

Now all work tends to become monotonous; all long-continued work is fatiguing; all work, just in proportion to its value, necessitates patience—the capacity to endure. But how is this capacity to be acquired and developed? If we are naturally impatient—as most of us are—how can we make ourselves patient? I answer, partly by reflection, and partly by practice.

I would have you all reflect often and long on the power of work. Think of what it has accomplished in the past. We unfortunately believe too much in genius and too little in toil. And yet every one who has been acknowledged by the world as a genius, has toiled just in proportion to his fame. The power of genius is in reality the power of work. The best definition I know of genius is that which calls it the infinite capacity for taking pains. You will find the truth of this definition illustrated by all the world's greatest men. Tennyson wrote "Come into the Garden, Maud" in five minutes, but spent two months in improving it. Goethe worked at "Faust" on and off till he died. Shakespeare, as Mr Swinburne has pointed out, laboured year after year in improving "Hamlet," not for the contemporary stage, but for posterity. Michael Angelo—you know the old story. A friend called one day upon the sculptor, and found him finishing a statue. Some time after, when he called again, Angelo was still engaged upon the same work. His friend, looking at the figure, said, "You have been idle since I saw you last." "By no means," replied Angelo; "I have retouched this part and polished that; I have softened this feature and brought out this muscle; I have given more expression to this lip and more energy to this limb." "Well, well," said his friend, "but all these are trifles." "It may be so," said the sculptor, "but recollect that trifles make perfection, and perfection is no trifle." And there is the same necessity for diligence in all other departments of work. You think that the laws of nature are discovered by inspiration. Well, inspiration it may be, but it is inspiration that moves very, very slowly. Faraday said the first task of the scientific investigator is to invent hypotheses, and his second task is to feel disgusted with them. Kepler found out the actual movements of the planets, but only after ninety-nine failures. Genius is something very different from cleverness; that is merely talent. It would be almost an insult to call the man of genius clever. The clever man will do a hundred things fairly well, while the genius does but the one. The talented man's productions are admired for a little while, and then they are forgotten. The productions of genius live for ever. But for work, the genius would very often rank below his fellows. Newton was the dunce of his school. Demosthenes was at first a stutterer. There is a story told of a teacher of music becoming indignant with a talented but lazy pupil, and saying to him that a good voice was really an obstacle to good singing. And I heard last year in Italy, that when Madame Albani first went to study under Signor Lamperti, she had so poor a voice that the Meister thought she would never succeed as a singer. On every page of history you will find illustrations of the fact that it is not ability but work which makes success.

Perhaps we are all agreed that success cannot be expected without work. But the worst of it is we all of us expect too much success for too little work. We look for the greatest effects from the smallest causes; and these effects we demand with an absolutely impossible celerity. We are ready enough to remind our impetuous neighbour that Rome wasn't built in a day. But our own private Rome, we think, is going to be an exception to the rule. And when we find it isn't, we become impatient and feel ready to throw up the game in despair. We are often dissatisfied, not only with the results of our work, but with the work itself. We think we have not accomplished anything when we have really done very well. I remember when I was writing my thesis for my first doctor's degree, every day I said to myself I have done practically nothing; and yet at the end of three weeks it was finished. That was quick work; but, looked at piecemeal, it seemed to be most hopelessly slow. We must learn to believe in the cumulative effects of work; and we must learn to wait. The child keeps digging up the seed he has planted, and is disappointed because it has not grown. It would have grown fast enough if he had but let it be. "All the performances of human art at which we look with praise or wonder," says Dr Johnson, "are the results of the resistless force of perseverance; it is by this that the quarry becomes a pyramid, and that distant countries are united by canals. If a man was to compare the effect of a single stroke of the pickaxe or of one impression of the spade with the general design and last result, he would be overwhelmed by the sense of their disproportion; yet these petty operations, incessantly continued, in time overcome the greatest difficulties; mountains are levelled and oceans bounded by the slender force of human beings." Sir Jonah Barrington used to tell a story of a carpenter who was making a magistrate's bench, and who was laughed at by his companions for the peculiar pains he took in planing and smoothing it. He smilingly observed that he did so to make it easy for himself, as he was resolved not to die till he had the right to sit upon it. And he was as good as his word. He lived to sit as a magistrate on the very bench he had sawed and planed. *There* was a man who believed in the cumulative effects of work; and his faith, like all rational faith, had its reward.

And we must not only be prepared to wait for success, but we must sometimes be prepared positively to fail. Failures are not agreeable, but they are often useful. At Cambridge the college authorities are very loath to give a man a scholarship in his first year. They think it makes him lazy; and so they always withhold it except in cases of extraordinary merit. I did not show that extraordinary merit, and I did not get the scholarship. I am very glad. My work was far better the second year than it would have been if I had succeeded the first. A failure is a most excellent tonic for any one who believes in the ultimate power of work.

And there is one thing more that should be said upon the subject, though it only applies to the few rare individuals who are greatly in advance of their age. These men must be content not only with temporary but even with permanent failure, so far as the verdict of their contemporaries is concerned. And as a rule such men do not mind. Much as they would like to be understood and appreciated by their own age, they are buoyed up by the thought that an authoritative judgment can be passed by posterity alone. When Kepler had finished his great work, he did not expect that it would be received with enthusiasm; he was quite prepared to find it ignored. He said in the ever-memorable words—and there is no finer instance of the power of faith—"I may well wait a hundred years for a reader, since God has waited six thousand years for a discoverer."

> Was die Schickung schickt, ertrage;
> Wer ausharret wird gekrönt.

So much for patience in regard to work. Now let me say a word about patience in trouble, suffering, affliction, or whatever we may please to call it, for which we can see no reason, which appears irremediable, and which does not seem at all likely to lead to anything either for ourselves or others in this world or the next. And here it is far harder to practise patience. Patient continuance in welldoing, when we have something to which we can look forward at the end, hard as it is, is comparatively easy. But how can you expect a man to be patient under what seems useless, needless, wasted suffering? How can you expect a man to be patient under bereavement, when he has lost one who can never be replaced? How can you expect a man to be patient when, on looking back over his past life, he sees that it has *all* been a failure? Faith in himself is of no use. He feels, he knows that he is helpless. Faith in the power of work is here equally impossible; work can now do nothing for him, except perhaps momentarily to drown his grief. Under such circumstances patience is absolutely impossible, apart from faith in God and immortality. And this faith is what so few of us really have. Though we constantly *say* we "believe in the resurrection of the dead and the life of the world to come," we chafe and fret when our wishes are thwarted as if there were no life but the present, as if the grave were the end of all things for us. When trouble comes upon us, we are as impatient as if we had never heard of God. We are always ready to preach patience; why cannot we practise what we preach? We can exercise faith for other men; shall we never exercise it for ourselves? Is it likely that in a well-ordered universe —and we profess to believe that the universe is well ordered—is is likely that *our* welfare alone has been overlooked? If it were our destiny to fight impotently against surrounding forces, which were bound in the end to destroy us, then there would be an excuse for our impatience. But if there be a God, a loving God, a God who is making all things to work together for good, then our fretful impatience is puerile and contemptible. Have we not the glorious hope of everlasting life?

Yes; but this very hope often makes us impatient. We should like, instead of a hope, to have possessed a demonstration. We should like to know exactly the kind of existence that awaits us in the future. We should like to be allowed in this life some communion with those whom we have loved and lost. And yet in the present state of our mental development, it may be quite impossible for us to understand any fuller or clearer revelation than that which has been given to us. Even if it were possible, it might be supremely inexpedient. There is probably no other discipline so useful for us as that of the comparative ignorance in which we are compelled to remain. At any rate I think we might bring ourselves to the sure and certain hope, that the Author of our being is caring for our future and doing in regard to it that which alone is best. Surely there is enough rationality in the universe, enough joy, enough beauty, enough glory, to discountenance the belief that the end of it all will be nothingness.

"Strive; yet I do not promise
   The prize you dream of to-day
Will not fade when you think to grasp it,
   And melt in your hand away.
But another and holier treasure,
   You would now perchance disdain,
Will come when your toil is over
   And pay you for all your pain.

Wait; yet I do not tell you
   The hour you long for now
Will not come with its radiance vanished
   And a shadow upon its brow.
Yet far through the misty future,
   With a crown of starry light,
An hour of joy you know not
   Is winging her silent flight.

The Sabbath.

"Remember the Sabbath-day, to keep it holy. Six days shalt thou labour and do all thy work: but the seventh day is the Sabbath of the Lord thy God: in it thou shalt not do any work, thou, nor thy son, nor thy daughter, thy man-servant, nor thy maid-servant, thy cattle, and thy stranger that is within thy gates."
—EXOD. xx. 8-10.

WILL you please listen to the following conversation between two gentlemen — Mr Orthodox, who keeps the Sabbath or thinks he keeps it, and Mr Heterodox, who doesn't keep it and doesn't wish to keep it.

Mr H. Why do you keep Sunday?

Mr O. Because of the fourth commandment.

Mr H. My good sir, that refers to Saturday.

Mr O. Yes; but the day has since been changed.

Mr H. Who changed it?

Mr O. Well, I don't know. I suppose the apostles. We read in the New Testament that they assembled together on the first day of the week, and this answers to the old meetings in the synagogues on the Jewish Sabbath.

Mr H. What business had the apostles to change the day ? What business had they to observe the first day when they were commanded to observe the seventh ?

Mr O. I don't know. But they were apostles; they were inspired ; it must have been all right.

Mr H. I should like to ask you another question. Do you believe that the Levitical regulations for the Sabbath are still binding ? that people should have no fires, no candles, no anything ?

Mr O. Certainly not. The rigour of the old Jewish Sabbath has been relaxed.

Mr H. Indeed ! Who relaxed it ?

Mr O. I don't know. I suppose the apostles.

Mr H. What makes you think so ?

Mr O. I don't know.

Mr H. How far has it been relaxed ?

Mr O. I can't exactly say.

Mr H. Well, how do you keep it ?

Mr O. I go to church twice.

Mr H. Is that all ?

Mr O. I read a chapter in the Bible.

Mr H. Is that all ?

Mr O. Well, I make the children learn hymns.

Mr H. Would you like to see the museums and picture-galleries open on Sunday ?

Mr O. No; certainly not.

Mr H. Why not?

Mr O. It would involve labour.

Mr H. Oh, I see; you don't approve of labour on Sunday. I suppose you give your own servants a holiday.

Mr O. Well, no.

Mr H. That, of course, is one of the obligations which have been relaxed!

We need not listen any more. We have heard enough to convince us that the views of Mr Orthodox upon this subject are in a state of hopeless confusion. I venture to say there are hundreds and thousands of persons who, if asked the same sort of questions, would give the same sort of replies. The fourth commandment, as a matter of fact, is only obeyed by one small sect in England —viz., the seventh-day Baptists. And yet an immense number of professing Christians believe that they ought to obey it, and what is still more curious, believe that they do obey it. How wonderful is man's power of self-deception! Just think of it. People fancy they are obeying a command to keep a certain day in one way, when they keep a different day in another way. It is as if they were told to wear a white dress on Monday, and imagined they were complying when they wore a black dress on Tuesday. How can Christianity ever be respected by the world at large when people like this are regarded as its representatives?

I. Now I want you to observe, in the first place, that the fourth commandment is distinguished from the other commandments in the Decalogue by being exclusively addressed to Jews. The reasons which were given for its observance are reasons which cannot have any weight with us. In Exodus xx. 11, it is based on the six days' theory of creation, which has long ago been exploded. "Remember the Sabbath, . . . for in six days the Lord made heaven and earth, the sea and all that in them is, and rested the seventh day: *wherefore* the Lord blessed the Sabbath-day, and hallowed it." In Deut. v. 15, it is based on the fact that those to whom it was addressed had been slaves. "Remember that thou wast a servant in the land of Egypt, and that the Lord thy God brought thee out thence through a mighty hand and by a stretched-out arm: *therefore* the Lord thy God commanded thee to keep the Sabbath-day."

II. The fourth commandment is distinguished from the rest by being addressed exclusively to the rich. It is a command given to the owners of men-servants and maid-servants, &c. It was evidently laid down in the interests of the poor.

Servants were in those days mere slaves; and under the Mosaic government many enactments were made in their favour. This was one. The fourth commandment was intended to secure for them a periodical respite from the excessive toil to which they were generally condemned.

III. The fourth commandment says nothing about worship. It is a command to rest. The meaning of to keep holy, or to sanctify, is simply to set apart for a particular purpose. It is used in other passages, where the purpose is purely secular. It is the same word which is translated in Jeremiah xxii. 7, "prepare"; and in this passage the word signifies setting apart for war. And so the Saturday was to be set apart for rest, as is shown by the context—"Remember the Sabbath-day to set it apart; in it thou shalt do no manner of work." Of course it is desirable to take advantage of any special opportunity afforded by any special days for worship and spiritual contemplation, but this is not keeping the fourth commandment. That commandment was kept by any one who abstained from work and let his servants abstain from work, even though he never once thought of God. It was broken by any one who allowed a single animal to labour, even though he himself spent the entire day in spiritual exercises. Such a man, under the Levitical dispensation, would have been put to death. In other words, the first commandment is not the fourth. It is quite possible to keep the first commandment and to break the fourth; or, *vice versa*, to keep the fourth and to break the first.

IV. Christ showed little respect for the traditional and conventional methods—the cant methods—of Sabbatarian observance which were common in His time. In fact they excited His contempt and indignation. Then, as now, people would do certain things that suited their own convenience; but there they would draw the line. Things profitable to themselves, things they liked or didn't mind, they put on one side of the line; things unprofitable to themselves, things they didn't care about, they put on the other side. On the plea of Sabbath observance, they could very often avoid the trouble of doing good. Christ most emphatically condemned all such conduct. For instance. "He was teaching in one of the synagogues on the Sabbath. And, behold, there was a woman which had a spirit of infirmity eighteen years, and was bowed together, and could in no wise lift up herself. And when Jesus saw her, He called her to Him, and said unto her, Woman, thou art loosed from thine infirmity. And He laid His hands on her: and immediately she was made straight, and glorified God. And the ruler of the synagogue answered with indignation, because that Jesus had healed on the Sabbath-day, and said unto the people, There are six days in which men ought to work: in them therefore come and be healed, and not on the Sabbath-day. The Lord then answered him and said, Thou hypocrite, doth not each one of you on the Sabbath loose his ox or his ass from the stall, and lead him away to watering. And ought not this woman to be loosed from this bond on the Sabbath-day?" Or read again the following: "It came to pass, that He went through the cornfields on the Sabbath-day; and His disciples began, as they went, to pluck the ears of corn. And the Pharisees said unto him, Behold, why do they on the Sabbath-day that which is not lawful? And He said unto them, Have ye never read what David did, when he had need, and was an hungered, he, and they that were with him? How he went into the house of God in the days of Abiathar the high priest, and did eat the showbread, which is not lawful to eat but for the priests, and gave also to them which were with him? And he said unto them, the Sabbath was made for man, and not man for the Sabbath."

V. St Paul puts the observance of the Sabbath on a level with the observance of the new moon. "Let no man judge you in meat or in drink, or in respect of an holy day, or of the new moon, or of the Sabbath, which are a shadow of things to come." "One man esteemeth one day above another, another esteemeth every day alike. Let every man be fully persuaded in his own mind."

VI. Neither Christ nor the apostles ever gave any instruction as to the observance of Sunday. The modern "Sabbath" is only referred to in Acts xx. 7, and in 1 Cor. xvi. 2. In these passages we simply read, "Upon the first day of the week, when the disciples were come together to break bread, Paul preached to them;" and "upon the first day of the week let every one of you lay by him in store, as God hath prospered him."

It follows, then, that the superstitious reverence for Sunday has absolutely no justification. On the strictest theory of inspiration, there is not a vestige of evidence that any divine command was ever given for the observance of any day but Saturday; and that day was set apart specially, not for worship, but for rest. From the single passage in the Acts just quoted, we are able to conjecture that the apostles were in the habit of meeting together on the first day of the week to commemorate the resurrection. But we also know, from what St Paul has said, that they attached no importance to any day as such. What the apostles and their immediate followers did after their morning service we do not know. But we do know that in post-apostolic times Christians went to their work after Church, very much as poor people do now upon the Continent. And from that time to this, there has been every possible diversity in the way in which Christians have kept, or have not kept, Sunday,—from Calvin who used to play at bowls, to a certain old lady of my acquaintance in Scotland, who, on returning from church, sends for the Catechism and the whip, and administers them alternately to her children for the rest of the day.

In regard to Sunday observance, there is only one point of agreement amongst professing Christians. They all keep it in a different manner from that in which the Jews kept Saturday. The Jews would not light a fire, would not walk more than a mile, would not work even a single animal; and, with that curious prodigality of punishment which goes with an early stage of civilisation, they visited all violation of the Sabbath law with death. To a pious Jew every modern Christian must appear a Sabbath-breaker; and every modern Christian *is* a Sabbath-breaker if the fourth commandment be binding upon him. It is high time that we made up our minds on this subject. Either the fourth commandment is binding on us or it is not. If it is, let us keep Saturday, or at any rate Sunday, in the way which the fourth commandment enjoins. If it is not, let us frankly say so. And in any case let us give up the canting hypocrisy of professing to obey a law which we know perfectly well we always disobey.

But though it is desirable to get rid of the superstitious reverence for Sunday, it is not desirable to do away with the observance of it as a day of rest. Though the fourth commandment in its original form referred, and could only refer, to the Jews, it was founded upon a principle of universal application—the principle, viz., of benevolence. It may seem surprising that Christ, who cared so much for the poor, should have apparently ignored the fourth commandment. For this there were two reasons. (1) It had led to formalism; and (2) all that was essentially good in it was implied in the golden rule. As to the particular day on which we should spare our servants, Christ said nothing. He did not care for such petty, paltry details. A day of rest is needed by men and by animals, but it cannot possibly matter which day be kept holy for this purpose. Like the Eucharist, it was left, under Christ's perfect law of liberty, to the individual judgment and conscience. Calvin suggested that the day should be changed to Thursday. Tyndale—I don't mean the heterodox professor of modern times but the orthodox reformer — suggested keeping one day in every ten. Of course it is desirable, if possible, that the same day should be observed throughout the same district. But there would be nothing to prevent different days being set apart for the purpose in different districts or in different towns, as is the case with the fast-days in Scotland. And sometimes a particular individual will be unable to keep the particular day which is kept by his neighbours and acquaintances. To me, for instance, Sunday is the hardest day of the week, and I am obliged to use my carriage. But I always let the horse and the coachman have Saturday to themselves. I am one of the very few Christians who, in this respect at least, adhere literally to the fourth commandment. Mr. Spurgeon is another. He once jocularly remarked that his horse was a Jew. So is mine. I am proud to find myself in such good company. But whatever be our own peculiar circumstances and condition, let us never forget that we are all bound to be thoughtfully considerate for others, especially for our dependants, for the poor, for the overworked. We are so apt to rush into extremes. We are often inclined to say, Sunday has been made into a fetish, a false value has been attached to it, we have outgrown such folly, all days in the week shall be alike for us. But it will always be well that there should be one day in the week, on which we make a special effort to alleviate the toil of the working classes, to lighten the burden of life for those who are less favourably circumstanced than ourselves.

REMARKS ON PREVIOUS SERMON.

AFTER preaching this sermon I received a great number of expostulatory letters. One was from a brother clergyman, "regretting that a minister, whose duty it was to instruct the children of the Foundling Hospital in the principles of Christianity, should," &c. Now I take this opportunity of saying, once for all, that I have absolutely nothing to do with the Foundling children. I am responsible for the Governors and adult congregation. But the children are more fortunate. They are in the hands of my friend and colleague, the chaplain. In fact at my suggestion the Governors have arranged that the smaller children shall be sent away before the sermon. And I often feel sorry for those who remain. They are obliged to keep perfectly quiet, which is no easy matter for little people at their age. But they manage to do it marvellously. I never hear a sound of any description from the children's gallery. I hope they will believe that I am very grateful to them.

Among the other letters was one which is so suggestive that I give it here in full.

"MY DEAR PROFESSOR,—You will forgive me, I hope, for daring to think what I say, and still more to say what I think about this morning's sermon. I look at the subject more or less from your side, and yet I could not help quarrelling very seriously with you. I went with you thoroughly to a certain point, and enjoyed the logical clearance,—and then you, not disappointed, but hurt me. You did not leave the observers of Sunday one *illogical* plank to stand upon. But surely you might have substituted a yet stronger, because reasonable, ground for their observance, instead of letting them through into the deep waters of general morality and individual judgment to sink or swim. How many *can* swim, I wonder ? Is not any, even an illogical and stupid, motive better left, as long as it has power to prompt in a right direction ? (On this I cannot make up my mind.) And could you not have taught people to distinguish between cant and feeling? Granted the expediency of showing up what was unfounded and absurd, which I do grant, was it quite fair to treat this as the *whole* motive, and ignore all the feelings and emotions and associations which to many are the strongest arguments in favour of Sunday observance ? The true meaning of a Sabbath, I take it, is felt by the orthodox, and requires to be brought to light, and then the absurd will disappear. Whereas if the absurd is merely cut up, the heart of the matter has not been reached at all. An undefined feeling remains, that somehow the deed is better than the creed, if one could only see why. And yet the latter having been shattered the former dies; the creed having been destroyed, the deed to which it prompted will by-and-by likewise vanish.

"It seems to me that the illogical, slipshod, orthodox reasoning in favour of Sunday observance, is only a weak *after*-attempt to justify a practice which does really rest upon a logical foundation. The observance itself, I cannot help thinking, has grown out of, and rests upon, something stronger than any arbitrary law, such as the fourth commandment may have been. The observance of Sunday, I cannot help believing, rests upon a deep-rooted, though but half-realised, sense of a great need in the nature of man,—a physical, spiritual and social need.

"I. *Physical.*—The general rightness of having a day of freedom from labour, which should benefit principally the working classes, was your chief argument, I think, in favour of Sabbath-keeping. This philanthropic scheme, you said, should be the outcome of the golden rule, and its application should be left to the individual judgment. Now I wonder how many shop and factory hands would get a holiday, how many people would have cold suppers anything like as often as once a-week, if individual judgment were not strengthened by general feeling, by custom, by combined action? The application of the golden rule at all in this matter seems to depend upon a recognition of the universal need of rest. Surely if the importance of this were enforced, the foolish obedience to the fourth commandment, to an obsolete and arbitrary law, would give place to a reasonable acquiescence in a custom which was seen to correspond to a universal and perpetual want.

"II. The observance of Sunday corresponds to a spiritual need, the need—viz., of spiritual refreshment and help. You said that the observance of the Sabbath was, according to the orthodox view, in obedience to the fourth commandment, but that this command made no reference to worship, and that therefore worship and the day of rest had no logical connection. That may be; but it surely does not matter whether the two things are logically connected or not. They have been practically associated for generations, and this association appears to me very natural and very sensible. The day of least physical and mental toil is the day best suited for spiritual refreshment, and spiritual refreshment consists essentially in spiritual *action*. 'Worship the Lord all the days of thy life' is a spiritual rule as grand and sweeping as the golden rule in morality, and as difficult of application. Unless we focus them on the particular, we can never effect anything by them. If we live content with

God's universal presence, we shall cease to be personally conscious of it. If we are satisfied with the ever-present possibility of prayer, it will soon become an impossibility. Without some reminders and constraints, without times and forms, we drift inevitably into forgetfulness and carelessness. 'Every day will do' soon becomes 'any day will do,' and finally 'no day.' And this is both unwise and wrong. Those to whom the divine presence is familiar in church are the likeliest to recognise it in the world. The spiritual sight only clears through constant and regular use. The conscious and voluntary union of the soul with God in daily life is hard enough with the help of Sundays! What would it be without? We do need a day apart in which the spirit may be braced in a purer atmosphere. The connection between the first and fourth commandment may possibly not be arbitrary after all, but based on a dim recognition of a harmony underlying both.

"III. The observance of Sunday is based on a social need. I cannot help believing strongly in the good of public worship and public observance of seasons. Apart from the possibility of the vast influence of one over many, afforded by the assemblage of a large congregation, public worship must increase the feeling of brotherhood to an untold degree. And how can we have public worship without publicly appointed and accepted times? As a question of mere expediency, it would surely be better that one arrangement should prevail over the widest possible area. Otherwise, if we travelled much, we might frequently come in for several Sundays in succession. This is only one of many inconveniences which would result. But on higher grounds—social and religious—a systematic Sabbath-keeping seems to me most desirable. In fact I cannot help thinking that without it the whole machinery of the Christian Church would fall to pieces, and its great work come to an end. Which particular day the choice falls upon appears immaterial. But the one that has been selected by common consent, and which has received the sanction of time, possesses many associations, such as the Resurrection, Whitsuntide, the meetings of the apostles; and these associations bring it peculiarly into harmony with the spirit of worship. The manner of rest and worship is of course quite a different question. And here I should say the decision must be almost entirely left to the individual, as soon as he is capable of forming a rational opinion on the subject. Since comparative rest is all that can be obtained by any one on any day, and the refreshment of the few must in any case give way to that of the many, I see no reason why galleries and gardens should not be open, and much reason why they should. It would be a fulfilment and not a violation of the meaning of the Christian Sabbath.

"Through all this rigmarole, if you ever have patience to read it [rigmarole, the young lady calls it; well, it is rigmarole that would do honour to a philosopher in his prime], can you gather what I felt to-day? that you were scathing not only a superstitious observance, but a custom based on a real need,—a need all the more pressing because it is so little felt in the present day; when it seems to me the one might have been destroyed and the other at the same time enforced. Forgive me, please, for all this. My excuse must be your own wish that people would make objections to your face and not behind your back, as I was forced by a horrid verger to do this morning.—Yours very sincerely, —— ——."

With this letter I most fully agree. My text for the previous sermon was the fourth commandment, "Remember Saturday to set it apart as a day of rest." My reason for saying nothing about worship was, not that I ignored its importance, but that the subject was not mentioned in the text.

Cotter Morison.

I WISH to speak to you this morning about Mr Cotter Morison's 'Service of Man.' This brilliant book produced a considerable impression in the reading world, and would doubtless have produced more had not the gifted author been obliged, on account of failing health, to hurry on its publication and give it to the world before it was complete. Mr Morison did not overrate the seriousness of his malady, for he has since died. The fact of his lamented death, however, need not prevent me from speaking of his book. I shall do so with all respect. Every one who knew him, liked and esteemed him; and it is impossible to read his treatise without feeling that the author was sincerely concerned for the welfare of the world, and sincerely convinced that the world needed to know and take to heart what he had to say.

Now, what he had to say, you will remember,

was this. He considered that religion in general, and Christianity in particular, had fostered immorality, and that it was incumbent on us therefore to substitute this service of man for the old service of God. Christianity, as he understands it, lays more stress upon creed than upon conduct, urges men to prepare themselves for the future life rather than the present, offers them salvation hereafter instead of commanding them to do their duty here. Christianity is the service of God, and with this, according to Mr Morison, the service of man is incompatible. We cannot, he thinks, serve God and man: we must choose between them.

Well now let us see. I would remark, in the first place, that though Mr Cotter Morison knows a good deal about the Christianity of Christendom, he knows scarcely anything—nothing fundamental —about the Christianity of Christ. His views of Christianity are derived from St Augustine, Dr Pusey, Luther, Mr Spurgeon, but not from Christ Himself. We must not find great fault with Mr Morison for this. The error into which he has fallen is a very common one; clergymen themselves are constantly guilty of it. The Christianity of the Church, the Christianity of a particular party in the Church, the Christianity of every most contemptible sect, is constantly identified with the Christianity of Jesus. People always will persist in believing that things are identical when they are called by the same name. But this is by no means necessarily the case. The name of Christianity has been applied to all kinds of totally different systems of religion,—systems agreeing in nothing except in their disagreement with the intentions of Christ Himself. The average Christianity of Christendom has probably been more opposed to the original Christianity of Christ than to many other religions called by entirely different names. This however Mr Morison did not see, and his failing to recognise so important a fact was fatal to his own book. It deprives the work of all, or nearly all, its force. Much of what he says is valid and effective against Augustinianism, Lutheranism, Calvinism, ecclesiasticism; but just because it applies to these things, it is irrelevant as regards Christ's Christianity. Nay, in attacking various spurious forms of Christianity, Mr Morison is really supporting, however unconsciously, the real Christianity of Christ.

Let us look, for example, at what he says about the doctrine of justification by faith. "Luther," he remarks, quoting Moehler, " not only taught that Christ had not come to impart a purer ethical code, but even maintained He had come to abolish the moral law, to liberate true believers from its curse, both for the past and for the future, and in that way to make them free. The evangelical liberty which Luther propounded announces that even the Decalogue shall not be brought into account against the believer, nor its violation be allowed to disturb his conscience, for he is exalted above it. The reformers referred to Christ, not as the strengthener and sanctifier, but exclusively as the forgiver of sins; they regarded the Mediator only in His capacity of pardoner." And this doctrine of justification by faith, though connected especially with the name of Luther, has been, in some form or other, very common throughout Christendom. As Mr Morison says, the Catholic Church has no advantage over the Protestant Church on this point. The Virgin takes the place of Christ as a free pardoner of the grossest sins, in consideration of an act of contrition or repentance. "It would not be easy," says Mr Morison, "to conceive a doctrine more injurious to morality than this Christian scheme."

The truth or falsity of this assertion will depend on the meaning you attach to the words contrition and repentance. If you intend merely verbal acknowledgment of wrong-doing, then the assertion is true. But if by contrition and repentance you mean heartfelt sorrow, so intense that he who experiences it is thereby converted, changed into a different being, hating what he used to love and loving what he used to hate, then the assertion is false. To forgive wrong-doing without heartfelt repentance would be to encourage immorality, and would be therefore ungodlike. But to refuse forgiveness after heartfelt repentance, would be equally ungodlike and equally fatal to morality; for if we believed ourselves at the mercy of an unforgiving tyrant, we should be stricken with the paralysis of despair, we should feel that all attempts at reformation would be useless.

And so of faith. This word may be, and has been, used in two completely different senses, just like the words contrition and repentance. The doctrine of justification by faith, as Luther understood it and as it has been very commonly understood, is not a doctrine of Christ. What Luther meant by faith you will best understand if you call to mind his opinion about the Epistle of St James. Luther did not like it; he called it an epistle of straw, and he wished to expunge it altogether from the Bible. He disliked the epistle for this reason. It laid stress on conduct. "What doth it profit, my brethren, though a man say he hath faith, and have not works? can faith save him? Faith, if it hath not works, is dead, being alone. Thou believest that God is one; thou doest well; the devils also believe and tremble. Wilt thou know, O vain man, that faith without works is dead? By works a man is justified and not by faith only." This didn't suit Luther, who was determined to maintain that men were justified by faith only. And by being justified he meant that righteousness was *imputed* to them by the Almighty while they were all the time unrighteous; and that when they died they would be taken to heaven, though the proper place for them was hell. If by faith then you mean what Luther meant—merely believing intellectually in the creeds, in the articles, or even in Jesus—I quite agree with Mr Morison that it is impossible to conceive a doctrine more injurious to morality than the doctrine of justification by faith.

But need I say that this is no doctrine of Christ's? It is quite true that in our translation of the Bible, even, I am sorry to see, in the Revised Version, Christ is represented as saying, "God so loved the world, that He gave His only begotten Son, that whosoever *believeth* in Him should not perish, but have everlasting life." But the word belief is the very worst word which could possibly have been selected for the purpose of expressing what the Saviour meant. "Except," He said, "ye eat my flesh and drink my blood, ye have no life in you." That is what Christ understood by faith. By this vehement metaphor He intended, of course, to signify the absorption of His own nature. No words could express a closer or more absolute union. They imply that the Master is to live in the disciples, and to manifest Himself by their conduct. And every real disciple must to some extent experience this strange transformation, must be able to say, with some amount of truth—"For me to live is Christ; it is not I who live, but Christ who liveth in me." It is really time that we gave up talking about belief in Christ. A better word would be trust. But even that is far too weak, unless we persistently bear in mind, that the trust which Christ asks of us is one which involves enthusiasm, self-surrender, love, passion, union.

And now, let us ask why was it that Christ demanded faith? Why? Just for the sake of helping us and stimulating us to that excellence of conduct which, according to Mr Morison, Christianity altogether ignores. Ignore conduct! Why, no teacher before or since ever laid such stress on it as Jesus of Nazareth. And it was because He laid so much stress upon conduct that He insisted, with equal importunity, upon the necessity for faith. Faith was the means, conduct was the end. "If ye love me," He said, "ye will keep my commandments." And what were His commandments? What sort of conduct was it that He wanted from us? Observance of ritual? Ascetic penances? Anything fanatical, useless, irrational? No; but precisely that service of man which Mr Morison so warmly and so nobly advocates. This is often represented as a Broad Church doctrine. If so, the evangelists were Broad Churchmen. Listen!

"A new commandment I give unto you, That ye love one another. By this shall men know that ye are my disciples, if ye have love one to another. . . . This is my commandment, That ye love one another. . . . I have chosen you, and ordained you, that ye should go and bring forth fruit. . . . These things I command you, That ye love one another."

"Ye shall know them by their fruits. Do men gather grapes of thorns, or figs of thistles? Even so, every good tree bringeth forth good fruit; but a corrupt tree bringeth forth evil fruit. A good tree cannot bring forth evil fruit, neither can a corrupt tree bring forth good fruit. Every tree that bringeth not forth good fruit is hewn down, and cast into the fire. Not every one that saith unto me, Lord, Lord, shall enter into the kingdom of heaven; but he that doeth the will of my Father which is in heaven. Many will say to me in that day, Lord, Lord, have we not prophesied in Thy name? and in Thy name have cast out devils? and in Thy name done many wonderful works? Then will I profess unto them, I never knew you: depart from me, ye that work iniquity."

"The kingdom of heaven is as a man travelling into a far country, who called his own servants, and delivered unto them his goods. And unto one he gave five talents, to another two, and to another one; to every man according to his several ability; and straightway took his journey. Then he that had received the five talents went and traded with the same, and made them other five talents. And likewise he that had received two, he also gained other two. But he that had received one went and digged in the earth, and hid his lord's money. After a long time the lord of those servants cometh, and reckoneth with them. And so he that had received five talents came and brought other five talents, saying, Lord, thou deliveredst unto me five talents: behold, I have gained beside them five talents more. His lord said unto him, Well done, thou good and faithful servant: thou hast been faithful over a few things, I will make thee ruler over many things: enter thou into the joy of thy lord. He also that had received two talents came and said, Lord, thou deliveredst unto me two talents: behold, I have gained two other talents beside them. His lord said unto him, Well done, good and faithful servant: thou hast been faithful over a few things, I will make thee ruler over many things: enter thou into the joy of thy lord. Then he which had received the one talent came and said, Lord, I knew thee that thou art an hard man, reaping where thou hast not sown, and gathering where thou hast not strawed: And I was afraid, and went and hid thy talent in the earth: lo, there thou hast that is thine. His lord answered and said unto him, Thou wicked and slothful servant, thou knewest that I reap where I sowed not, and gather where I have not strawed: thou oughtest therefore to have put my money to the exchangers, and then at my coming I should have received mine own with usury. Take therefore the talent from him, and give it unto him which hath ten talents. For unto every one that hath shall be given, and he shall have abundance: but from him that hath not shall be taken away even that which he hath. And cast ye the unprofitable servant into outer darkness."

"When the Son of man shall come in His glory, and all the holy angels with Him, then shall He sit upon the throne of His glory: and before Him shall be gathered all nations: and He shall separate them one from another, as a shepherd divideth his sheep from the goats : and He shall set the sheep on His right hand, but the goats on the left. Then shall the King say unto them on His right hand, Come, ye blessed of my Father, inherit the kingdom prepared for you from the foundation of the world: For I was an hungered, and ye gave me meat: I was thirsty, and ye gave me drink : I was a stranger, and ye took me in: naked, and ye clothed me: I was sick, and ye visited me ; I was in prison, and ye came unto me. Then shall the righteous answer Him, saying, Lord, when saw we Thee an hungered, and fed Thee? or thirsty, and gave Thee drink? When saw we Thee a stranger, and took Thee in? or naked, and clothed Thee? And the King shall answer and say unto them, Verily I say unto you, Inasmuch as ye have done it unto one of the least of these my brethren, ye have done it unto me. Then shall He say also to them on the left hand, Depart from me, ye cursed, into everlasting fire, prepared for the devil and his angels : For I was an hungered, and ye gave me no meat: I was thirsty, and ye gave me no drink : I was a stranger, and ye took me not in: naked, and ye clothed me not: sick, and in prison, and ye visited me not. Then shall they also answer him, saying, Lord, when saw we Thee an hungered, or athirst, or a stranger, or naked, or sick, or in prison, and did not minister unto Thee? Then shall He answer them, saying, Verily I say unto you, Inasmuch as ye did it not to one of the least of these, ye did it not to me. And these shall go away into everlasting punishment: but the righteous into life eternal."

In the face of all this, it is simply preposterous to say that Christ laid more stress on creed than on conduct, that He urged men to prepare themselves for the future life rather than the present, and that He considered salvation to be of more importance than morality. Christ left behind Him no creed at all. He identified salvation with morality. He asserted, over and over again in the most unmistakable terms, that the only way in which men could prepare for the future life was by doing their duty in the present. So far as this world is concerned, so far as regards what is most fundamental in Christianity, Mr Morison is at one with Christ. But it is the eternal glory of the Nazarene to have taught what unfortunately Mr Morison could not accept, but what perhaps he now understands—that the salvation begun here is to be continued hereafter; that the service of man, whether we know it or not, is in reality the service of God.

" Abou Ben Adhem (may his tribe increase)
Awoke one night from a deep dream of peace,
And saw within the moonlight in his room,
Making it rich and like a lily in bloom,
An angel writing in a book of gold.
Exceeding peace had made Ben Adhem bold,
And to the presence in the room he said,
' What writest thou ?'—The vision raised its head
And with a look made of all sweet accord,
Answered, 'The names of those who love the Lord.'
' And is mine one ?' said Abou.   ' Nay, not so,'
Replied the angel.   Abou spoke more low
But cheerly still, and said, ' I pray thee, then,
Write me as one that loves his fellow-men.'

The angel wrote and vanished.   The next night
It came again with a great wakening light,
And showed the names whom love of God had bless'd,
And lo ! Ben Adhem's name led all the rest ! "

THE END.

PRINTED BY WILLIAM BLACKWOOD AND SONS.

WORKS BY PROFESSOR MOMERIE.

I.

PERSONALITY;

THE BEGINNING AND END OF METAPHYSICS,

AND A NECESSARY ASSUMPTION IN ALL POSITIVE PHILOSOPHY.

Third Edition, revised. Crown 8vo, 3s.

"This is a little book, but it contains more sound philosophy than many pretentious treatises....... In an admirably lucid way the author scatters to the winds the baseless assumptions of the sense philosophy."—*British Quarterly Review.*

"It is not often that we have to complain of the brevity of a sermon or of a treatise on philosophy; but in the case of a little book of the latter kind, recently published anonymously, we have found the arguments so cogent, the style so clear, and the matter at issue so important, that we heartily wish that the writer had allowed himself room for the fuller treatment of his subject....... We confidently refer our readers to this well-reasoned volume."—*Modern Review.*

"Professor Momerie's remarks on the doctrines of the defenders of empiricism present a close, and thoroughly scientific, examination of the views these thinkers put forth as to the nature of sensation, perception, and cognition....... The arguments are throughout conducted with marked logical power, and the conclusions are very important in relation to the present aspect of philosophical thought in England."—*Scotsman.*

"The work under our notice will well repay the careful reading of those who wish to have at their command plain answers to modern positivism."—*Ecclesiastical Gazette.*

"His discussion of these questions stamps Dr Momerie as an acute metaphysician, a philosophical scholar, and a powerful dialectician."—*Glasgow Herald.*

"When published anonymously received a very hearty welcome by all who were interested in the advent of a new writer of great power, of happy diction, and of independent thinking."—*Montrose Standard.*

II.

THE ORIGIN OF EVIL;

AND OTHER SERMONS.

Fifth Edition. Crown 8vo, 5s.

"Professor Momerie has done well to publish his sermons; they are good reading....... A real contribution to the side of common-sense religion."—*Saturday Review.*

"We decidedly recommend them to persons perplexed by the speculations of modern science."—*Spectator.*

"This is a remarkable volume of sermons. Though it consists of only about 300 pages, it contains an amount of thought and learning which might have been expanded into a bulky folio."—*Glasgow Mail.*

"These sermons are some of the very best produced in this country within the last hundred years."—*Inquirer.*

"The author is an original thinker, whose sympathies are very wide."—*Guardian.*

"Those who preach may learn much from their perusal."—*Christian World.*

"Out of the common run, they give one a refreshing sense of novelty and power."—*Glasgow Herald.*

"Die Vorträge zeigen allenthalben eine schöne Harmonie zwischen Schriftwahrheit und Lebenswahrheit."—*Deutsches Litteraturblatt.*

"Der Verfasser behandelt in diesen Vorträgen wichtige Fragen aus dem Gebiet des christlichen Lebens. Wir heben besonders die über das Leiden hervor, in denen der Verfasser tiefe beherzigenswerthe Gedanken ausspricht. Wir nehmen keinen Anstand, diese Vorträge zum Besten zu rechnen, was über diesen Gegenstand gesagt worden."—*Christliches Bücherschatz.*

"The author of the 'Origin of Evil' will go sadly astray if he does not make his mark on the age."—*London Figaro.*

"We should almost like to have heard these sermons preached. We are willing to read them carefully, and recommend them to others for like reading, even though, in almost every instance, we dissent from the author's pleading."—*National Reformer.*

"These sermons are everything that sermons ought *not* to be."—*English Independent.*

III.

DEFECTS OF MODERN CHRISTIANITY;
AND OTHER SERMONS.

Third Edition. Crown 8vo, 5s.

"Throughout Mr Momerie's attractive little volume the morning air of the new world breathes through the dry leaves of the old theology."—*Westminster Review.*

"There is an intellectuality, spirituality, and a simplicity in Mr Momerie's sermons, that should make them models for young preachers."—*Christian Union.*

"Professor Momerie, by his former books, has already laid the foundation of a reputation as a philosophical thinker and an able expositor of religious subjects. The present volume is marked by equal ability, intellectual force, independent and original thinking, and will confirm the favourable opinion which he has already produced.......Whatever views readers may detect as different from their own, they will not fail to admire the author's powerful enforcement of the practical side of Christianity.......There follows, as the second part of the volume, nine lectures on the Book of Job; and we have not read before, within the same compass, a more masterly and interesting exposition of that great poem.......There are also three admirable sermons on 'The Connection between Reason and Faith,' which will repay repeated reading.......The volume deserves to be widely read; and whether readers agree or not in all respects with the author, they will not rise from the perusal without feeling that Christianity is something grander than they have ordinarily realised it to be, and that the Christian life is the bravest and most beautiful life possible."—*Aberdeen Journal.*

"Very fresh and striking."—*Globe.*

"Although he is a polished and accomplished scholar, he simply defies the conventionalities of churches and schools."—*Literary World.*

IV.

THE BASIS OF RELIGION;

BEING AN EXAMINATION OF 'NATURAL RELIGION.'

Second Edition. Crown 8vo, 2s. 6d.

" As a controversialist, Professor Momerie is no less candid than he is remorselessly severe."—*Scotsman.*

" As a revelation of the pretentiousness of that philosophy [Positivism] Dr Momerie's powerful essay is very valuable."—*Fifeshire Journal.*

" The result of profound study and earnest thought.......This attempt to sketch out a basis for rational theology is fitted to the needs of the times. ......Professor Momerie has won for himself a name as one of the most powerful and original thinkers of the day."—*Globe.*

" Professor Momerie has wide views of men and things, resembling in this quality the author of 'Ecce Homo' himself, and he has attacked from the Cambridge University pulpit the book 'Natural Religion,' accusing it of considerable vagueness of conception and of considerable misconception of critical points of its own argument. The present book presents the substance of these sermons in the form of a brief essay.......We would recommend our readers to see for themselves how those confusions of thought, by which the school of writers—of whom the author of 'Natural Religion' is an eminent representative—seek to save religion when supernaturalism has disappeared, are exposed. We are certain they will be charmed with the accurate philosophical thinking of Professor Momerie, with his unpretentious display of keen logical reasoning, conveyed in lucid and forcible language, which arrays and adorns it like a well-fitting garment."—*Eskdale Advertiser.*

"Greater force is given to this essay, since the author is himself an advanced thinker."—*Christian Union.*

V.

AGNOSTICISM.

Second Edition. Crown 8vo, 5s.

"To readers who do not demand that 'the scheme of salvation in its fulness' should be enunciated in every sermon, this volume, which is happily free from rhetoric, and for the most part from any ostentation of the reading which it indicates, will be interesting from its acuteness, learning, and insight."—*Saturday Review*.

"This is a really good book. It is profound in thought, large and comprehensive in view, liberal in spirit, and delightfully clear and simple in style. We wish that theologians and philosophers in general would write in Professor Momerie's manner...... Following the chapters on Agnosticism, there are ten other chapters on the book of Ecclesiastes. They form an admirable and scholarly analysis of that strange and melancholy book."—*The Inquirer*.

"We are thankful for so masterly, so comprehensive, and so complete a vindication of the principles of Christian Theism, with its powerful refutation of the main positions of Agnosticism. The book meets a real and widespread need, in a style as trenchant and effective as it is popular."—*Freeman*.

"Dr Momerie's breadth of intellect and sympathy, his clear thinking and well-chastened style, as well as his deep religiousness, which will, no doubt, after a time assume a more positively evangelical form, eminently adapt him to be a teacher to his generation. He has freed himself, by we know not what process, from many of the prejudices of the older schools; but he can search into the very soul of unbelieving sophistry, and the spirit of his exhortation is always ennobling and heavenward."—*Methodist Times*.

"It is long since we have met with a volume of sermons which will so well repay a careful study."—*Ecclesiastical Gazette*.

"The work of a majestic intellect."—*Fifeshire Journal*.

VI.

PREACHING AND HEARING;

AND OTHER SERMONS.

Second Edition. Crown 8vo, 4s. 6d.

"The author, himself one of the most eloquent preachers of the day, is eminently qualified to do justice to his subject. He has brought to it an experience and scholarly proficiency which few men could have done."—*Christian Union.*

"For such preaching as this, and for all the ample learning and wise thought by which it is fortified, the Church of God has every reason to be thankful."—*Literary World.*

"Marked by all the force, acuteness, and eloquence which we have learnt to expect from him, and in addition by a knowledge of men and manners not generally associated with philosophical research.......His literary style is another proof, if proof were needed, of the vast resources of the simple Anglo-Saxon."—*Fifeshire Journal.*

"His sermons are unlike any sermons we can call to mind."—*Guardian.*

"If such sermons were often to be heard from the pulpit, preachers would not have to complain of empty pews or inattentive listeners."—*Rock.*

"Their delivery was quite startling."—*Swansea Journal.*

"Those who would know what pulpit boldness in the present day really means should make these sermons their study."—*Christian World.*

"The present volume is more directly popular in style, and amply maintains the reputation of the writer."—*Inquirer.*

VII.

BELIEF IN GOD.

Second Edition.   Crown 8vo, 3s.

"One of the most brilliant arguments for the Divine existence." —*Christian World.*

"In some respects Professor Momerie is the ablest preacher of his day. ......He is ever endeavouring to present recondite problems in the simplest, clearest language, and in this he is eminently successful.......It is not too abstruse even for mere smatterers in philosophical discussion. Considering its scope, it is indeed astonishingly lucid."—*Dundee Advertiser.*

"No preacher need be ashamed to face the most scientific sceptic with this little book in his hand."—*Literary World.*

"From the time that Professor Momerie published anonymously the volume on 'The Origin of Evil,' his writings have been devoured with exceptional keenness by intelligent readers. Many were the conjectures as to who the author of that work was, but it was universally allowed that the anonymous writer was destined to leave his mark upon the mind of the country; he was a daring and fresh thinker, and was possessed of rare unravelling power. This little volume bears the impress of his majestic intellect...... It is a model of lucid style, clear and consecutive reasoning, fairness to an honourable opponent, and humility in victory."—*Perthshire Advertiser.*

"'Belief in God' was originally written for the 'Helps to Belief' Series, but the editor, thinking it too abstruse, recommended considerable alterations. We are devoutly thankful the gifted Professor refused to mutilate his work, and withdrew it from the series."—*Nonconformist.*

"His criticism of Herbert Spencer's theory of the Unknowable is very acute."—*Glasgow Herald.*

"It is spread out into only eighty pages, but those eighty pages contain more material for thought than many another volume or series of volumes contain in eight hundred."—*Inquirer.*

WILLIAM BLACKWOOD & SONS, EDINBURGH AND LONDON.

IN ONE VOLUME. THE LIBRARY EDITION OF

STORMONTH'S DICTIONARY

OF THE

ENGLISH LANGUAGE,

PRONOUNCING, ETYMOLOGICAL, AND EXPLANATORY.

Embracing Scientific and other Terms, numerous Familiar Terms, and a Copious Selection of Old English Words. To which are appended Lists of Scripture and other Proper Names, Abbreviations, and Foreign Words and Phrases.

BY THE REV. JAMES STORMONTH.

The PRONUNCIATION carefully revised by the Rev. P. H. PHELP, M.A. CANTAB.

Royal 8vo, handsomely bound in half-morocco, **31s. 6d.**

Opinions of the British and American Press.

Times.—"This may serve in great measure the purposes of an English cyclopedia. It gives lucid and succinct definitions of the technical terms in science and art, in law and medicine. We have the explanation of words and phrases that puzzle most people, showing wonderfully comprehensive and out-of-the-way research. . . . We need only add, that the dictionary appears in all its departments to have been brought down to meet the latest demands of the day, and that it is admirably printed."

Pall Mall Gazette.—"The pronunciation of every word is given, the symbols employed for marking the sounds being commendably clear. . . . After the pronunciation comes the etymology. It has, we think, been well managed here. And the matter is, on the whole, as judiciously chosen as it is skilfully compressed and arranged."

Scotsman.—"There can be no question that the work when completed will form one of the best and most serviceable works of reference of its class. . . . It is admirably adapted to meet the requirements of every ordinary reader, and there are few occasions of special reference to which it will not be found adequate. The definitions are necessarily brief, but they are almost always clear and pointed. . . . A word of praise is due to the beauty and clearness of the printing."

STORMONTH'S DICTIONARY—*Continued.*

Opinions of the British and American Press—*Continued.*

Civil Service Gazette.—"We have had occasion to notice the peculiar features and merits of 'Stormonth's Dictionary,' and we need not repeat our commendations both of the judicious plan and the admirable execution. . . . This is a pre-eminently good, comprehensive, and authentic English lexicon, embracing not only all the words to be found in previous dictionaries, but all the modern words—scientific, new coined, and adopted from foreign languages, and now naturalised and legitimised."

Notes and Queries.—"The whole constitutes a work of high utility."

Dublin Irish Times.—"The book has the singular merit of being a dictionary of the highest order in every department and in every arrangement, without being cumbersome; whilst for ease of reference there is no dictionary we know of that equals it. . . . For the library table it is also, we must repeat, precisely the sort of volume required, and indispensable to every large reader or literary worker."

Liverpool Mercury.—"Every page bears the evidence of extensive scholarship and laborious research, nothing necessary to the elucidation of present-day language being omitted. . . . As a book of reference for terms in every department of English speech, this work must be accorded a high place—in fact, it is quite a library in itself. . . . It is a marvel of accuracy."

New York Tribune.—"The work exhibits all the freshness and best results of modern lexicographic scholarship, and is arranged with great care, so as to facilitate reference."

New York Mail and Express.—"Is the nearest approach to the ideal popular dictionary that has yet appeared in our language."

New York Sun.—"A well-planned and carefully-executed work, which has decided merits of its own, and for which there is a place not filled by any of its rivals."

Boston Journal.—"A critical and accurate dictionary, the embodiment of good scholarship, and the result of modern researches. . . . It holds an unrivalled place in bringing forth the result of modern philological criticism."

Boston Gazette.—"There can be but little doubt that, when completed, the work will be one of the most serviceable and most accurate that English lexicography has yet produced for general use."

Toronto Globe.—"In every respect this is one of the best works of the kind in the language."

WILLIAM BLACKWOOD & SONS, EDINBURGH AND LONDON.

CATALOGUE

OF

MESSRS BLACKWOOD & SONS' PUBLICATIONS.

PHILOSOPHICAL CLASSICS FOR ENGLISH READERS.
Edited by WILLIAM KNIGHT, LL.D.,
Professor of Moral Philosophy in the University of St Andrews.

In crown 8vo Volumes, with Portraits, price 3s. 6d.

Now ready—

1. **Descartes.** By Professor MAHAFFY, Dublin.
2. **Butler.** By Rev. W. LUCAS COLLINS, M.A.
3. **Berkeley.** By Professor CAMPBELL FRASER, Edinburgh.
4. **Fichte.** By Professor ADAMSON, Owens College, Manchester.
5. **Kant.** By Professor WALLACE, Oxford.
6. **Hamilton.** By Professor VEITCH, Glasgow.
7. **Hegel.** By Professor EDWARD CAIRD, Glasgow.
8. **Leibniz.** By J. THEODORE MERZ.
9. **Vico.** By Professor FLINT, Edinburgh.
10. **Hobbes.** By Professor CROOM ROBERTSON, London.
11. **Hume.** By the Editor.
12. **Spinoza.** By the Very Rev. Principal CAIRD, Glasgow.
13. **Bacon.** PART I. By Professor Nichol, Glasgow.

In preparation—
BACON. PART II.—Philosophy. By Professor Nichol, Glasgow.

FOREIGN CLASSICS FOR ENGLISH READERS.
Edited by Mrs OLIPHANT.

In crown 8vo, 2s. 6d.

CONTENTS.

DANTE. By the Editor.
VOLTAIRE. By Lieut.-General Sir E. B. Hamley, K.C.B.
PASCAL. By Principal Tulloch.
PETRARCH. By Henry Reeve, C.B.
GOETHE. By A. Hayward, Q.C.
MOLIÈRE. By the Editor and F. Tarver, M.A.
MONTAIGNE. By Rev. W. L. Collins, M.A.
RABELAIS. By Walter Besant, M.A.
CALDERON. By E. J. Hasell.
SAINT SIMON. By Clifton W. Collins, M.A.
CERVANTES. By the Editor.
CORNEILLE AND RACINE. By Henry M. Trollope.
MADAME DE SÉVIGNÉ. By Miss Thackeray.
LA FONTAINE, AND OTHER FRENCH FABULISTS. By Rev. W. Lucas Collins, M.A.
SCHILLER By James Sime, M.A., Author of 'Lessing: his Life and Writings.'
TASSO. By E. J. Hasell.
ROUSSEAU. By Henry Grey Graham.

Now Complete.
ANCIENT CLASSICS FOR ENGLISH READERS.
Edited by the Rev. W. LUCAS COLLINS, M.A.

Complete in 28 Vols. crown 8vo, cloth, price 2s. 6d. each. And may also be had in 14 Volumes, strongly and neatly bound, with calf or vellum back, £3, 10s.

Saturday Review.—"It is difficult to estimate too highly the value of such a series as this in giving 'English readers' an insight, exact as far as it goes, into those olden times which are so remote and yet to many of us so close."

CATALOGUE

OF

MESSRS BLACKWOOD & SONS'

PUBLICATIONS.

ALISON. History of Europe. By Sir ARCHIBALD ALISON, Bart., D.C.L.
1. From the Commencement of the French Revolution to the Battle of Waterloo.
   LIBRARY EDITION, 14 vols., with Portraits. Demy 8vo, £10, 10s.
   ANOTHER EDITION, in 20 vols. crown 8vo, £6.
   PEOPLE'S EDITION, 13 vols. crown 8vo, £2, 11s.
2. Continuation to the Accession of Louis Napoleon.
   LIBRARY EDITION, 8 vols. 8vo, £6, 7s. 6d.
   PEOPLE'S EDITION, 8 vols. crown 8vo, 34s.
3. Epitome of Alison's History of Europe. Twenty-ninth Thousand, 7s. 6d.
4. Atlas to Alison's History of Europe. By A. Keith Johnston.
   LIBRARY EDITION, demy 4to, £3, 3s.
   PEOPLE'S EDITION, 31s. 6d.

—— Life of John Duke of Marlborough. With some Account of his Contemporaries, and of the War of the Succession. Third Edition, 2 vols. 8vo. Portraits and Maps, 30s.

—— Essays: Historical, Political, and Miscellaneous. 3 vols. demy 8vo, 45s.

AIRD. Poetical Works of Thomas Aird. Fifth Edition, with Memoir of the Author by the Rev. JARDINE WALLACE, and Portrait, Crown 8vo, 7s. 6d.

ALLARDYCE. The City of Sunshine. By ALEXANDER ALLARDYCE. Three vols. post 8vo, £1, 5s. 6d.

—— Memoir of the Honourable George Keith Elphinstone, K.B., Viscount Keith of Stonehaven, Marischal, Admiral of the Red. 8vo, with Portrait, Illustrations, and Maps, 21s.

ALMOND. Sermons by a Lay Head-master. By HELY HUTCHINSON ALMOND, M.A. Oxon., Head-master of Loretto School. Crown 8vo, 5s.

ANCIENT CLASSICS FOR ENGLISH READERS. Edited by Rev. W. LUCAS COLLINS, M.A. Complete in 28 vols., cloth, 2s. 6d. each; or in 14 vols., tastefully bound, with calf or vellum back, £3, 10s.

Contents of the Series.

HOMER: THE ILIAD, by the Editor.—HOMER: THE ODYSSEY, by the Editor.—HERODOTUS, by George C. Swayne, M.A.—XENOPHON, by Sir Alexander Grant, Bart., LL.D. EURIPIDES, by W. B. Donne—ARISTOPHANES, by the Editor.—PLATO, by Clifton W. Collins, M.A.—LUCIAN, by the Editor.—ÆSCHYLUS, by the Right Rev. the Bishop of Colombo.—SOPHOCLES, by Clifton W. Collins, M.A.—HESIOD AND THEOGNIS, by the Rev. J. Davies, M.A.—GREEK ANTHOLOGY, by Lord Neaves.—VIRGIL, by the Editor. —HORACE, by Sir Theodore Martin, K.C.B.—JUVENAL, by Edward Walford, M.A.— PLAUTUS AND TERENCE, by the Editor.—THE COMMENTARIES OF CÆSAR, by Anthony Trollope.—TACITUS, by W. B. Donne.—CICERO, by the Editor.—PLINY'S LETTERS, by the Rev. Alfred Church, M.A., and the Rev. W. J. Brodribb, M.A.—LIVY, by the Editor.—OVID, by the Rev. A. Church, M.A.—CATULLUS, TIBULLUS, AND PROPERTIUS, by the Rev. Jas. Davies, M.A.—DEMOSTHENES, by the Rev. W. J. Brodribb, M.A.— ARISTOTLE, by Sir Alexander Grant, Bart., LL.D.—THUCYDIDES, by the Editor.— LUCRETIUS, by W. H. Mallock, M.A.—PINDAR, by the Rev. F. D. Morice, M.A.

AYLWARD. The Transvaal of To-day: War, Witchcraft, Sports, and Spoils in South Africa. By ALFRED AYLWARD, Commandant, Transvaal Republic. Second Edition. Crown 8vo, 6s.

AYTOUN. Lays of the Scottish Cavaliers, and other Poems. By W. EDMONDSTOUNE AYTOUN, D.C.L., Professor of Rhetoric and Belles-Lettres in the University of Edinburgh. Cheap Edition, printed from a new type, and tastefully bound. Fcap. 8vo, 3s. 6d.

Another Edition, being the Thirtieth. Fcap. 8vo, cloth extra, 7s. 6d.

——— An Illustrated Edition of the Lays of the Scottish Cavaliers. From designs by Sir NOEL PATON. Small 4to, 21s., in gilt cloth.

——— Bothwell: a Poem. Third Edition. Fcap., 7s. 6d.

——— Poems and Ballads of Goethe. Translated by Professor AYTOUN and Sir THEODORE MARTIN, K.C.B. Third Edition. Fcap., 6s.

——— Bon Gaultier's Book of Ballads. By the SAME. Fourteenth and Cheaper Edition. With Illustrations by Doyle, Leech, and Crowquill. Fcap. 8vo, 5s.

——— The Ballads of Scotland. Edited by Professor AYTOUN. Fourth Edition. 2 vols. fcap. 8vo, 12s.

——— Memoir of William E. Aytoun, D.C.L. By Sir THEODORE MARTIN, K.C.B. With Portrait. Post 8vo, 12s.

BACH. On Musical Education and Vocal Culture. By ALBERT B. BACH. Fourth Edition. 8vo, 7s. 6d.

——— The Principles of Singing. A Practical Guide for Vocalists and Teachers. With Course of Vocal Exercises. Crown 8vo, 6s.

——— The Art of Singing. With Musical Exercises for Young People. Crown 8vo, 3s.

BALLADS AND POEMS. By MEMBERS OF THE GLASGOW BALLAD CLUB. Crown 8vo, 7s. 6d.

BANNATYNE. Handbook of Republican Institutions in the United States of America. Based upon Federal and State Laws, and other reliable sources of information. By DUGALD J. BANNATYNE, Scotch Solicitor, New York; Member of the Faculty of Procurators, Glasgow. Crown 8vo, 7s. 6d.

BEDFORD. The Regulations of the Old Hospital of the Knights of St John at Valetta. From a Copy Printed at Rome, and preserved in the Archives of Malta; with a Translation, Introduction, and Notes Explanatory of the Hospital Work of the Order. By the Rev. W. K. R. BEDFORD, one of the Chaplains of the Order of St John in England. Royal 8vo, with Frontispiece, Plans, &c., 7s. 6d.

BELLAIRS. The Transvaal War, 1880-81. Edited by Lady BELLAIRS. With a Frontispiece and Map. 8vo, 15s.

BELLAIRS. Gossips with Girls and Maidens, Betrothed and Free. By Lady BELLAIRS. New Edition. Crown 8vo, 5s.

BESANT. The Revolt of Man. By WALTER BESANT, M.A. Eighth Edition. Crown 8vo, 3s. 6d.

——— Readings in Rabelais. Crown 8vo, 7s. 6d.

BEVERIDGE. Culross and Tulliallan; or Perthshire on Forth. Its History and Antiquities. With Elucidations of Scottish Life and Character from the Burgh and Kirk-Session Records of that District. By DAVID BEVERIDGE. 2 vols. 8vo, with Illustrations, 42s.

——— Between the Ochils and the Forth; or, from Stirling Bridge to Aberdour. Crown 8vo, 6s.

BLACK. Heligoland and the Islands of the North Sea. By WILLIAM GEORGE BLACK. Crown 8vo, 4s. 6d.

BLACKIE. Lays and Legends of Ancient Greece. By JOHN STUART BLACKIE, Emeritus Professor of Greek in the University of Edinburgh. Second Edition. Fcap. 8vo. 5s.

——— The Wisdom of Goethe. Fcap. 8vo. Cloth, extra gilt, 6s.

BLACKWOOD'S MAGAZINE, from Commencement in 1817 to May 1888. Nos. 1 to 866, forming 142 Volumes.

——— Index to Blackwood's Magazine. Vols. 1 to 50. 8vo, 15s.

——— Tales from Blackwood. Forming Twelve Volumes of Interesting and Amusing Railway Reading. Price One Shilling each, in Paper Cover. Sold separately at all Railway Bookstalls. They may also be had bound in cloth, 18s., and in half calf, richly gilt, 30s. Or 12 volumes in 6, Roxburghe, 21s., and half red morocco, 28s.

——— Tales from Blackwood. New Series. Complete in Twenty-four Shilling Parts. Handsomely bound in 12 vols., cloth, 30s. In leather back, Roxburghe style, 37s. 6d. In half calf, gilt, 52s. 6d. In half morocco, 55s.

——— Standard Novels. Uniform in size and legibly Printed. Each Novel complete in one volume.

FLORIN SERIES, Illustrated Boards. Or in Cloth Boards, 2s. 6d.

TOM CRINGLE'S LOG. By Michael Scott.
THE CRUISE OF THE MIDGE. By the Same.
CYRIL THORNTON. By Captain Hamilton.
ANNALS OF THE PARISH. By John Galt.
THE PROVOST, &c. By John Galt.
SIR ANDREW WYLIE. By John Galt.
THE ENTAIL. By John Galt.
MISS MOLLY. By Beatrice May Butt.
REGINALD DALTON. By J. G. Lockhart.
PEN OWEN. By Dean Hook.
ADAM BLAIR. By J. G. Lockhart.
LADY LEE'S WIDOWHOOD. By General Sir E. B. Hamley.
SALEM CHAPEL. By Mrs Oliphant.
THE PERPETUAL CURATE. By Mrs Oliphant.
MISS MARJORIBANKS. By Mrs Oliphant.
JOHN : A Love Story. By Mrs Oliphant.

SHILLING SERIES, Illustrated Cover. Or in Cloth Boards, 1s. 6d.

THE RECTOR, and THE DOCTOR'S FAMILY. By Mrs Oliphant.
THE LIFE OF MANSIE WAUCH. By D. M. Moir.
PENINSULAR SCENES AND SKETCHES. By F. Hardman.
SIR FRIZZLE PUMPKIN, NIGHTS AT MESS, &c.
THE SUBALTERN.
LIFE IN THE FAR WEST. By G. F. Ruxton.
VALERIUS : A Roman Story. By J. G. Lockhart.

BLACKMORE. The Maid of Sker. By R. D. BLACKMORE, Author of 'Lorna Doone,' &c. New Edition. Crown 8vo, 6s.

BLAIR. History of the Catholic Church of Scotland. From the Introduction of Christianity to the Present Day. By ALPHONS BELLESHEIM, D.D., Canon of Aix-la-Chapelle. Translated, with Notes and Additions, by D. OSWALD HUNTER BLAIR, O.S.B., Monk of Fort Augustus. To be completed in 4 vols. 8vo. Vols. I. and II. 25s.

BOSCOBEL TRACTS. Relating to the Escape of Charles the Second after the Battle of Worcester, and his subsequent Adventures. Edited by J. HUGHES, Esq., A.M. A New Edition, with additional Notes and Illustrations, including Communications from the Rev. R. H. BARHAM, Author of the 'Ingoldsby Legends.' 8vo, with Engravings, 16s.

LIST OF BOOKS PUBLISHED BY

BROOKE, Life of Sir James, Rajah of Sarāwak. From his Personal Papers and Correspondence. By SPENSER ST JOHN, H.M.'s Minister-Resident and Consul-General Peruvian Republic; formerly Secretary to the Rajah. With Portrait and a Map. Post 8vo, 12s. 6d.

BROUGHAM. Memoirs of the Life and Times of Henry Lord Brougham. Written by HIMSELF. 3 vols. 8vo, £2, 8s. The Volumes are sold separately, price 16s. each.

BROWN. The Forester: A Practical Treatise on the Planting, Rearing, and General Management of Forest-trees. By JAMES BROWN, LL.D., Inspector of and Reporter on Woods and Forests. Fifth Edition, revised and enlarged. Royal 8vo, with Engravings, 36s.

BROWN. The Ethics of George Eliot's Works. By JOHN CROMBIE BROWN. Fourth Edition. Crown 8vo, 2s. 6d.

BROWN. A Manual of Botany, Anatomical and Physiological. For the Use of Students. By ROBERT BROWN, M.A., Ph.D. Crown 8vo, with numerous Illustrations, 12s. 6d.

BUCHAN. Introductory Text-Book of Meteorology. By ALEXANDER BUCHAN, M.A., F.R.S.E., Secretary of the Scottish Meteorological Society, &c. Crown 8vo, with 8 Coloured Charts and other Engravings, pp. 218. 4s. 6d.

BUCHANAN. The Shirè Highlands (East Central Africa). By JOHN BUCHANAN, Planter at Zomba. Crown 8vo, 5s.

BURBIDGE. Domestic Floriculture, Window Gardening, and Floral Decorations. Being practical directions for the Propagation, Culture, and Arrangement of Plants and Flowers as Domestic Ornaments. By F. W. BURBIDGE. Second Edition. Crown 8vo, with numerous Illustrations, 7s. 6d.

——— Cultivated Plants: Their Propagation and Improvement. Including Natural and Artificial Hybridisation, Raising from Seed, Cuttings, and Layers, Grafting and Budding, as applied to the Families and Genera in Cultivation. Crown 8vo, with numerous Illustrations, 12s. 6d.

BURTON. The History of Scotland: From Agricola's Invasion to the Extinction of the last Jacobite Insurrection. By JOHN HILL BURTON, D.C.L., Historiographer-Royal for Scotland. New and Enlarged Edition, 8 vols., and Index. Crown 8vo, £3, 3s.

——— History of the British Empire during the Reign of Queen Anne. In 3 vols. 8vo. 36s.

——— The Scot Abroad. Third Edition. Crown 8vo, 10s. 6d.

——— The Book-Hunter. New Edition. Crown 8vo, 7s. 6d.

BUTE. The Roman Breviary: Reformed by Order of the Holy Œcumenical Council of Trent; Published by Order of Pope St Pius V.; and Revised by Clement VIII. and Urban VIII.; together with the Offices since granted. Translated out of Latin into English by JOHN, Marquess of Bute, K.T. In 2 vols. crown 8vo, cloth boards, edges uncut. £2, 2s.

——— The Altus of St Columba. With a Prose Paraphrase and Notes. In paper cover, 2s. 6d.

BUTLER. Pompeii: Descriptive and Picturesque. By W. BUTLER. Post 8vo, 5s.

BUTT. Miss Molly. By BEATRICE MAY BUTT. Cheap Edition, 2s.

——— Eugenie. Crown 8vo, 6s. 6d.

CAIRD. Sermons. By JOHN CAIRD, D.D., Principal of the University of Glasgow. Sixteenth Thousand. Fcap. 8vo, 5s.

——— Religion in Common Life. A Sermon preached in Crathie Church, October 14, 1855, before Her Majesty the Queen and Prince Albert. Published by Her Majesty's Command. Cheap Edition, 3d.

CAMPBELL. Sermons Preached before the Queen at Balmoral. By the Rev. A. A. CAMPBELL, Minister of Crathie. Published by Command of Her Majesty. Crown 8vo, 4s. 6d.

CAMPBELL. Records of Argyll. Legends, Traditions, and Recollections of Argyllshire Highlanders, collected chiefly from the Gaelic. With Notes on the Antiquity of the Dress, Clan Colours or Tartans of the Highlanders. By LORD ARCHIBALD CAMPBELL. Illustrated with Nineteen full-page Etchings. 4to, printed on hand-made paper, £3, 3s.

CANTON. A Lost Epic, and other Poems. By WILLIAM CANTON. Crown 8vo, 5s.

CAPPON. Victor Hugo. A Memoir and a Study. By JAMES CAPPON, M.A. Post 8vo, 10s. 6d.

CARRICK. Koumiss; or, Fermented Mare's Milk: and its Uses in the Treatment and Cure of Pulmonary Consumption, and other Wasting Diseases. With an Appendix on the best Methods of Fermenting Cow's Milk. By GEORGE L. CARRICK, M.D., L.R.C.S.E. and L.R.C.P.E., Physician to the British Embassy, St Petersburg, &c. Crown 8vo, 10s. 6d.

CAUVIN. A Treasury of the English and German Languages. Compiled from the best Authors and Lexicographers in both Languages. Adapted to the Use of Schools, Students, Travellers, and Men of Business; and forming a Companion to all German-English Dictionaries. By JOSEPH CAUVIN, LL.D. & Ph.D., of the University of Göttingen, &c. Crown 8vo, 7s. 6d.

CAVE-BROWN. Lambeth Palace and its Associations. By J. CAVE-BROWN, M.A., Vicar of Detling, Kent, and for many years Curate of Lambeth Parish Church. With an Introduction by the Archbishop of Canterbury. Second Edition, containing an additional Chapter on Medieval Life in the Old Palaces. 8vo, with Illustrations, 21s.

CHARTERIS. Canonicity; or, Early Testimonies to the Existence and Use of the Books of the New Testament. Based on Kirchhoffer's 'Quellensammlung.' Edited by A. H. CHARTERIS, D.D., Professor of Biblical Criticism in the University of Edinburgh. 8vo, 18s.

CHRISTISON. Life of Sir Robert Christison, Bart., M.D., D.C.L. Oxon., Professor of Medical Jurisprudence in the University of Edinburgh. Edited by his Sons. In two vols. 8vo. Vol. I.—Autobiography. 16s. Vol. II.—Memoirs. 16s.

CHURCH SERVICE SOCIETY. A Book of Common Order: Being Forms of Worship issued by the Church Service Society. Fifth Edition. 6s.

CLOUSTON. Popular Tales and Fictions: their Migrations and Transformations. By W. A. CLOUSTON, Editor of 'Arabian Poetry for English Readers,' 'The Book of Sindibad,' &c. 2 vols. post 8vo, roxburghe binding, 25s.

COCHRAN. A Handy Text-Book of Military Law. Compiled chiefly to assist Officers preparing for Examination; also for all Officers of the Regular and Auxiliary Forces. Specially arranged according to the Syllabus of Subjects of Examination for Promotion, Queen's Regulations, 1883. Comprising also a Synopsis of part of the Army Act. By Major F. COCHRAN, Hampshire Regiment, Garrison Instructor, North British District. Crown 8vo, 7s. 6d.

COLQUHOUN. The Moor and the Loch. Containing Minute Instructions in all Highland Sports, with Wanderings over Crag and Corrie, Flood and Fell. By JOHN COLQUHOUN. Seventh Edition. With Illustrations. Complete in 1 vol. 8vo.

CONGREVE. Tales of Country Life in La Gruyère. From the French of Pierre Sciobéret. By L. DORA CONGREVE. Crown 8vo, 7s. 6d.

COTTERILL. Suggested Reforms in Public Schools. By C. C. COTTERILL, M.A., Assistant Master at Fettes College, Edin. Crown 8vo, 3s. 6d.

COX. The Opening of the Line: A Strange Story of Dogs and their Doings. By PONSONBY COX. Profusely Illustrated by J. H. O. BROWN. 4to, 1s.

COUNTESS IRENE. By the Author of 'Lauterdale and Caterina.' 3 vols. post 8vo, 25s. 6d.

CRANSTOUN. The Elegies of Albius Tibullus. Translated into English Verse, with Life of the Poet, and Illustrative Notes. By JAMES CRANSTOUN, LL.D., Author of a Translation of 'Catullus.' Crown 8vo, 6s. 6d.

—— The Elegies of Sextus Propertius. Translated into English Verse, with Life of the Poet, and Illustrative Notes. Crown 8vo, 7s. 6d.

CRAWFORD. Saracinesca. By F. MARION CRAWFORD, Author of 'Mr Isaacs,' 'Dr Claudius,' 'Zoroaster,' &c. &c. Third Edition. Crown 8vo, 6s.

CRAWFORD. The Doctrine of Holy Scripture respecting the Atonement. By the late THOMAS J. CRAWFORD, D.D., Professor of Divinity in the University of Edinburgh. Fourth Edition. 8vo, 12s.

—— The Fatherhood of God, Considered in its General and Special Aspects, and particularly in relation to the Atonement, with a Review of Recent Speculations on the Subject. Third Edition, Revised and Enlarged. 8vo, 9s.

—— The Preaching of the Cross, and other Sermons. 8vo, 7s. 6d.

—— The Mysteries of Christianity. Crown 8vo, 7s. 6d.

CUSHING. The Blacksmith of Voe. A Novel. By Paul Cushing, Author of 'Misogyny and the Maiden,' 'A Woman with a Secret,' &c. 3 vols. crown 8vo, 25s. 6d.

DAVIES. Norfolk Broads and Rivers; or, The Waterways, Lagoons, and Decoys of East Anglia. By G. CHRISTOPHER DAVIES, Author of 'The Swan and her Crew.' Illustrated with Seven full-page Plates. New and Cheaper Edition. Crown 8vo, 6s.

DAYNE. In the Name of the Tzar. A Novel. By J. BELFORD DAYNE. Crown 8vo, 6s.

DESCARTES. The Method, Meditations, and Principles of Philosophy of Descartes. Translated from the Original French and Latin. With a New Introductory Essay, Historical and Critical, on the Cartesian Philosophy. By JOHN VEITCH, LL.D., Professor of Logic and Rhetoric in the University of Glasgow. A New Edition, being the Ninth. Price 6s. 6d.

DOBSON. History of the Bassandyne Bible. The First Printed in Scotland. With Notices of the Early Printers of Edinburgh. By WILLIAM T. DOBSON, Author of 'Literary Frivolities,' 'Poetical Ingenuities,' 'Royal Characters of Scott,' &c. Post 8vo, with Facsimiles and other Illustrations. 7s. 6d.

DOGS, OUR DOMESTICATED: Their Treatment in reference to Food, Diseases, Habits, Punishment, Accomplishments. By 'MAGENTA.' Crown 8vo, 2s. 6d.

DU CANE. The Odyssey of Homer, Books I.-XII. Translated into English Verse. By Sir CHARLES DU CANE, K.C.M.G. 8vo, 10s. 6d.

DUDGEON. History of the Edinburgh or Queen's Regiment Light Infantry Militia, now 3rd Battalion The Royal Scots; with an Account of the Origin and Progress of the Militia, and a Brief Sketch of the old Royal Scots. By Major R. C. DUDGEON, Adjutant 3rd Battalion The Royal Scots. Post 8vo, with Illustrations. 10s. 6d.

DUNCAN. Manual of the General Acts of Parliament relating to the Salmon Fisheries of Scotland from 1828 to 1882. By J. BARKER DUNCAN. Crown 8vo, 5s.

DUNSMORE. Manual of the Law of Scotland, as to the Relations between Agricultural Tenants and their Landlords, Servants, Merchants, and Bowers. By W. DUNSMORE. 8vo, 7s. 6d.

DUPRÉ. Thoughts on Art, and Autobiographical Memoirs of Giovanni Dupré. Translated from the Italian by E. M. PERUZZI, with the permission of the Author. New Edition. With an Introduction by W. W. Story. Crown 8vo, 10s. 6d.

ELIOT. George Eliot's Life, Related in her Letters and Journals. Arranged and Edited by her husband, J. W. CROSS. With Portrait and other Illustrations. Third Edition. 3 vols. post 8vo, 42s.

ELIOT. Works of George Eliot (Cabinet Edition). Handsomely printed in a new type, 21 volumes, crown 8vo, price £5, 5s. The Volumes are also sold separately, price 5s. each, viz.:—
Romola. 2 vols.—Silas Marner, The Lifted Veil, Brother Jacob. 1 vol.—Adam Bede 2 vols.—Scenes of Clerical Life. 2 vols.—The Mill on the Floss. 2 vols.—Felix Holt. 2 vols.—Middlemarch. 3 vols.—Daniel Deronda. 3 vols.—The Spanish Gypsy. 1 vol.—Jubal, and other Poems, Old and New. 1 vol.—Theophrastus Such. 1 vol.—Essays. 1 vol.

—— George Eliot's Life. (Cabinet Edition.) With Portrait and other Illustrations. 3 vols. crown 8vo, 15s.

—— George Eliot's Life. With Portrait and other Illustrations. New Edition, in one volume. Crown 8vo, 7s. 6d.

—— Novels by GEORGE ELIOT. Cheap Edition. Adam Bede. Illustrated. 3s. 6d., cloth.—The Mill on the Floss. Illustrated. 3s. 6d., cloth.—Scenes of Clerical Life. Illustrated. 3s., cloth.—Silas Marner: The Weaver of Raveloe. Illustrated. 2s. 6d., cloth.—Felix Holt, the Radical. Illustrated. 3s. 6d., cloth.—Romola. With Vignette. 3s. 6d., cloth.

—— Middlemarch. Crown 8vo, 7s. 6d.

—— Daniel Deronda. Crown 8vo, 7s. 6d.

—— Essays. By GEORGE ELIOT. New Edition. Crown 8vo, 5s.

—— Impressions of Theophrastus Such. New Edition. Crown 8vo, 5s.

—— The Spanish Gypsy. New Edition. Crown 8vo, 5s.

—— The Legend of Jubal, and other Poems, Old and New. New Edition. Crown 8vo, 5s., cloth.

—— Wise, Witty, and Tender Sayings, in Prose and Verse. Selected from the Works of GEORGE ELIOT. Seventh Edition. Fcap. 8vo, 6s.

—— The George Eliot Birthday Book. Printed on fine paper, with red border, and handsomely bound in cloth, gilt. Fcap. 8vo, cloth, 3s. 6d. And in French morocco or Russia, 5s.

ESSAYS ON SOCIAL SUBJECTS. Originally published in the 'Saturday Review.' A New Edition. First and Second Series. 2 vols. crown 8vo, 6s. each.

EWALD. The Crown and its Advisers; or, Queen, Ministers, Lords, and Commons. By ALEXANDER CHARLES EWALD, F.S.A. Crown 8vo, 5s.

FAITHS OF THE WORLD, The. A Concise History of the Great Religious Systems of the World. By various Authors. Being the St Giles' Lectures—Second Series. Crown 8vo, 5s.

FARRER. A Tour in Greece in 1880. By RICHARD RIDLEY FARRER. With Twenty-seven full-page Illustrations by LORD WINDSOR. Royal 8vo, with a Map, 21s.

FERRIER. Philosophical Works of the late James F. Ferrier, B.A. Oxon., Professor of Moral Philosophy and Political Economy, St Andrews. New Edition. Edited by Sir ALEX. GRANT, Bart., D.C.L., and Professor LUSHINGTON. 3 vols. crown 8vo, 34s. 6d.

—— Institutes of Metaphysic. Third Edition. 10s. 6d.

—— Lectures on the Early Greek Philosophy. Third Edition, 10s. 6d.

—— Philosophical Remains, including the Lectures on Early Greek Philosophy. 2 vols., 24s.

FLETCHER. Lectures on the Opening Clauses of the Litany, delivered in St Paul's Church, Edinburgh. By JOHN B. FLETCHER, M.A. Crown 8vo, 4s.

FLINT. The Philosophy of History in Europe. By ROBERT FLINT, D.D., LL.D., Professor of Divinity, University of Edinburgh. Vol. I. 8vo. [*New Edition in preparation.*]

FLINT. Theism. Being the Baird Lecture for 1876. By ROBERT FLINT, D.D., LL.D., Professor of Divinity, University of Edinburgh. Sixth Edition. Crown 8vo, 7s. 6d.

—— Anti-Theistic Theories. Being the Baird Lecture for 1877. Third Edition. Crown 8vo, 10s. 6d.

FORBES. Insulinde: Experiences of a Naturalist's Wife in the Eastern Archipelago. By Mrs H. O. FORBES. Post 8vo, with a Map. 8s. 6d.

FOREIGN CLASSICS FOR ENGLISH READERS. Edited by Mrs OLIPHANT. Price 2s. 6d. *For List of Volumes published, see page 2.*

GALT. Annals of the Parish. By JOHN GALT. Fcap. 8vo, 2s.

—— The Provost. Fcap. 8vo, 2s.

—— Sir Andrew Wylie. Fcap. 8vo, 2s.

—— The Entail; or, The Laird of Grippy. Fcap. 8vo, 2s.

GENERAL ASSEMBLY OF THE CHURCH OF SCOTLAND.

—— Family Prayers. Authorised by the General Assembly of the Church of Scotland. A New Edition, crown 8vo, in large type, 4s. 6d. Another Edition, crown 8vo, 2s.

—— Prayers for Social and Family Worship. For the Use of Soldiers, Sailors, Colonists, and Sojourners in India, and other Persons, at home and abroad, who are deprived of the ordinary services of a Christian Ministry. Cheap Edition, 1s. 6d.

—— The Scottish Hymnal Appendix. 1. Longprimer type, 1s. 2. Nonpareil type, cloth limp, 4d.; paper cover, 2d.

—— Scottish Hymnal with Appendix Incorporated. Published for Use in Churches by Authority of the General Assembly. 1. Large type, cloth, red edges, 2s. 6d.; French morocco, 4s. 2. Bourgeois type, limp cloth, 1s.; French morocco, 2s. 3. Nonpareil type, cloth, red edges, 6d.; French morocco, 1s. 4d. 4. Paper covers, 3d. 5. Sunday-School Edition, paper covers, 1d. 6. Children's Hymnal, paper covers, 1d. No. 1, bound with the Psalms and Paraphrases, French morocco, 7s. 6d. No. 2, bound with the Psalms and Paraphrases, cloth, 2s.; French morocco, 3s.

GERARD. Reata: What's in a Name. By E. D. GERARD. New Edition. Crown 8vo, 6s.

—— Beggar my Neighbour. New Edition. Crown 8vo, 6s.

—— The Waters of Hercules. New Edition. Crown 8vo, 6s.

—— The Land beyond the Forest. Facts, Figures, and Fancies from Transylvania. By E. GERARD, Author of 'Reata,' &c. In Two Volumes. With Maps and Illustrations. 25s.

GERARD. Stonyhurst Latin Grammar. By Rev. JOHN GERARD. Fcap. 8vo, 3s.

GILL. Free Trade: an Inquiry into the Nature of its Operation. By RICHARD GILL. Crown 8vo, 7s. 6d.

GOETHE'S FAUST. Part I. Translated into English Verse by Sir THEODORE MARTIN, K.C.B. Second Edition, post 8vo, 6s. Ninth Edition, fcap., 3s. 6d.

—— Part II. Translated into English Verse by the SAME. Second Edition, revised. Fcap. 8vo, 6s.

GOETHE. Poems and Ballads of Goethe. Translated by Professor AYTOUN and Sir THEODORE MARTIN, K.C.B. Third Edition, fcap. 8vo, 6s.

GORDON CUMMING. At Home in Fiji. By C. F. GORDON CUMMING, Author of 'From the Hebrides to the Himalayas.' Fourth Edition, post 8vo. With Illustrations and Map. 7s. 6d.

—— A Lady's Cruise in a French Man-of-War. New and Cheaper Edition. 8vo. With Illustrations and Map. 12s. 6d.

GORDON-CUMMING. Fire-Fountains. The Kingdom of Hawaii: Its Volcanoes, and the History of its Missions. By C. F. GORDON-CUMMING, Author of 'From the Hebrides to the Himalayas.' With Map and numerous Illustrations. 2 vols. 8vo, 25s.
——— Granite Crags: The Yō-semité Region of California. Illustrated with 8 Engravings. New and Cheaper Edition. 8vo, 8s. 6d.
——— Wanderings in China. New and Cheaper Edition. In 1 vol. 8vo, with Illustrations, 10s.
GRAHAM. The Life and Work of Syed Ahmed Khan, C.S.I. By Lieut.-Colonel G. F. I. GRAHAM, B.S.C. 8vo, 14s.
GRANT. Bush-Life in Queensland. By A. C. GRANT. New Edition. Crown 8vo, 6s.
GRIFFITHS. Locked Up. By Major ARTHUR GRIFFITHS. Author of 'The Wrong Road,' 'Chronicles of Newgate,' &c. With Illustrations by C. J. STANILAND, R.I. Crown 8vo, 2s. 6d.
HALDANE. Subtropical Cultivations and Climates. A Handy Book for Planters, Colonists, and Settlers. By R. C. HALDANE. Post 8vo, 9s.
HAMERTON. Wenderholme: A Story of Lancashire and Yorkshire Life. By PHILIP GILBERT HAMERTON, Author of 'A Painter's Camp.' A New Edition. Crown 8vo, 6s.
HAMILTON. Lectures on Metaphysics. By Sir WILLIAM HAMILTON, Bart., Professor of Logic and Metaphysics in the University of Edinburgh. Edited by the Rev. H. L. MANSEL, B.D., LL.D., Dean of St Paul's; and JOHN VEITCH, M.A., Professor of Logic and Rhetoric, Glasgow. Seventh Edition. 2 vols. 8vo, 24s.
——— Lectures on Logic. Edited by the SAME. Third Edition. 2 vols., 24s.
——— Discussions on Philosophy and Literature, Education and University Reform. Third Edition, 8vo, 21s.
——— Memoir of Sir William Hamilton, Bart., Professor of Logic and Metaphysics in the University of Edinburgh. By Professor VEITCH of the University of Glasgow. 8vo, with Portrait, 18s.
——— Sir William Hamilton: The Man and his Philosophy. Two Lectures Delivered before the Edinburgh Philosophical Institution, January and February 1883. By the SAME. Crown 8vo, 2s.
HAMLEY. The Operations of War Explained and Illustrated. By Lieut.-General Sir EDWARD BRUCE HAMLEY, K.C.B. Fourth Edition, revised throughout. 4to, with numerous Illustrations, 30s.
——— Thomas Carlyle: An Essay. Second Edition. Crown 8vo. 2s. 6d.
——— The Story of the Campaign of Sebastopol. Written in the Camp. With Illustrations drawn in Camp by the Author. 8vo, 21s.
——— On Outposts. Second Edition. 8vo, 2s.
——— Wellington's Career; A Military and Political Summary. Crown 8vo, 2s.
——— Lady Lee's Widowhood. Crown 8vo, 2s. 6d.
——— Our Poor Relations. A Philozoic Essay. With Illustrations, chiefly by Ernest Griset. Crown 8vo, cloth gilt, 3s. 6d.
HAMLEY. Guilty, or Not Guilty? A Tale. By Major-General W. G. HAMLEY, late of the Royal Engineers. New Edition. Crown 8vo, 3s. 6d.
——— Traseaden Hall. "When George the Third was King." New and Cheaper Edition. Crown 8vo, 6s.
HARBORD. Definitions and Diagrams in Astronomy and Navigation. By the Rev. J. B. HARBORD, M.A., Assistant Director of Education, Admiralty. 1s.
HASELL. Bible Partings. By E. J. HASELL. Crown 8vo, 6s.
——— Short Family Prayers. By Miss HASELL. Cloth, 1s.

HAY. The Works of the Right Rev. Dr George Hay, Bishop of
Edinburgh. Edited under the Supervision of the Right Rev. Bishop STRAIN.
With Memoir and Portrait of the Author. 5 vols. crown 8vo, bound in extra
cloth, £1, 1s. Or, sold separately—viz.:
The Sincere Christian Instructed in the Faith of Christ from the Written Word.
2 vols., 8s.—The Devout Christian Instructed in the Law of Christ from the Written
Word. 2 vols. 8s.—The Pious Christian Instructed in the Nature and Practice of the
Principal Exercises of Piety. 1 vol., 4s.

HEATLEY. The Horse-Owner's Safeguard. A Handy Medical
Guide for every Man who owns a Horse. By G. S. HEATLEY, M.R.C.V.S.
Crown 8vo, 5s.

——— The Stock-Owner's Guide. A Handy Medical Treatise for
every Man who owns an Ox or a Cow. Crown 8vo, 4s. 6d.

HEMANS. The Poetical Works of Mrs Hemans. Copyright Editions.—One Volume, royal 8vo, 5s.—The Same, with Illustrations engraved on
Steel, bound in cloth, gilt edges, 7s. 6d.—Six Volumes in Three, fcap., 12s. 6d.
SELECT POEMS OF MRS HEMANS. Fcap., cloth, gilt edges, 3s.

HOLE. A Book about Roses: How to Grow and Show Them. By
the Very Rev. Dean HOLE. Tenth Edition, revised. Crown 8vo, 3s. 6d.

HOME PRAYERS. By Ministers of the Church of Scotland and
Members of the Church Service Society. Second Edition. Fcap. 8vo, 3s.

HOMER. The Odyssey. Translated into English Verse in the
Spenserian Stanza. By PHILIP STANHOPE WORSLEY. Third Edition, 2 vols.
fcap., 12s.

——— The Iliad. Translated by P. S. WORSLEY and Professor
CONINGTON. 2 vols. crown 8vo, 21s.

HOSACK. Mary Queen of Scots and Her Accusers. Containing a
Variety of Documents never before published. By JOHN HOSACK, Barrister-at-Law. A New and Enlarged Edition, with a Photograph from the Bust on
the Tomb in Westminster Abbey. 2 vols. 8vo, £1, 1s.

HUTCHINSON. Hints on the Game of Golf. By HORACE G.
HUTCHINSON. Fourth Edition. Fcap. 8vo, cloth, 1s. 6d.

IDDESLEIGH. Lectures and Essays. By the late EARL OF
IDDESLEIGH, G.C.B., D.C.L., &c. 8vo, 16s.

INDEX GEOGRAPHICUS: Being a List, alphabetically arranged,
of the Principal Places on the Globe, with the Countries and Subdivisions of
the Countries in which they are situated, and their Latitudes and Longitudes.
Applicable to all Modern Atlases and Maps. Imperial 8vo, pp. 676, 21s.

JAMIESON. Discussions on the Atonement: Is it Vicarious?
By the Rev. GEORGE JAMIESON, A.M., B.D., D.D., Author of 'Profound Problems in Philosophy and Theology.' 8vo, 16s.

JEAN JAMBON. Our Trip to Blunderland; or, Grand Excursion
to Blundertown and Back. By JEAN JAMBON. With Sixty Illustrations
designed by CHARLES DOYLE, engraved by DALZIEL. Fourth Thousand.
Handsomely bound in cloth, gilt edges, 6s. 6d. Cheap Edition, cloth, 3s. 6d.
In boards, 2s. 6d.

JENNINGS. Mr Gladstone: A Study. By LOUIS J. JENNINGS,
M.P., Author of 'Republican Government in the United States,' 'The Croker
Memoirs,' &c. Popular Edition. Crown 8vo, 1s.

JERNINGHAM. Reminiscences of an Attaché. By HUBERT
E. H. JERNINGHAM. Second Edition. Crown 8vo, 5s.

——— Diane de Breteuille. A Love Story. Crown 8vo, 2s. 6d.

JOHNSTON. The Chemistry of Common Life. By Professor
J. F. W. JOHNSTON. New Edition, Revised, and brought down to date. By
ARTHUR HERBERT CHURCH, M.A. Oxon.; Author of 'Food: its Sources,
Constituents, and Uses;' 'The Laboratory Guide for Agricultural Students;'
'Plain Words about Water,' &c. Illustrated with Maps and 102 Engravings
on Wood. Complete in one volume, crown 8vo, pp. 618, 7s. 6d.

JOHNSTON. Elements of Agricultural Chemistry and Geology. Fourteenth Edition, Revised, and brought down to date. By Sir CHARLES A. CAMERON, M.D., F.R.C.S.I., &c. Fcap. 8vo, 6s. 6d.
—— Catechism of Agricultural Chemistry and Geology. An entirely New Edition, revised and enlarged, by Sir CHARLES A. CAMERON, M.D., F.R.C.S.I.,&c. Eighty-sixth Thousand, with numerous Illustrations, 1s.

JOHNSTON. Patrick Hamilton: a Tragedy of the Reformation in Scotland, 1528. By T. P. JOHNSTON. Crown 8vo, with Two Etchings by the Author, 5s.

KENNEDY. Sport, Travel, and Adventures in Newfoundland and the West Indies. By Captain W. R. KENNEDY, R.N. With Illustrations by the Author. Post 8vo, 14s.

KING. The Metamorphoses of Ovid. Translated in English Blank Verse. By HENRY KING, M.A., Fellow of Wadham College, Oxford, and of the Inner Temple, Barrister-at-Law. Crown 8vo, 10s. 6d.

KINGLAKE. History of the Invasion of the Crimea. By A. W. KINGLAKE. Cabinet Edition. Seven Volumes, illustrated with Maps and Plans, crown 8vo, at 6s. each. The Volumes respectively contain:—
I. THE ORIGIN OF THE WAR between the Czar and the Sultan. II. RUSSIA MET AND INVADED. III. THE BATTLE OF THE ALMA. IV. SEBASTOPOL AT BAY. V. THE BATTLE OF BALACLAVA. VI. THE BATTLE OF INKERMAN. VII. WINTER TROUBLES.
—— History of the Invasion of the Crimea. Vol. VI. Winter Troubles. Demy 8vo, with a Map, 16s.
—— History of the Invasion of the Crimea. Vols. VII. and VIII. From the Morrow of Inkerman to the Death of Lord Raglan. With an Index to the Whole Work. With Maps and Plans. Demy 8vo, 28s.
—— Eothen. A New Edition, uniform with the Cabinet Edition of the 'History of the Invasion of the Crimea,' price 6s.

KNOLLYS. The Elements of Field-Artillery. Designed for the Use of Infantry and Cavalry Officers. By HENRY KNOLLYS, Captain Royal Artillery; Author of 'From Sedan to Saarbrück,' Editor of 'Incidents in the Sepoy War,' &c. With Engravings. Crown 8vo, 7s. 6d.

LAING. Select Remains of the Ancient Popular and Romance Poetry of Scotland. Originally Collected and Edited by DAVID LAING, LL.D. Re-edited, with Memorial-Introduction, by JOHN SMALL, M.A. With a Portrait of Dr Laing. 4to, 25s.

LAVERGNE. The Rural Economy of England, Scotland, and Ireland. By LEONCE DE LAVERGNE. Translated from the French. With Notes by a Scottish Farmer. 8vo, 12s.

LAWLESS. Hurrish: a Study. By the Hon. EMILY LAWLESS, Author of 'A Chelsea Householder,' 'A Millionaire's Cousin.' Third and cheaper Edition, crown 8vo, 6s.

LEE. A Phantom Lover: A Fantastic Story. By VERNON LEE. Crown 8vo, 1s.

LEE. Glimpses in the Twilight. Being various Notes, Records, and Examples of the Supernatural. By the Rev. GEORGE F. LEE, D.C.L. Crown 8vo. 8s. 6d.

LEES. A Handbook of Sheriff Court Styles. By J. M. LEES, M.A., LL.B., Advocate, Sheriff-Substitute of Lanarkshire. New Ed., 8vo, 21s.
—— A Handbook of the Sheriff and Justice of Peace Small Debt Courts. 8vo, 7s. 6d.

LETTERS FROM THE HIGHLANDS. Reprinted from 'The Times.' Fcap. 8vo, 4s. 6d.

LIGHTFOOT. Studies in Philosophy. By the Rev. J. LIGHTFOOT, M.A., D.Sc., Vicar of Cross Stone, Todmorden. Crown 8vo, 4s. 6d.

LINDAU. The Philosopher's Pendulum, and other Stories. By RUDOLPH LINDAU. Crown 8vo, 7s. 6d.

LITTLE. Madagascar: Its History and People. By the Rev. HENRY W. LITTLE, some years Missionary in East Madagascar. Post 8vo, 10s. 6d.

LOCKHART. Doubles and Quits. By LAURENCE W. M. LOCKHART. With Twelve Illustrations. Fourth Edition. Crown 8vo, 6s.

—— Fair to See: a Novel. Eighth Edition. Crown 8vo, 6s.

—— Mine is Thine: a Novel. Eighth Edition. Crown 8vo, 6s.

LORIMER. The Institutes of Law: A Treatise of the Principles of Jurisprudence as determined by Nature. By JAMES LORIMER, Regius Professor of Public Law and of the Law of Nature and Nations in the University of Edinburgh. New Edition, revised throughout, and much enlarged. 8vo, 18s.

—— The Institutes of the Law of Nations. A Treatise of the Jural Relation of Separate Political Communities. In 2 vols. 8vo. Volume I., price 16s. Volume II., price 20s.

M'COMBIE. Cattle and Cattle-Breeders. By WILLIAM M'COMBIE, Tillyfour. New Edition, enlarged, with Memoir of the Author. By JAMES MACDONALD, Editor of the 'Live-Stock Journal.' Crown 8vo, 3s. 6d.

MACRAE. A Handbook of Deer-Stalking. By ALEXANDER MACRAE, late Forester to Lord Henry Bentinck. With Introduction by HORATIO ROSS, Esq. Fcap. 8vo, with two Photographs from Life. 3s. 6d.

M'CRIE. Works of the Rev. Thomas M'Crie, D.D. Uniform Edition. Four vols. crown 8vo, 24s.

—— Life of John Knox. Containing Illustrations of the History of the Reformation in Scotland. Crown 8vo, 6s. Another Edition, 3s. 6d.

—— Life of Andrew Melville. Containing Illustrations of the Ecclesiastical and Literary History of Scotland in the Sixteenth and Seventeenth Centuries. Crown 8vo, 6s.

—— History of the Progress and Suppression of the Reformation in Italy in the Sixteenth Century. Crown 8vo, 4s.

—— History of the Progress and Suppression of the Reformation in Spain in the Sixteenth Century. Crown 8vo, 3s. 6d.

—— Lectures on the Book of Esther. Fcap. 8vo, 5s.

MACDONALD. A Manual of the Criminal Law (Scotland) Procedure Act, 1887. By NORMAN DORAN MACDONALD. Revised by the LORD ADVOCATE. 8vo, cloth. 10s. 6d.

MACGREGOR. Life and Opinions of Major-General Sir Charles MacGregor, K.C.B., C.S.I., C.I.E., Quartermaster-General of India. From his Letters and Diaries. Edited by LADY MACGREGOR. With Portraits and Maps to illustrate Campaigns in which he was engaged. In 2 vols. 8vo.
[*In the press.*

M'INTOSH. The Book of the Garden. By CHARLES M'INTOSH, formerly Curator of the Royal Gardens of his Majesty the King of the Belgians, and lately of those of his Grace the Duke of Buccleuch, K.G., at Dalkeith Palace. Two large vols. royal 8vo, embellished with 1350 Engravings. £4, 7s. 6d.
Vol. I. On the Formation of Gardens and Construction of Garden Edifices. 776 pages, and 1073 Engravings, £2, 10s.
Vol. II. Practical Gardening. 868 pages, and 279 Engravings, £1, 17s. 6d.

MACKAY. A Manual of Modern Geography; Mathematical, Physical, and Political. By the Rev. ALEXANDER MACKAY, LL.D., F.R.G.S. 11th Thousand, revised to the present time. Crown 8vo, pp. 688. 7s. 6d.

—— Elements of Modern Geography. 53d Thousand, revised to the present time. Crown 8vo, pp. 300, 3s.

—— The Intermediate Geography. Intended as an Intermediate Book between the Author's 'Outlines of Geography' and 'Elements of Geography.' Thirteenth Edition, revised. Crown 8vo, pp. 238, 2s.

—— Outlines of Modern Geography. 176th Thousand, revised to the present time. 18mo, pp. 118, 1s.

MACKAY. First Steps in Geography. By the Rev. ALEXANDER MACKAY, LL.D., F.R.G.S. 86th Thousand. 18mo, pp. 56. Sewed, 4d.; cloth, 6d.
—— Elements of Physiography and Physical Geography. With Express Reference to the Instructions recently issued by the Science and Art Department. 30th Thousand, revised. Crown 8vo, 1s. 6d.
—— Facts and Dates; or, the Leading Events in Sacred and Profane History, and the Principal Facts in the various Physical Sciences. The Memory being aided throughout by a Simple and Natural Method. For Schools and Private Reference. New Edition. Crown 8vo, 3s. 6d.
MACKAY. An Old Scots Brigade. Being the History of Mackay's Regiment, now incorporated with the Royal Scots. With an Appendix containing many Original Documents connected with the History of the Regiment. By JOHN MACKAY (late) OF HERRIESDALE. Crown 8vo, 5s.
MACKAY. The Founders of the American Republic. A History of Washington, Adams, Jefferson, Franklin, and Madison. With a Supplementary Chapter on the Inherent Causes of the Ultimate Failure of American Democracy. By CHARLES MACKAY, LL.D. Post 8vo, 10s. 6d.
MACKELLAR. More Leaves from the Journal of a Life in the Highlands, from 1862 to 1882. Translated into Gaelic by Mrs MARY MACKELLAR. By command of Her Majesty the Queen. Crown 8vo, with Illustrations. 10s. 6d.
MACKENZIE. Studies in Roman Law. With Comparative Views of the Laws of France, England, and Scotland. By LORD MACKENZIE, one of the Judges of the Court of Session in Scotland. Sixth Edition, Edited by JOHN KIRKPATRICK, Esq., M.A. Cantab.; Dr Jur. Heidelb.; LL.B. Edin.; Advocate. 8vo, 12s.
MAIN. Three Hundred English Sonnets. Chosen and Edited by DAVID M. MAIN. Fcap. 8vo, 6s.
MAIR. A Digest of Laws and Decisions, Ecclesiastical and Civil relating to the Constitution, Practice, and Affairs of the Church of Scotland. With Notes and Forms of Procedure. By the Rev. WILLIAM MAIR, D.D., Minister of the Parish of Earlston. Crown 8vo, 7s. 6d.
MAITLAND. Parva. By E. FULLER MAITLAND (E. F. M.) Fcap. 8vo. 5s.
MARMORNE. The Story is told by ADOLPHUS SEGRAVE, the youngest of three Brothers. Third Edition. Crown 8vo, 6s.
MARSHALL. French Home Life. By FREDERIC MARSHALL. Second Edition. 5s.
MARSHMAN. History of India. From the Earliest Period to the Close of the India Company's Government; with an Epitome of Subsequent Events. By JOHN CLARK MARSHMAN, C.S.I. Abridged from the Author's larger work. Second Edition, revised. Crown 8vo, with Map, 6s. 6d.
MARTIN. Goethe's Faust. Part I. Translated by Sir THEODORE MARTIN, K.C.B. Second Ed., crown 8vo, 6s. Ninth Ed., fcap. 8vo, 3s. 6d.
—— Goethe's Faust. Part II. Translated into English Verse. Second Edition, revised. Fcap. 8vo, 6s.
—— The Works of Horace. Translated into English Verse, with Life and Notes. 2 vols. New Edition, crown 8vo, 21s.
—— Poems and Ballads of Heinrich Heine. Done into English Verse. Second Edition. Printed on *papier vergé*, crown 8vo, 8s.
—— Catullus. With Life and Notes. Second Ed., post 8vo, 7s. 6d.
—— The Vita Nuova of Dante. With an Introduction and Notes. Second Edition, crown 8vo, 5s.
—— Aladdin: A Dramatic Poem. By ADAM OEHLENSCHLAEGER. Fcap. 8vo, 5s.
—— Correggio: A Tragedy. By OEHLENSCHLAEGER. With Notes. Fcap. 8vo, 3s.

LIST OF BOOKS PUBLISHED BY

MARTIN. King Rene's Daughter: A Danish Lyrical Drama. By HENRIK HERTZ. Second Edition, fcap., 2s. 6d.

MARTIN. On some of Shakespeare's Female Characters. In a Series of Letters. By HELENA FAUCIT, LADY MARTIN. Dedicated by permission to Her Most Gracious Majesty the Queen. Third Edition. 8vo, with Portrait, 7s. 6d.

MATHESON. Can the Old Faith Live with the New? or the Problem of Evolution and Revelation. By the Rev. GEORGE MATHESON, D.D. Second Edition. Crown 8vo, 7s. 6d.

—— The Psalmist and the Scientist; or, Modern Value of the Religious Sentiment. Crown 8vo, 7s. 6d.

MAURICE. The Balance of Military Power in Europe. An Examination of the War Resources of Great Britain and the Continental States. By Colonel Maurice, R.A., Professor of Military Art and History at the Royal Staff College. Crown 8vo, with a Map. 6s.

MEIKLEJOHN. An Old Educational Reformer—Dr Bell. By J. M. D. MEIKLEJOHN, M.A., Professor of the Theory, History, and Practice of Education in the University of St Andrews. Crown 8vo, 3s. 6d.

—— The Golden Primer. With Coloured Illustrations by Walter Crane. Small 4to, boards, 5s.

—— The English Language: Its Grammar, History, and Literature. With Chapters on Versification, Paraphrasing, and Punctuation. Second Edition. Crown 8vo, 4s. 6d.

MICHEL. A Critical Inquiry into the Scottish Language. With the view of Illustrating the Rise and Progress of Civilisation in Scotland. By FRANCISQUE-MICHEL, F.S.A. Lond. and Scot., Correspondant de l'Institut de France, &c. In One handsome Quarto Volume, printed on hand-made paper, and appropriately bound in Roxburghe style. Price 66s.

MICHIE. The Larch: Being a Practical Treatise on its Culture and General Management. By CHRISTOPHER Y. MICHIE, Forester, Cullen House. Crown 8vo, with Illustrations. New and Cheaper Edition, enlarged, 5s.

MILNE. The Problem of the Churchless and Poor in our Large Towns. With special reference to the Home Mission Work of the Church of Scotland. By the Rev. ROBT. MILNE, M.A., D.D., Ardler. Crown 8vo, 5s.

MINTO. A Manual of English Prose Literature, Biographical and Critical: designed mainly to show Characteristics of Style. By W. MINTO, M.A., Professor of Logic in the University of Aberdeen. Third Edition, revised. Crown 8vo, 7s. 6d.

—— Characteristics of English Poets, from Chaucer to Shirley. New Edition, revised. Crown 8vo, 7s. 6d.

—— The Crack of Doom. 3 vols. post 8vo, 25s. 6d.

MITCHELL. Biographies of Eminent Soldiers of the last Four Centuries. By Major-General JOHN MITCHELL, Author of 'Life of Wallenstein.' With a Memoir of the Author. 8vo, 9s.

MOIR. Life of Mansie Wauch, Tailor in Dalkeith. With 8 Illustrations on Steel, by the late GEORGE CRUIKSHANK. Crown 8vo, 3s. 6d. Another Edition, fcap. 8vo, 1s. 6d.

MOMERIE. Defects of Modern Christianity, and other Sermons. By the Rev. A. W. MOMERIE, M.A., D.Sc., LL.D., Professor of Logic and Metaphysics in King's College, London. Third Edition. Crown 8vo, 5s.

—— The Basis of Religion. Being an Examination of Natural Religion. Second Edition. Crown 8vo, 2s. 6d.

—— The Origin of Evil, and other Sermons. Fifth Edition, enlarged. Crown 8vo, 5s.

—— Personality. The Beginning and End of Metaphysics, and a Necessary Assumption in all Positive Philosophy. Third Edition. Crown 8vo, 3s.

—— Agnosticism. Second Edition, Revised. Crown 8vo, 5s.

—— Preaching and Hearing; and Other Sermons. Second Edition. Crown 8vo, 4s. 6d.

MOMERIE. Belief in God. Second Edition. Crown 8vo, 3s.

MONTAGUE. Campaigning in South Africa. Reminiscences of an Officer in 1879. By Captain W. E. MONTAGUE, 94th Regiment, Author of 'Claude Meadowleigh,' &c. 8vo, 10s. 6d.

MONTALEMBERT. Memoir of Count de Montalembert. A Chapter of Recent French History. By Mrs OLIPHANT, Author of the 'Life of Edward Irving,' &c. 2 vols. crown 8vo, £1, 4s.

MURDOCH. Manual of the Law of Insolvency and Bankruptcy : Comprehending a Summary of the Law of Insolvency, Notour Bankruptcy, Composition-contracts, Trust-deeds, Cessios, and Sequestrations; and the Winding-up of Joint-Stock Companies in Scotland ; with Annotations on the various Insolvency and Bankruptcy Statutes; and with Forms of Procedure applicable to these Subjects. By JAMES MURDOCH, Member of the Faculty of Procurators in Glasgow. Fifth Edition, Revised and Enlarged, 8vo, £1, 10s.

MY TRIVIAL LIFE AND MISFORTUNE: A Gossip with no Plot in Particular. By A PLAIN WOMAN. New Edition, crown 8vo, 6s.

By the SAME AUTHOR.

POOR NELLIE. New and Cheaper Edition. Complete in one volume, crown 8vo, 6s.

NEAVES. Songs and Verses, Social and Scientific. By an Old Contributor to 'Maga.' By the Hon. Lord NEAVES. Fifth Ed., fcap. 8vo, 4s.

—— The Greek Anthology. Being Vol. XX. of 'Ancient Classics for English Readers.' Crown 8vo, 2s. 6d.

NICHOLSON. A Manual of Zoology, for the Use of Students. With a General Introduction on the Principles of Zoology. By HENRY ALLEYNE NICHOLSON, M.D., D.Sc., F.L.S., F.G.S., Regius Professor of Natural History in the University of Aberdeen. Seventh Edition, rewritten and enlarged. Post 8vo, pp. 956, with 555 Engravings on Wood, 18s.

—— Text-Book of Zoology, for the Use of Schools. Fourth Edition, enlarged. Crown 8vo, with 188 Engravings on Wood, 7s. 6d.

—— Introductory Text-Book of Zoology, for the Use of Junior Classes. Sixth Edition, revised and enlarged, with 166 Engravings, 3s.

—— Outlines of Natural History, for Beginners ; being Descriptions of a Progressive Series of Zoological Types. Third Edition, with Engravings, 1s. 6d.

—— A Manual of Palæontology, for the Use of Students. With a General Introduction on the Principles of Palæontology. Second Edition. Revised and greatly enlarged. 2 vols. 8vo, with 722 Engravings, £2, 2s.

—— The Ancient Life-History of the Earth. An Outline of the Principles and Leading Facts of Palæontological Science. Crown 8vo, with 276 Engravings, 10s. 6d.

—— On the "Tabulate Corals" of the Palæozoic Period, with Critical Descriptions of Illustrative Species. Illustrated with 15 Lithograph Plates and numerous Engravings. Super-royal 8vo, 21s.

—— Synopsis of the Classification of the Animal Kingdom. 8vo, with 106 Illustrations, 6s.

—— On the Structure and Affinities of the Genus Monticulipora and its Sub-Genera, with Critical Descriptions of Illustrative Species. Illustrated with numerous Engravings on wood and lithographed Plates. Super-royal 8vo, 18s.

NICHOLSON. Communion with Heaven, and other Sermons. By the late MAXWELL NICHOLSON, D.D., Minister of St Stephen's, Edinburgh. Crown 8vo, 5s. 6d.

—— Rest in Jesus. Sixth Edition. Fcap. 8vo, 4s. 6d.

NICHOLSON. A Treatise on Money, and Essays on Present Monetary Problems. By JOSEPH SHIELD NICHOLSON, M.A., D.Sc., Professor of Commercial and Political Economy and Mercantile Law in the University of Edinburgh. 8vo, 10s. 6d.

OLIPHANT. Masollam : a Problem of the Period. A Novel. By LAURENCE OLIPHANT. 3 vols. post 8vo, 25s. 6d.

OLIPHANT. Scientific Religion; or, Higher Possibilities of Life and Practice through the Operation of Natural Forces. By LAURENCE OLIPHANT. Second Edition. 8vo, 16s.

———— Altiora Peto. New and Cheaper Edition. Crown 8vo, boards, 2s. 6d.

———— Piccadilly: A Fragment of Contemporary Biography. With Eight Illustrations by Richard Doyle. Eighth Edition, 4s. 6d. Cheap Edition, in paper cover, 2s. 6d.

———— Traits and Travesties; Social and Political. Post 8vo, 10s. 6d.

———— The Land of Gilead. With Excursions in the Lebanon. With Illustrations and Maps. Demy 8vo, 21s.

———— The Land of Khemi. Post 8vo, with Illustrations, 10s. 6d.

———— Haifa: Life in Modern Palestine. 2d Edition. 8vo, 7s. 6d.

———— Episodes in a Life of Adventure; or, Moss from a Rolling Stone. Fourth Edition. Post 8vo, 6s.

———— Fashionable Philosophy, and other Sketches. In paper cover, 1s.

———— Sympneumata: or, Evolutionary Functions now Active in Man. Edited by LAURENCE OLIPHANT. Post 8vo, 10s. 6d.

OLIPHANT. The Story of Valentine; and his Brother. By Mrs OLIPHANT. 5s., cloth.

———— Katie Stewart. 2s. 6d.

OSBORN. Narratives of Voyage and Adventure. By Admiral SHERARD OSBORN, C.B. 3 vols. crown 8vo, 12s.

OSSIAN. The Poems of Ossian in the Original Gaelic. With a Literal Translation into English, and a Dissertation on the Authenticity of the Poems. By the Rev. ARCHIBALD CLERK. 2 vols. imperial 8vo, £1, 11s. 6d.

OSWALD. By Fell and Fjord; or, Scenes and Studies in Iceland. By E. J. OSWALD. Post 8vo, with Illustrations. 7s. 6d.

OUTRAM. Lyrics: Legal and Miscellaneous. By the late GEORGE OUTRAM, Esq., Advocate. New Edition, with Explanatory Notes. Edited by J. H. Stoddart, LL.D.; and Illustrated by William Ralston and A. S. Boyd. Fcap. 8vo, 5s.

PAGE. Introductory Text-Book of Geology. By DAVID PAGE, LL.D., Professor of Geology in the Durham University of Physical Science, Newcastle, and Professor LAPWORTH of Mason Science College, Birmingham. With Engravings & Glossarial Index. Twelfth Edition. Revised and Enlarged. 3s. 6d.

———— Advanced Text-Book of Geology, Descriptive and Industrial. With Engravings, and Glossary of Scientific Terms. Sixth Edition, revised and enlarged, 7s. 6d.

———— Introductory Text-Book of Physical Geography. With Sketch-Maps and Illustrations. Edited by CHARLES LAPWORTH, LL.D., F.G.S., &c., Professor of Geology and Mineralogy in the Mason Science College, Birmingham. 12th Edition. 2s. 6d.

———— Advanced Text-Book of Physical Geography. Third Edition, Revised and Enlarged by Prof. LAPWORTH. With Engravings. 5s.

PATON. Spindrift. By Sir J. NOEL PATON. Fcap., cloth, 5s.

———— Poems by a Painter. Fcap., cloth, 5s.

PATTERSON. Essays in History and Art. By R. HOGARTH PATTERSON. 8vo, 12s.

———— The New Golden Age, and Influence of the Precious Metals upon the World. 2 vols. 8vo, 31s. 6d.

PAUL. History of the Royal Company of Archers, the Queen's Body-Guard for Scotland. By JAMES BALFOUR PAUL, Advocate of the Scottish Bar. Crown 4to, with Portraits and other Illustrations. £2, 2s.

PEILE. Lawn Tennis as a Game of Skill. With latest revised Laws as played by the Best Clubs. By Captain S. C. F. PEILE, B.S.C. Fourth Edition, fcap. cloth, 1s. 6d.

PETTIGREW. The Handy Book of Bees, and their Profitable Management. By A. PETTIGREW. Fourth Edition, Enlarged, with Engravings. Crown 8vo, 3s. 6d.

PHILOSOPHICAL CLASSICS FOR ENGLISH READERS. Companion Series to Ancient and Foreign Classics for English Readers. Edited by WILLIAM KNIGHT, LL.D., Professor of Moral Philosophy, University of St Andrews. In crown 8vo volumes, with portraits, price 3s. 6d.
[For list of Volumes published, see page 2.

POLLOK. The Course of Time : A Poem. By ROBERT POLLOK, A.M. Small fcap. 8vo, cloth gilt, 2s. 6d. The Cottage Edition, 32mo, sewed, 8d. The Same, cloth, gilt edges, 1s. 6d. Another Edition, with Illustrations by Birket Foster and others, fcap., gilt cloth, 3s. 6d., or with edges gilt, 4s.

PORT ROYAL LOGIC. Translated from the French ; with Introduction, Notes, and Appendix. By THOMAS SPENCER BAYNES, LL.D., Professor in the University of St Andrews. Tenth Edition, 12mo, 4s.

POTTS AND DARNELL. Aditus Faciliores : An easy Latin Construing Book, with Complete Vocabulary. By A. W. POTTS, M.A., LL.D., Head-Master of the Fettes College, Edinburgh, and sometime Fellow of St John's College, Cambridge; and the Rev. C. DARNELL, M.A., Head-Master of Cargilfield Preparatory School, Edinburgh, and late Scholar of Pembroke and Downing Colleges, Cambridge. Ninth Edition, fcap. 8vo, 3s. 6d.

—————— Aditus Faciliores Graeci. An easy Greek Construing Book, with Complete Vocabulary. Fourth Edition, fcap. 8vo, 3s.

PRINGLE. The Live-Stock of the Farm. By ROBERT O. PRINGLE. Third Edition. Revised and Edited by JAMES MACDONALD, Editor of the 'Live-Stock Journal,' &c. Crown 8vo, 7s. 6d.

PUBLIC GENERAL STATUTES AFFECTING SCOTLAND from 1707 to 1847, with Chronological Table and Index. 3 vols. large 8vo, £3, 3s.

PUBLIC GENERAL STATUTES AFFECTING SCOTLAND, COLLECTION OF. Published Annually with General Index.

RAMSAY. Rough Recollections of Military Service and Society. By Lieut.-Col. BALCARRES D. WARDLAW RAMSAY. Two vols. post 8vo, 21s.

RAMSAY. Scotland and Scotsmen in the Eighteenth Century. Edited from the MSS. of JOHN RAMSAY, Esq. of Ochtertyre, by ALEXANDER ALLARDYCE, Author of 'Memoir of Admiral Lord Keith, K.B.,' &c. 2 vols. 8vo, 31s. 6d.

RANKIN. A Handbook of the Church of Scotland. By JAMES RANKIN, D.D., Minister of Muthill; Author of 'Character Studies in the Old Testament,' &c. An entirely New and much Enlarged Edition. Crown 8vo, with 2 Maps, 7s. 6d.

RANKINE. A Treatise on the Rights and Burdens incident to the Ownership of Lands and other Heritages in Scotland. By JOHN RANKINE M.A., Advocate, Professor of Scots Law in the University of Edinburgh. Second Edition, Revised and Enlarged. 8vo, 45s.

RECORDS OF THE TERCENTENARY FESTIVAL OF THE UNIVERSITY OF EDINBURGH. Celebrated in April 1884. Published under the Sanction of the Senatus Academicus. Large 4to, £2, 12s. 6d.

RICE. Reminiscences of Abraham Lincoln. By Distinguished Men of his Time. Collected and Edited by ALLEN THORNDIKE RICE, Editor of the 'North American Review.' Large 8vo, with Portraits, 21s.

RIMMER. The Early Homes of Prince Albert. By ALFRED RIMMER, Author of 'Our Old Country Towns,' &c. Beautifully Illustrated with Tinted Plates and numerous Engravings on Wood. 8vo, 10s. 6d.

ROBERTSON. Orellana, and other Poems. By J. LOGIE ROBERTSON, M.A. Fcap. 8vo. Printed on hand-made paper. 6s.

—————— The White Angel of the Polly Ann, and other Stories. A Book of Fables and Fancies. Fcap. 8vo, 3s. 6d.

—————— Our Holiday Among the Hills. By JAMES and JANET LOGIE ROBERTSON. Fcap. 8vo, 3s. 6d.

ROSCOE. Rambles with a Fishing-rod. By E. S. ROSCOE. Crown

ROSS. Old Scottish Regimental Colours. By ANDREW ROSS, S.S.C., Hon. Secretary Old Scottish Regimental Colours Committee. Dedicated by Special Permission to Her Majesty the Queen. Folio, handsomely bound in cloth, £2, 12s. 6d.

RUSSELL. The Haigs of Bemersyde. A Family History. By JOHN RUSSELL. Large 8vo, with Illustrations. 21s.

RUSSELL. Fragments from Many Tables. Being the Recollections of Some Wise and Witty Men and Women. By GEO. RUSSELL. In 1 vol. Cr. 8vo.

RUSTOW. The War for the Rhine Frontier, 1870: Its Political and Military History. By Col. W. RUSTOW. Translated from the German, by JOHN LAYLAND NEEDHAM, Lieutenant R.M. Artillery. 3 vols. 8vo, with Maps and Plans, £1, 11s. 6d.

RUTLAND. Notes of an Irish Tour in 1846. By the DUKE OF RUTLAND, G.C.B. (Lord JOHN MANNERS). New Edition. Crown 8vo, 2s. 6d.

RUTLAND. Gems of German Poetry. Translated by the DUCHESS OF RUTLAND (Lady JOHN MANNERS). Small quarto, 3s. 6d.

———— Impressions of Bad-Homburg. Comprising a Short Account of the Women's Associations of Germany under the Red Cross. By the DUCHESS OF RUTLAND (Lady JOHN MANNERS). Crown 8vo, 1s. 6d.

———— Some Personal Recollections of the Later Years of the Earl of Beaconsfield, K.G. Sixth Edition, 6d.

———— Employment of Women in the Public Service. 6d.

———— Some of the Advantages of Easily Accessible Reading and Recreation Rooms, and Free Libraries. With Remarks on Starting and Maintaining Them. Second Edition, crown 8vo, 1s.

———— A Sequel to Rich Men's Dwellings, and other Occasional Papers. Crown 8vo, 2s. 6d.

———— Encouraging Experiences of Reading and Recreation Rooms. Aims of Guilds, Nottingham Social Guild, Existing Institutions, &c., &c. Crown 8vo, 1s.

SCHILLER. Wallenstein. A Dramatic Poem. By FREDERICK VON SCHILLER. Translated by C. G. A. LOCKHART. Fcap. 8vo, 7s. 6d.

SCOTCH LOCH FISHING. By "Black Palmer." Crown 8vo, interleaved with blank pages, 4s.

SCOTTISH METAPHYSICS. Reconstructed in accordance with the Principles of Physical Science. By the Writer of 'Free Notes on Herbert Spencer's First Principles.' Crown 8vo, 5s.

SELLAR. Manual of the Education Acts for Scotland. By ALEXANDER CRAIG SELLAR, M.P. Eighth Edition. Revised and in great part rewritten by J. EDWARD GRAHAM, B.A. Oxon., Advocate. Containing the Technical Schools Act, 1887, and all Acts bearing on Education in Scotland. With Rules for the conduct of Elections, with Notes and Cases. 8vo, 10s. 6d.

SELLER AND STEPHENS. Physiology at the Farm; in Aid of Rearing and Feeding the Live Stock. By WILLIAM SELLER, M.D., F.R.S.E., Fellow of the Royal College of Physicians, Edinburgh, formerly Lecturer on Materia Medica and Dietetics; and HENRY STEPHENS, F.R.S.E., Author of 'The Book of the Farm,' &c. Post 8vo, with Engravings, 16s.

SETH. Scottish Philosophy. A Comparison of the Scottish and German Answers to Hume. Balfour Philosophical Lectures, University of Edinburgh. By ANDREW SETH, M.A., Professor of Logic, Rhetoric, and Metaphysics in the University of St Andrews. Crown 8vo, 5s.

———— Hegelianism and Personality. Balfour Philosophical Lectures. Second Series. Crown 8vo, 5s.

SETON. A Budget of Anecdotes. Chiefly relating to the Current Century. Compiled and Arranged by GEORGE SETON, Advocate, M.A. Oxon. New and Cheaper Edition, fcap. 8vo. Boards, 1s. 6d.

SHADWELL. The Life of Colin Campbell, Lord Clyde. Illustrated by Extracts from his Diary and Correspondence. By Lieutenant-General SHADWELL, C.B. 2 vols. 8vo. With Portrait, Maps, and Plans. 36s.

SHAND. Half a Century; or, Changes in Men and Manners. By ALEX. INNES SHAND, Author of 'Against Time,' &c. Second Ed., 8vo, 12s. 6d.

SHAND. Letters from the West of Ireland. By ALEX. INNES
SHAND. Reprinted from the 'Times.' Crown 8vo, 5s.
SHARPE. Letters from and to Charles Kirkpatrick Sharpe.
Edited by ALEXANDER ALLARDYCE, Author of 'Memoir of Admiral Lord Keith, K.B.,' &c. With a Memoir by the Rev. W. K. R. BEDFORD. In two vols. 8vo. Illustrated with Etchings and other Engravings.
SIM. Margaret Sim's Cookery. With an Introduction by L. B. WALFORD, Author of 'Mr Smith: A Part of His Life,' &c. Crown 8vo, 5s.
SKELTON. Maitland of Lethington; and the Scotland of Mary Stuart. A History. By JOHN SKELTON, C.B., LL.D. Author of 'The Essays of Shirley.' Demy 8vo, 12s. 6d.
SMITH. Italian Irrigation: A Report on the Agricultural Canals of Piedmont and Lombardy, addressed to the Hon. the Directors of the East India Company; with an Appendix, containing a Sketch of the Irrigation System of Northern and Central India. By Lieut.-Col. R. BAIRD SMITH, F.G.S., Bengal Engineers. Second Edition. 2 vols. 8vo, with Atlas, 30s.
SMITH. Thorndale; or, The Conflict of Opinions. By WILLIAM SMITH, Author of 'A Discourse on Ethics,'&c. New Edition. Cr. 8vo, 10s. 6d.
—— Gravenhurst; or, Thoughts on Good and Evil. Second Edition, with Memoir of the Author. Crown 8vo, 8s.
SMITH. Greek Testament Lessons for Colleges, Schools, and Private Students, consisting chiefly of the Sermon on the Mount and the Parables of our Lord. With Notes and Essays. By the Rev. J. HUNTER SMITH, M.A., King Edward's School, Birmingham. Crown 8vo, 6s.
SMITH. Writings by the Way. By JOHN CAMPBELL SMITH, M.A., Sheriff-Substitute. Crown 8vo, 9s.
SMITH. The Secretary for Scotland. Being a Statement of the Powers and Duties of the new Scottish Office. With a Short Historical Introduction and numerous references to important Administrative Documents. By W. C. SMITH, LL.B., Advocate. 8vo. 6s.
SOLTERA. A Lady's Ride Across Spanish Honduras. By MARIA SOLTERA. With Illustrations. Post 8vo, 12s. 6d.
—— The Fat of the Land. A Novel. 3 vols. post 8vo, 25s. 6d.
SORLEY. The Ethics of Naturalism. Being the Shaw Fellowship Lectures, 1884. By W. R. Sorley, M.A., Fellow of Trinity College, Cambridge, and Examiner in Philosophy in the University of Edinburgh. Crown 8vo, 6s.
SPEEDY. Sport in the Highlands and Lowlands of Scotland with Rod and Gun. By TOM SPEEDY. Second Edition, Revised and Enlarged. With Illustrations by Lieut.-Gen. Hope Crealocke, C.B., C.M.G., and others. 8vo, 15s.
SPROTT. The Worship and Offices of the Church of Scotland; or, the Celebration of Public Worship, the Administration of the Sacraments, and other Divine Offices, according to the Order of the Church of Scotland. By GEORGE W. SPROTT, D.D., Minister of North Berwick. Crown 8vo. 6s.
STARFORTH. Villa Residences and Farm Architecture: A Series of Designs. By JOHN STARFORTH, Architect. 102 Engravings. Second Edition, medium 4to, £2, 17s. 6d.
STATISTICAL ACCOUNT OF SCOTLAND. Complete, with Index, 15 vols. 8vo, £16, 16s.
Each County sold separately, with Title, Index, and Map, neatly bound in cloth, forming a very valuable Manual to the Landowner, the Tenant, the Manufacturer, the Naturalist, the Tourist, &c.
STEPHENS. The Book of the Farm; detailing the Labours of the Farmer, Farm-Steward, Ploughman, Shepherd, Hedger, Farm-Labourer, Field-Worker, and Cattleman. By HENRY STEPHENS, F.R.S.E. A New and Enlarged Edition. Revised and in great part rewritten by JAMES MACDONALD, Author of 'Food from the Far West,' Joint-Author of 'Polled Cattle,' 'Hereford Cattle,' &c., &c. Assisted by many of the leading agricultural authorities of the day. Illustrated with numerous Portraits of Animals and Engravings of Implements. [In preparation.
—— The Book of Farm Buildings; their Arrangement and Construction. By HENRY STEPHENS, F.R.S.E., Author of 'The Book of the Farm:' and ROBERT SCOTT BURN. Illustrated with 1045 Plates and En-

STEPHENS. The Book of Farm Implements and Machines. By J. SLIGHT and R. SCOTT BURN, Engineers. Edited by HENRY STEPHENS. Large 8vo, uniform with 'The Book of the Farm,' £2, 2s.

STEVENSON. British Fungi. (Hymenomycetes.) By Rev. JOHN STEVENSON, Author of 'Mycologia Scotia,' Hon. Sec. Cryptogamic Society of Scotland. 2 vols. post 8vo, with Illustrations, price 12s. 6d. each.
Vol. I. AGARICUS—BOLBITIUS. Vol. II. CORTINARIUS—DACRYMYCES.

STEWART. Advice to Purchasers of Horses. By JOHN STEWART, V.S., Author of 'Stable Economy.' New Edition. 2s. 6d.

—— Stable Economy. A Treatise on the Management of Horses in relation to Stabling, Grooming, Feeding, Watering, and Working. By JOHN STEWART, V.S. Seventh Edition, fcap. 8vo, 6s. 6d.

STORMONTH. Etymological and Pronouncing Dictionary of the English Language. Including a very Copious Selection of Scientific Terms. For Use in Schools and Colleges, and as a Book of General Reference. By the Rev. JAMES STORMONTH. The Pronunciation carefully Revised by the Rev. P. H. PHELP, M.A. Cantab. Ninth Edition, Revised throughout. Crown 8vo, pp. 800. 7s. 6d.

—— Dictionary of the English Language, Pronouncing, Etymological, and Explanatory. Revised by the Rev. P. H. PHELP. Library Edition. Imperial 8vo, handsomely bound in half morocco, 31s. 6d.

—— The School Etymological Dictionary and Word-Book. Combining the advantages of an ordinary pronouncing School Dictionary and an Etymological Spelling-book. Fourth Edition. Fcap. 8vo, pp. 254. 2s.

STORY. Nero; A Historical Play. By W. W. STORY, Author of 'Roba di Roma.' Fcap. 8vo, 6s.

—— Vallombrosa. Post 8vo, 5s.

—— He and She; or, A Poet's Portfolio. Fcap. 8vo, in parchment, 3s. 6d.

—— Poems. 2 vols. fcap., 7s. 6d.

—— Fiammetta. A Summer Idyl. Crown 8vo, 7s. 6d.

STRICKLAND. Life of Agnes Strickland. By her SISTER. Post 8vo, with Portrait engraved on Steel, 12s. 6d.

STURGIS. John-a-Dreams. A Tale. By JULIAN STURGIS. New Edition, crown 8vo, 3s. 6d.

—— Little Comedies, Old and New. Crown 8vo, 7s. 6d.

SUTHERLAND. Handbook of Hardy Herbaceous and Alpine Flowers, for general Garden Decoration. Containing Descriptions, in Plain Language, of upwards of 1000 Species of Ornamental Hardy Perennial and Alpine Plants, adapted to all classes of Flower-Gardens, Rockwork, and Waters; along with Concise and Plain Instructions for their Propagation and Culture. By WILLIAM SUTHERLAND, Landscape Gardener; formerly Manager of the Herbaceous Department at Kew. Crown 8vo, 7s. 6d.

TAYLOR. The Story of My Life. By the late Colonel MEADOWS TAYLOR, Author of 'The Confessions of a Thug,' &c. &c. Edited by his Daughter. New and cheaper Edition, being the Fourth. Crown 8vo, 6s.

THOLUCK. Hours of Christian Devotion. Translated from the German of A. Tholuck, D.D., Professor of Theology in the University of Halle. By the Rev. ROBERT MENZIES, D.D. With a Preface written for this Translation by the Author. Second Edition, crown 8vo, 7s. 6d.

THOMSON. Handy Book of the Flower-Garden: being Practical Directions for the Propagation, Culture, and Arrangement of Plants in Flower-Gardens all the year round. Embracing all classes of Gardens, from the largest to the smallest. With Engraved Plans, illustrative of the various systems of Grouping in Beds and Borders. By DAVID THOMSON, Gardener to his Grace the Duke of Buccleuch, K.T., at Drumlanrig. Fourth and Cheaper Edition, crown 8vo, 5s.

THOMSON. The Handy Book of Fruit-Culture under Glass : being a series of Elaborate Practical Treatises on the Cultivation and Forcing of Pines, Vines, Peaches, Figs, Melons, Strawberries, and Cucumbers. With Engravings of Hothouses, &c., most suitable for the Cultivation and Forcing of these Fruits. By DAVID THOMSON, Gardener to his Grace the Duke of Buccleuch, K.T., at Drumlanrig. Second Ed. Cr. 8vo, with Engravings, 7s. 6d.

THOMSON. A Practical Treatise on the Cultivation of the Grape-Vine. By WILLIAM THOMSON, Tweed Vineyards. Ninth Edition, 8vo, 5s.

THOMSON. Cookery for the Sick and Convalescent. With Directions for the Preparation of Poultices, Fomentations, &c. By BARBARA THOMSON. Fcap. 8vo, 1s. 6d.

THOTH. A Romance. Crown 8vo, 4s. 6d.

TOM CRINGLE'S LOG. A New Edition, with Illustrations. Crown 8vo, cloth gilt, 5s. Cheap Edition, 2s.

TRANSACTIONS OF THE HIGHLAND AND AGRICULTURAL SOCIETY OF SCOTLAND. Published annually, price 5s.

TULLOCH. Rational Theology and Christian Philosophy in England in the Seventeenth Century. By JOHN TULLOCH, D.D., Principal of St Mary's College in the University of St Andrews; and one of her Majesty's Chaplains in Ordinary in Scotland. Second Edition. 2 vols. 8vo, 16s.

—— Modern Theories in Philosophy and Religion. 8vo, 15s.

—— Luther, and other Leaders of the Reformation. Third Edition, enlarged. Crown 8vo, 3s. 6d.

—— Memoir of Principal Tulloch, D.D., LL.D., one of Her Majesty's Chaplains for Scotland. By Mrs Oliphant, Author of 'Memoirs of Count de Montalembert,' 'Life of Edward Irving,' 8vo, with a Portrait.

TWO STORIES OF THE SEEN AND THE UNSEEN. 'THE OPEN DOOR,' 'OLD LADY MARY.' Crown 8vo, cloth, 2s. 6d.

VEITCH. Institutes of Logic. By JOHN VEITCH, LL.D., Professor of Logic and Rhetoric in the University of Glasgow. Post 8vo, 12s. 6d.

—— The Feeling for Nature in Scottish Poetry. From the Earliest Times to the Present Day. 2 vols. fcap. 8vo, in Roxburghe binding. 15s.

VIRGIL. The Æneid of Virgil. Translated in English Blank Verse by G. K. RICKARDS, M.A., and Lord RAVENSWORTH. 2 vols. fcap. 8vo, 10s.

WALFORD. The Novels of L. B. WALFORD. New and Uniform Edition. Crown 8vo, each 5s. *Sold separately.*
MR SMITH: A PART OF HIS LIFE.—COUSINS.— PAULINE.—TROUBLESOME DAUGHTERS.—DICK NETHERBY.—THE BABY'S GRANDMOTHER.—HISTORY OF A WEEK.

—— Four Biographies from 'Blackwood': Jane Taylor, Hannah More, Elizabeth Fry, Mary Somerville. Crown 8vo, 5s.

WARDEN. Poems. By FRANCIS HEYWOOD WARDEN. With a Notice by Dr Vanroth. Crown 8vo, 5s.

WARREN'S (SAMUEL) WORKS. People's Edition, 4 vols. crown 8vo, cloth, 15s. 6d. Or separately :—
Diary of a Late Physician. Cloth, 2s. 6d.; boards, 2s.
Ten Thousand A-Year. Cloth, 3s. 6d.; boards, 2s. 6d.
Now and Then. The Lily and the Bee. Intellectual and Moral Development of the Present Age. 4s. 6d.
Essays: Critical, Imaginative, and Juridical. 5s.

WARREN. The Five Books of the Psalms. With Marginal Notes. By Rev. SAMUEL L. WARREN, Rector of Esher, Surrey; late Fellow, Dean, and Divinity Lecturer, Wadham College, Oxford. Crown 8vo, 5s.

WATSON. Christ's Authority; and other Sermons. By the late ARCHIBALD WATSON, D.D., Minister of the Parish of Dundee, and one of Her Majesty's Chaplains for Scotland. With Introduction by the Very Rev. PRINCIPAL CAIRD, Glasgow. Crown 8vo, 7s. 6d.

WEBSTER. The Angler and the Loop-Rod. By DAVID WEBSTER. Crown 8vo, with Illustrations, 7s. 6d.

WELLINGTON. Wellington Prize Essays on "the System of Field Manœuvres best adapted for enabling our Troops to meet a Continental Army." Edited by Lieut.-General Sir EDWARD BRUCE HAMLEY, K.C.B. 8vo, 12s. 6d.

WESTMINSTER ASSEMBLY. Minutes of the Westminster Assembly, while engaged in preparing their Directory for Church Government, Confession of Faith, and Catechisms (November 1644 to March 1649). Edited by the Rev. Professor ALEX. T. MITCHELL, of St Andrews, and the Rev. JOHN STRUTHERS, LL.D. With a Historical and Critical Introduction by Professor Mitchell. 8vo, 15s.

WHITE. The Eighteen Christian Centuries. By the Rev. JAMES WHITE. Seventh Edition, post 8vo, with Index, 6s.

——— History of France, from the Earliest Times. Sixth Thousand, post 8vo, with Index, 6s.

WHITE. Archæological Sketches in Scotland—Kintyre and Knapdale. By Colonel T. P. WHITE, R.E., of the Ordnance Survey. With numerous Illustrations. 2 vols. folio, £4, 4s. Vol. I., Kintyre, sold separately, £2, 2s.

——— The Ordnance Survey of the United Kingdom. A Popular Account. Crown 8vo, 5s.

WILLS AND GREENE. Drawing-room Dramas for Children. By W. G. WILLS and the Hon. Mrs GREENE. Crown 8vo, 6s.

WILSON. Works of Professor Wilson. Edited by his Son-in-Law, Professor FERRIER. 12 vols. crown 8vo, £2, 8s.

——— Christopher in his Sporting-Jacket. 2 vols., 8s.

——— Isle of Palms, City of the Plague, and other Poems. 4s.

——— Lights and Shadows of Scottish Life, and other Tales. 4s.

——— Essays, Critical and Imaginative. 4 vols., 16s.

——— The Noctes Ambrosianæ. 4 vols., 16s.

——— Homer and his Translators, and the Greek Drama. Crown 8vo, 4s.

WILSON. From Korti to Khartum: A Journal of the Desert March from Korti to Gubat, and of the Ascent of the Nile in General Gordon's Steamers. By Colonel Sir CHARLES W. WILSON, K.C.B., K.C.M.G., R.E. Seventh Edition. Crown 8vo, 2s. 6d.

WINGATE. Annie Weir, and other Poems. By DAVID WINGATE. Fcap. 8vo, 5s.

——— Lily Neil. A Poem. Crown 8vo, 4s. 6d.

WORDSWORTH. The Historical Plays of Shakspeare. With Introductions and Notes. By CHARLES WORDSWORTH, D.C.L., Bishop of S. Andrews. 3 vols. post 8vo, each price 7s. 6d.

WORSLEY. Poems and Translations. By PHILIP STANHOPE WORSLEY, M.A. Edited by EDWARD WORSLEY. Second Edition, enlarged. Fcap. 8vo, 6s.

YATE. England and Russia Face to Face in Asia. A Record of Travel with the Afghan Boundary Commission. By Lieutenant A. C. YATE, Bombay Staff Corps, Special Correspondent of the 'Pioneer,' 'Daily Telegraph,' &c., &c., with the Afghan Boundary Commission. 8vo, with Maps and Illustrations, 21s.

YATE. Northern Afghanistan; or, Letters from the Afghan Boundary Commission. By Major C. E. Yate, C.S.I., Bombay Staff Corps. 8vo, with Maps. 18s.

YOUNG. A Story of Active Service in Foreign Lands. Compiled from letters sent home from South Africa, India, and China, 1856-1882. By Surgeon-General A. Graham Young, Author of 'Crimean Cracks.' Crown 8vo, Illustrated, 7s. 6d.

YULE. Fortification: for the Use of Officers in the Army, and Readers of Military History. By Col. YULE, Bengal Engineers. 8vo, with numerous Illustrations, 10s. 6d.

8/88.